12.(a) OVER...ME

1'ADAPT ($60-

CW01657333

Dear Michael,

Ciao Dottore.

Its been a long time and I trust you are well.

Forgive my abrupt intrusion on your normal business.

Though, the period between its execution and pertinent transaction date has elapsed the 7 years we have on this rare instance counter-parties that exceed the term Whicer Unlikely but possible as

XAM is registered with the BVI and Loop has and had registered employees (THROUGHT) $ the period. Luckily the NDA was to Phil Adler who, equally remains in the biz,

: JE SUIS

I ← : LE MATRICE

: CJ

: HSBC

LAMMY. : MATRIX CHURCHILL

Modernism on Sea

WHAMMY.

V.

← Dflex. FLEX

T
O
U
C
H.

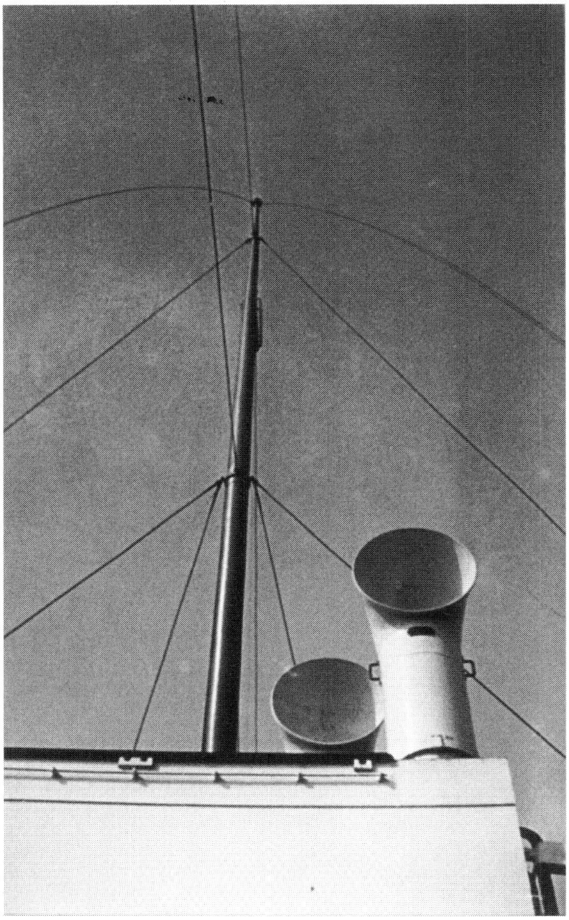

The nautical shapes of modernism:
Atlantic Voyage by Paul Nash, 1931

The Bafidi Code
by,
Del Boy

O
F
A
H.

MODERNISM *on Sea*

Art and Culture at the British Seaside

EDITED BY

Lara Feigel and Alexandra Harris

Peter Lang Oxford

First published in 2009
by Peter Lang Ltd,
International Academic Publishers,
Evenlode Court, Main Road,
Long Hanborough, Witney,
Oxfordshire OX29 8SZ
England

www.peterlang.com

Lara Feigel and Alexandra Harris
have asserted their moral right under
the Copyright, Designs and Patents Act
of 1988 to be identified as the Editors of
this Work.

© Peter Lang Ltd 2009

All rights reserved. No part of this book
may be reprinted or reproduced or
utilized in any form, by any electronic,
mechanical or other means, now
known or hereafter invented, including
photocopying and recording, or in any
information storage or retrieval system,
without the prior permission, in writing,
of the Publishers.

A catalogue record for this book is
available from the British Library
ISBN 978-1-90616-524-6

DESIGN Kara Trapani, Peter Lang Ltd
DRAWINGS Alexandra Harris
Printed in Great Britain by the
MPG Books Group

Contents

Part VI Modernism and After

Acknowledgements

We would like to thank our research assistant Miranda Stern for all her help and good humour, and to thank Barrie Bullen, John Craig Gray, Hugh Fowler-Wright and Clarissa Lewis for their generosity and support. The project was made possible by funding from the University of Sussex, Oxford English Faculty, Christ Church Oxford and the AHRC, to all of whom we are very grateful. Our thanks also go to Kara Trapani for her inspired designs, to Jennifer Speake for her meticulous copy-editing, and to our superb editor Hannah Godfrey for her enthusiasm throughout.

Illustrations

Frontispiece: Paul Nash, *Atlantic Voyage*, 1931, photograph, Government Art Collection. © Crown copyright: UK Government Art Collection / estate of Paul Nash.

Plates

Figures

Introduction

Lara Feigel and Alexandra Harris

Modernism is usually seen as the most urban and frenetic of artistic movements. A typical journey through high modernism would start in the cafés and arcades of Paris, whirl along the banks of the Liffey and stop the traffic in Bloomsbury before blasting into a Berlin nightclub. But a discerning artistic pilgrim would do well to pause on the cliffs and promenades of the English coast. *Modernism on Sea* puts the case for a new geography of avant-gardism, acknowledging that the most intriguing cultural hubs of modern times include Swanage, Margate, Morecambe and Hythe. This book takes a series of expeditions in the footsteps of the twentieth century's great seaside artists and it argues that there exists in this country a rich, continuous tradition of seaside art that has never properly been pieced together.

Convalescing at Margate in 1921, T.S. Eliot spent long hours sitting in a blustery shelter looking out over the yellowed winter sea. His sense of desolation went into the poem he was writing and which would become 'The Fire Sermon' section of *The Waste Land*. His location mattered, and he acknowledged it explicitly:

> On Margate Sands.
> I can connect
> Nothing with nothing.[1]

Eliot's great lament for a broken postwar world belonged to Margate as much as it belonged to London Bridge. But if the seaside was, for Eliot, a site of modernist emptiness, it has seemed for subsequent writers more like a place of excess. Reaching Hastings, in his 2004 novel *Dining on Stones*, Iain Sinclair finds himself haunted by Eliot and needing to refute him. 'I couldn't help myself', says a narrator almost delirious with the joy of allusion, 'everything connected with everything'.[2] And so these two writers, nearly a century apart, continue their argument on the shingle: just one instance of the dialogues which have shaped the modern beach.

It is possible to imagine an epic journey through the artistic and literary histories of the British coast, all 9040 miles of it. The tour might be made on foot, now that a continuous coastal path is to be opened, giving access to the cliffs right around the island. It would certainly be long and varied. It would find Elizabeth Bowen at Broadstairs, Folkestone and Hythe; Graham Greene, Patrick Hamilton and Walter Sickert at Brighton; Paul Nash enjoying the surrealist attraction of Swanage; John Betjeman admiring Victorian piers in Devon and Cornwall; Alfred Wallis, Barbara Hepworth, Roger Hilton and Virginia Woolf at St Ives; Anthony Gormley's iron figures at Crosby; Jeanette Winterson remembering Blackpool; W.G. Sebald spinning histories from the ruins of deserted Norfolk; Graham Swift on the reclaimed fenlands of Cambridgeshire; Benjamin Britten and many others at Aldeburgh; and (coming full circle back to Kent) John Piper and Derek Jarman scouring the shingle of Dungeness. In reality, of course, this book can only send out feelers, making day-trips rather than odysseys. It is personal and partial, reflecting the interests of its contributors, but we hope that it will be suggestive.

Our starting point was on the East Sussex coast, at Bexhill-on-Sea, home to one of Britain's first and finest modernist buildings, the De La Warr Pavilion. In 2005 we went on a small-scale pilgrimage to see this newly restored landmark of International Style design. Standing on the windy, deserted beach, we looked up at the chic white curves of the Pavilion, which had been commissioned in 1933 by the forward-thinking Earl De La Warr, and designed by the émigré architects Erich Mendelsohn and Serge Chermayeff. We couldn't help being struck by the incongruities. Bexhill is a genteel, conservative seaside town, offering peaceful retirement homes and excellent teashops. The Pavilion in its midst is commandingly beautiful, but seems awkwardly out of place, caught between its roles as modernist icon and local community centre. Visitors from across Britain come to admire its cantilevered glass staircase and elegant sun terraces, but they do not stay long. When the last train has taken the pilgrims back to London, the local pensioners gather to watch cabaret entertainers and nostalgically re-enact the seaside tea-dances of their youth.

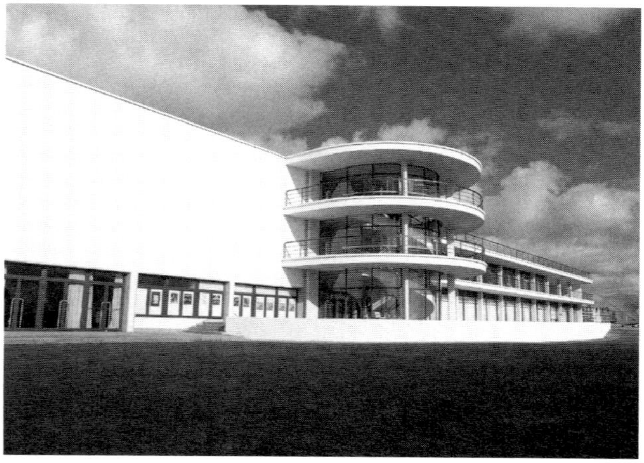

Figure 1
One of Britain's first and finest modernist buildings: the De La Warr Pavilion at Bexhill-on-Sea

What better place, we thought, to discuss the complex imaginative life of the coast. And so *Modernism on Sea* began as an interdisciplinary conference at the Pavilion. It brought together a community of beachcombing scholars, writers, readers and thinkers to explore twentieth-century artistic responses to the seaside. Why, we asked, is modernism so often linked with the life of the city and so rarely with the shore? The devoted observer of modern life would certainly find plenty to interest him on the esplanade: sunbathing, crowd-mingling, sexual licence, surreal juxtapositions, the modernist architecture of the lido; or, in more metaphorical terms, the experience of being on the edge, caught between the vast sea and the small human pleasures of the shore. Once we started looking, we realised that Bexhill and Romney Marsh were unsung artistic centres. And we felt that the continuity between interwar seaside artists and those working today was so strong that we should try to bring the story right up to the present without putting too many neat categorical barriers in the way.

John K. Walton, whose work on the development of resorts has set the standard for social histories of the seaside, has found sadly little to engage him in the literature of the sands. He laments that 'there has not, in fact, been a great novel set primarily, or even to a large extent, at the twentieth-century British seaside: nothing to match Mann's *Buddenbrooks* or the seaside dimension in Proust'.[3] This literary void seems astonishing, given our coast-consciousness as an island nation. But one does not have to look very far to start filling in the hole. It is true that the greatness of the British seaside is not the greatness of Mann or Proust: its aesthetics are different. But if we pay closer attention to those unique aesthetics we will find a rich literary heritage, a continuous tradition of painting and sculpture, and some of the most innovative architecture in Europe.

Seaside Style

One of the best guides to England's coastal heritage is John Piper, who wrote appreciatively, all through the 1930s, about the marriage of tradition and modernity in nautical style. Looking at the simple, functional shapes of lighthouses and fishermen's huts, he found a language of design which was rooted in the vernacular of particular English places, but which was consonant, too, with the pared-down world of contemporary abstraction. The modern painter, he thought, might have much to learn at the beach. In her essay in this volume, Frances Spalding, Piper's biographer, asks what Piper found there, and how he promoted to others his generous and distinctive nautical vision.

The seaside shapes the work of artists, and in turn artists shape the seaside with their own preoccupations. Piper was interested in the coast's elastic capacity to harmonise strong forms with messy detritus; he was always drawn to the pot-luck offerings of low tide, and loved to describe the 'water-logged sand shoes, banana skins, cuttle fish, dead seagulls, sides of boxes with THIS SIDE UP on them'.[4] He admired both the quiet simplicity of a whitewashed cottage and the chatty, show-off exuberance of Victorian villas.

The novelist Elizabeth Bowen, too, had a great feel for stucco flourishes. Having been brought from Ireland to the south coast of England at the age of seven, Bowen found seaside architecture an astonishing contrast to the imposing plainness of Dublin's eighteenth-century terraces. 'I was surfeited with the classical when we sailed for England' she remembered, 'where release, to the point of delirium, awaited me.'[5] Traces of that delirium survive in the relish with which, near the end of her life, she evoked those extravagantly whimsical seaside houses:

> I found myself in a paradise of white balconies, ornate porches, verandahs festooned with Dorothy Perkins roses, bow windows protuberant as balloons, dream-childish attic bedrooms with tentlike ceilings, sublimated ivory-fretwork inglenooks inset with jujubes of tinted glass, built-in overmantels with flight upon flight of brackets round oval mirrors, oxidised bronze door-handles with floral motifs [...] [6]

Bowen could be brutally snobbish about this profusion. She always took care to detach her more discerning adult self from the children in her writing who are allowed to admire fantastic verandahs and bows.

This scepticism about florid seaside style was felt much more deeply by the émigré European architects (Mendelsohn and Chermayeff foremost amongst them) who lived in England during the 1930s and who wondered how the seaside might be transformed into a modernist utopia. To them, the nineteenth-century bric-a-brac was not only claustrophobic but untrustworthy. Why was so much decoration needed? Perhaps something rotten was being covered up, in which case it was time to expose the underlying structure of things.

This is precisely what the Bexhill Pavilion aimed to do, with its glass walls and open vistas. Early photographs show the building rising serene behind the Edwardian onion-shaped domes that were still in place along the esplanade. These relics were soon cleared away, allowing uninterrupted views of the cruise-liner curves. And meanwhile Chermayeff was suggesting further ways to tidy up Britain's seaside towns. Writing in the *Architectural Review* in 1936, under the pseudonym of Peter Maitland, he complained about haphazard development and inefficient amenities. He was particularly scathing about 'the genteel teashop in the side-street, where you have neither the view of the sea you have come to enjoy, nor enough to eat, and where all the gaps are filled with mustard and cress'.[7] These are just the kind of teashops where Bowen's characters have their most intense conversations, but Chermayeff was more in favour of food served 'efficiently and quickly' from a snack bar near the beach. The resorts, he thought, should be divided into 'zones', so that holiday flats were separate from residents' housing, and family bathing separate from adult.

Chermayeff had a strong vision of the clean, efficient seaside, and there were many who supported him. But accident and ornament could not be kept at bay. It was not long before the Bexhill curves were obscured again. After the war, when modernist taste was in recession, attempts were made to give the Pavilion a feel of cosiness – just the sort of cluttered intimacy the building was designed to resist. Out came the carpets, deep-piled and patterned. Concrete pillars were clad in wood to give an olde-worlde feel, and trailing plants were draped over any offensively sharp edges. It was a travesty, but a tremendously human one, and admirable in its way. It takes some audacity to fly so determinedly in the face of so authoritative a building. Twenty-first-century restoration work restored the Pavilion to its mid-1930s glory. But even then the effect was precariously achieved. Moments before the Queen arrived for the royal opening, a pot of brown paint was spilt over the white façade, as if the robust forces of mess were staging a high-profile campaign against the rule of whiteness.[8]

Seaside Society

These questions of aesthetics have a complex, fascinating relationship with the radical social changes of the interwar years. Swathes of the British coast became a pleasure beach as the number of seaside holidaymakers steadily multiplied. The working classes took advantage of the cheaper, faster train services and the improved pay and holiday conditions to escape for a day or week beside the sea. In 1937, seven million people were reported to visit Blackpool alone. Commercial art exploited the seaside exodus – here was a captive audience with time and some money to while away. In his essay, Svetlin Stratiev details the history of the humble seaside postcard, which developed complex survival techniques to evade censors and attract visitors, creating and perpetuating a unique brand of bawdy seaside humour.

In turn, the new crowds at the seaside provoked the enthusiasm and scorn of the literary establishment. Edwina Keown sets T.S. Eliot's fear of the emergent middle classes against Elizabeth Bowen's more appreciative account of their vigour, and it becomes clear that Bowen's mixed feelings about stucco connected with her acute readings of the seaside's social politics.

By the 1930s, the working classes had taken over the beaches from the middle classes and the essay on the 1930s seaside holiday explores the literary ambivalence towards the seaside crowds. Where Auden enthused about the freedom offered by the beach, Graham Greene set the lax morality of the seaside mob against the more stringent morality of his Catholic anti-hero, Pinkie. One of *Brighton Rock*'s most disturbing implications is that murder is in better taste than a careless one-night stand. The ambivalence towards the crowds intensified in the lead-up to war, when for writers like Patrick Hamilton the carefree frivolity of the popular seaside came to seem irresponsible and even dangerous.

In the 1930s, the seaside was defined as much by the 'side' as by the sea itself. In 1937, the 1930s people-watching group Mass-Observation went to Blackpool to observe the working classes at play and found that for most of the summer visitors the seaside ended with the promenade. Where nineteenth-century bathers had visited the coast chiefly to take the waters, 1930s holidaymakers were determined to return home with a suntan. Fred Gray's essay investigates the lure of the sun at the interwar seaside, exploring its influence on coastal architecture in this period. He argues that iconic seaside buildings like the De La Warr Pavilion catered for a growing number of seaside visitors who sought open spaces and sun terraces to bare their (occasionally naked) bodies to the sun (see Plate 1). Gone were the evenings spent staring at the crashing waves; this was a generation of seasiders who lounged by day and danced by night. A host of ever-new, ever-glittering amusements proliferated to fulfil their requirements – and their holiday fantasies. And the essays in the seaside holiday section show that artists throughout the twentieth century have taken advantage of the glamour, creating a literature and cinema of attractions as excessive as the seaside it depicts.

If the visitors kept close to the attractions and amenities of the coastline, many of the buildings they inhabited looked as if they might be about to set sail. As Bruce Peter points out, modern architecture was profoundly indebted to ship design, and the Pavilion which stayed put in Bexhill was nonetheless paying tribute to the vast liners which sailed between Europe and America. Peter offers a tour of the twentieth century's most advanced cabins and sundecks, demonstrating that modernism afloat set the standard for modernism on dry land.

Seaside Memories

The feel for the coast can be a very personal thing. The attachment runs deep, and it is rare for two people to feel quite the same way about a particular stretch. Ted Hughes once wanted to show Sylvia Plath what an English beach could be:

> an altogether other England –
> An Avalon for which I had the wavelength.[9]

What he reported regretfully in his poem 'The Beach' was that the wavelength was not shared. Plath felt no connection with the car park on the Front at Woolacombe on a bleak November day:

> You refused to get out.
> You sat behind your mask, inaccessible –
> Staring towards the ocean that had failed you.
> I walked to the water's edge. A dull wave
> Managed to lift and flop.[10]

This is one of Hughes's places: rainy, English, unsensational. But the ocean has failed him too because it has so flatly refused to perform for his wife. What she had wanted from the coast was a great scouring and cleansing, which the splashy Devon pot-holes were not going to provide. The image of Plath and Hughes together in their damp car at Woolacombe, needing such different things from the sea, is powerfully indicative of the coast's capacity to separate out (and draw together) differing literary sensibilities.

Ben Morgan's essay on Plath in this volume responds to her sense of the sea as a sublime symbolic force, making and unmaking itself in rhythms which might provide form for her poetry. The words which recur in Morgan's essay (flux, rupture, dissolution) take us a long way from the cheery bandstands of Bexhill or the puddles of Woolacombe, and Plath was well aware of how these variant ideas of the seaside might play up against each other. This awareness came, partly, from reading and criticising Virginia Woolf. As Morgan shows, Plath responded keenly to a version of Woolf as a mystic seer, submerged in clarifying waters (most notably the Woolf of *The Waves*) but was troubled when Woolf's prose turned heavier, 'needing the earth'.[11] Yet what Plath had identified was part of Woolf's great gift: to feel the pull of the universalising sea at one and the same time as the pull of the grubby, jolly, populous shore. This is why, so often, Woolf will describe a deserted beach, sublime in its inhumanity, before watching as the peace is shattered by a child running, splashing and shouting into the waves. David Bradshaw's essay pays attention to these opposing forces in Woolf's seaside writing, tracing her imagery of underwater amorphousness, and its complex relationship with the imagery of landlocked solidity.

It sounds like a particularly Woolfian preoccupation, but this potent relationship between sea and land emerges as one of the most recurrent dynamics of modern literature. It is there all through the writing of Stevie Smith, for example, as William May demonstrates in his essay on her characteristic responsiveness to both the shabbiness and the sublimity of the seaside holiday. Smith is a great poet of the bucket and spade, but her jolliness is always close to melancholy. Her faithful narrator Pompey is moved to tears when she looks out to sea, watching 'all that great wilderness of thought, coming rolling from the deep deep sea'.[12]

Seasides awaken Stevie Smith's intense sense of 'nostalgie', as they do for Osbert and Sacheverell Sitwell among many others. Deborah Parsons develops an aesthetics of nostalgia, examining the intricate workings of memory in the Sitwells' long-neglected autobiographical works, which reach back, longingly, to sunlit childhoods on the sands at Scarborough. The Sitwells were acutely concerned with the juncture between Edwardian gentility and modern times, and accordingly their writing about Scarborough reminds us how often modernism (for all its futuristic bravado) was shaped by memories of an older world. So the pierrot troupes which performed in *fin-de-siècle* Scarborough were at the root of Sacheverell's life-long fascination with the commedia dell'arte, and those pierrots find their way into the modernist work not only of Sitwell but of Picasso and Diaghilev – and of Walter Sickert, whose melancholy identification with the pierrots at Brighton is explored here by Nicola Moorby. It begins to seem no wonder that the Camden Town Group swapped London for Brighton in 1915: the seaside offers ordinariness and sublimity, nostalgia and contemporaneity, in measures quite as compelling as Fitzroy Square.

In 1915 Sickert looked sadly at the empty deckchairs of Brighton; in 1942 Osbert Sitwell looked back on a Scarborough that had been fractured by the first war and was being shattered, irreparably, by the second. Although much of it became a military zone in wartime, the seaside still had a role to play. It was crucial to wartime propaganda and became a symbol of 'what we are fighting for'. The War Ministry's propaganda films produced by John Grierson's Crown Film Unit abound in images of the coast as a symbol of Britain's proud isolation and its triumphant naval past.

Seaside Century

For a short time after the war, it seemed that the seaside might provide the model for a new, reconstructed Britain. Paul Rennie makes a fascinating case for the influence of seaside style on the Festival of Britain, with its promenades, bunting and democratic mixing of people. But the future was not so coastally oriented as it might have seemed in 1951. It would never regain the glamour and the wealth of the 1930s and in the late twentieth century, as seaside towns sought to reinvent themselves and fight off atrophy, it is not surprising that they turned again to the 1930s. Morecambe and Bexhill were not alone in restoring their great modernist buildings as they attempted to attract twenty-first-century visitors.

Thomas Heatherwick has described his 2008 East Beach Café in Littlehampton as responding to the 'raw beauty' of the seaside, and the building resembles a piece of driftwood, swept into the shore. Yet the clean lines of the pale blue exterior mark the building out as part of the nautical tradition, and the menu includes old-fashioned potted shrimps. Like his predecessors, Heatherwick sees the seaside as a place where the classes come together and has designed his café as an establishment where 'you can eat a Mr Whippy or drink Dom Pérignon'.

Postmodernism on Sea has paid pastiche-filled homage to its predecessors. Andrew Kötting's 1996 film *Gallivant* is a joyful montage of seaside past and present, punctuated with scenes from 1930s public information films and with reminiscences by Kötting's grandmother Gladys about her youth at the Bexhill seaside. Kötting, like us, takes the Pavilion as his starting point, and he examines its role as a cultural landmark in his essay in this volume. He appends a critique of *Gallivant* by Iain Sinclair, who specifically lauds his friend's montage of 'found' past and filmed present, and whose own fiction lingers on the deserted balconies of 1930s seafront apartments, peering into the 'cracked swimming pool', recording 'glimpses of revenants, tourist class, on a ghost ship'.[13] Graham Swift's *Last Orders* (1996) looked back to prewar Margate as a place where dreams were made ('The Pier, the Jetty, the Sands. Dreamland'), and where dreams were broken.[14] When he made a film based on Swift's novel, director Fred Schepisi used nostalgic Technicolor for flashback shots of the younger Jack and his wife at the seaside, and each frame made its nod to iconic images of prewar holiday advertisements. The contemporary shots of the grey coast seem to have discoloured just as the film has, now that the seaside has passed its prime.

Michael Bracewell sees the English seaside as the site of an elegiac romanticism. For Bracewell, the contemporary seaside visitor goes to the coast partly in search of ghosts. In faded seaside resorts, the cultural tourist encounters a spectral pageant of 1930s sun-worshippers and of 1960s pop icons parading past the steamy cafes and the overgrown rides. Bracewell's essay suggests that Morecambe is as potent a subject for the romantic artist as the nearby Lake District and celebrates the English seaside town as 'a melancholy but intoxicating Venice of the national vernacular'.

Where Bracewell evokes the pop glamour of Morecambe, Alan Powers heads away from the resorts to the marshes and shingle of Aldeburgh. He asks what it was that drew Benjamin Britten to this small coastal town and shows how this mutable landscape, constantly dramatising its struggle against 'the destructive element', became home to art that was (politically, sexually and aesthetically) treading new and ever-shifting ground. Powers's essay pays tribute to a local festival which sprang from the love of a particular place, but which has become part of the national consciousness. And he affirms that the romantic English tradition which celebrates what Piper called the 'changeable climate of our sea-washed country' is still a strong, deep vein in our arts.[15]

This book is about the English coast, but it is a coast in dialogue with countries across the sea. It was appropriate that if International Style buildings were to be erected anywhere in England it should have been on the south coast, where they could look across to France and, beyond that, to the

Mediterranean. These were buildings in exile, designed by exiled architects who imaginatively linked England back to the continent.

A later exile, the German writer W.G. Sebald, looked out to Dogger Bank and reflected that this was once where 'the delta of the Rhine flowed out into the sea and where green forests grew from silting sands'.[16] England had once been attached to Europe and, in *The Rings of Saturn*, his novel of a journey around Norfolk, Sebald set about recording the continuity of lives criss-crossing between these lands which had only physically been severed. No illusions of Little England's detachment can survive a reading of Sebald, whose writing is about our responsibilities to the past, and to a world wider than the familiar radius of our daily lives. His English coastline is connected to remote places by supple, intricate chains of association which he moulds into bridges so elaborate that it might be possible to walk over them. So the trains which once brought holidaymakers to Blyth were in fact built for the emperor of China; the shape of the imperial dragon is still just about discernible beneath the paintwork. From the lost village of Dunwich grows a vast temple of Xanadu. And walking the deserted marshes around Walberswick, Sebald observes that this might be the shore of the Caspian Sea, or the Gulf of Lion-tung.

In German, Sebald's novel was subtitled *Eine Englische Wallfahrt*, 'An English Pilgrimage'. It is one of many journeys in modern literature which attest to the strong feelings of ritual and pilgrimage which the coast can arouse. We feel, like Masefield, the call of the sea; we go back again and again to the same seasides, enacting the same ceremonies of toe-dipping, pebble-collecting and fossil-hunting. The last essay in this book is about the sustaining nature of these repetitions, these small dialogues which we keep having with the elements and which go on, mile after mile, around England's edges.

Part I

SEASIDE HOLIDAYS

Lara Feigel

Lara Feigel is a Lecturer in Modern Literary Studies at King's College, London. She is currently working on a monograph emerging from her doctoral thesis at the University of Sussex on the influence of cinema on politically committed British literature, 1930–45. She is also researching a project on modernist autobiography and self-portraiture and another on the role of literature in the reconstruction of Europe after the Second World War, focusing on the work of International PEN and Unesco. She is a co-editor (with John Sutherland and Natasha Spender) of the journals of Stephen Spender (Faber, 2009) and the editor of *A Nosegay: A Literary Journey from the Fragrant to the Fetid* (Old Street Publishing, 2006).

Kiss Me Quick

The Aesthetics of Excess in 1930s Literature and Film

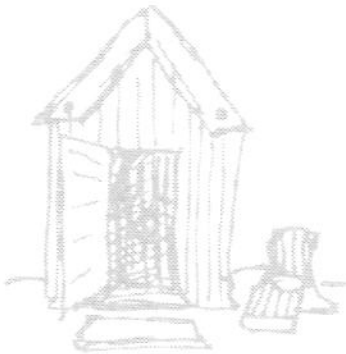

THE POPULAR SEASIDE RESORT was an enticing setting for the 1930s filmmaker or writer, offering a world of heady opulence and excess. The workers who flocked towards the sea left behind the grime of the northern factories and the chaos of the London streets to linger on the promenade, swoon in the ballroom and whirl in ecstasy on the flying machine. The seaside filmmaker could dizzy his audience as it bounced with the camera along the rollercoaster while the seaside writer could detail the vulgarity of the pleasure beach.

This surplus was in sharp contrast to the everyday landscape of the 1930s, and artists made the most of the montage possibilities offered by the disjunction. That 'low dishonest decade' is traditionally viewed as an era when the hedonism of the 1920s had given way to upper-class anxieties about fascism and mass poverty and to working-class fears of unemployment. It was a time when George Orwell lived as a tramp in London and W.H. Auden wrote film scripts about coalmining. But even the unemployed could forget their cares in the Fun House, and filmmakers and writers alike embraced the artistic potential of the workers at play. The madness of the coast could be brought into the service equally of Walter Greenwood, offering his workers a brief moment of happiness at the seaside in *Love on the Dole* (1933), or of Graham Greene, whose tale of damnation and murder is lit up against a backdrop of Guinness, oysters and song in *Brighton Rock* (1938).

The contrast between the dinginess of the urban home and the sparkling possibilities of the coast are made explicit in the 1936 GPO documentary film, *The Way to the Sea*, produced by Paul Rotha and scripted by Auden. The GPO film unit, spearheaded by the socialist filmmaker John Grierson, typically produced formally innovative accounts of working-class heroism and hardship like *Coal Face* (1935) or Marxist accounts of production processes such as *Night Mail* (1936). *The Way to the Sea* was typical of the Griersonian tradition in documenting the process of shipbuilding from 286 AD to the present and reminding the audience that the seaside day-trip is only rendered possible by industry. Nonetheless, the focus of the film and of Auden's commentary in particular is on the freedom possible at the seaside.

For the writer or filmmaker who was prepared to countenance the crude, the popular seaside resort offered the chance to develop an aesthetics of pleasure. In particular, it enabled artists to represent the working classes without pity or disdain. This aesthetics of pleasure is perhaps most evident in *Hindle Wakes*, a film made by Maurice Elvey in 1927, very early in the tradition examined here. Elvey follows two working girls from the cotton mills to Blackpool and uses the techniques of avant-garde cinema to capture the delights of Blackpool on screen.

Predictably, not all of the artistic establishment was enticed by the seaside or able to tolerate its vulgarity. As the workers flocked to Blackpool or Brighton, the intellectuals questioned the morality of the popular seaside and bristled in fear at the 'masses'. The sheer size of the seaside crowd was problematic for an artistic culture that had embraced the working classes but was having problems coming to terms with them en masse. In 1937, the anthropologists at Mass-Observation made the same journey from cotton mill to Blackpool that Elvey had made so enthusiastically ten years earlier, with less celebratory results. Mass-Observation had been founded earlier that year by the anthropologist Tom Harrisson, the poet Charles Madge and the GPO filmmaker Humphrey Jennings and aimed at producing a 'science of ourselves', hoping to analyse Britain in order that it could be 'understood and thus constantly transformed'.[1] They began by setting up camp in Bolton ('Worktown') to survey the mass habits of the workers in the cotton mills, and in the summer they followed the Worktowners to the seaside to observe them at play, surreptitiously noting down such pertinent details as their choice of breakfast cereals and their proclivities for sitting down or standing up while kissing. What they found led them to question the individuality attained by the working classes during the only week of the year when they had the chance to be themselves. Mass-Observation's anxiety about the masses reflected a widespread intellectual fear of mass culture. For writers like J.B. Priestley, the crowds at Blackpool were unpleasant, and for Graham Greene and Patrick Hamilton, Brighton's teaming pier and promenade were a more menacing phenomenon.

But even once it was framed as cheap and tawdry, the popular seaside resort was artistically potent. Greene was drawn to the seediness of Brighton long before he started *Brighton Rock*, repeatedly visiting the town in an attempt to soak up its peculiar atmosphere, at once hedonistic and sinister, and his 1938 novel draws its power from its gaudy seaside setting. This essay argues that the 1930s saw the birth of an art of excess, situated at the seaside. The garish overabundance possible at the seaside resort could be represented as ecstatic freedom, when framed by the gruelling cares of the industrial north, or as tawdry escapism, framed by Catholic asceticism or impending war. Equally, the seaside crowd could be a welcoming hub that allowed each individual to find a home, or a de-individuating mob that denied culture and sensitivity. The seaside artist often felt called upon to answer moral questions about the desirability of crowd experience in an era when fascist governments in Europe were aspiring to just the crowd mentality that the British took on at the seaside. Nonetheless, in a decade otherwise dominated by political earnestness, the popular seaside resort enabled an alternative artistic tradition that was opulent and crude but, above all, pleasurable.

The Way to the Sea: The Rise of Mass Leisure Time in the 1930s

The popularity of the week in Blackpool or the day-trip to Portsmouth or Brighton was a new phenomenon in the late 1920s and 1930s, rendered possible by two factors: time and transport. During the early twentieth century, workers gained in free time, with 6.3 million workers experiencing cuts in weekly hours in 1919.[2] By 1930, workers were guaranteed one day off each week and a week's (unpaid) holiday each year. In the mid-1930s, the yearly holiday was seen as a right of citizenship, with Harold Laski and Clement Atlee organising a committee to subsidise holidays for the unemployed.[3]

For left-wing writers and filmmakers like Auden and Rotha, the new leisure time was a sign of a civilised shift towards a more socialist society. In *The Way to the Sea* Auden and the director J.B. Holmes capitalise on the 1930s penchant for fast montage sequences, typically used to contrast upper-class and working-class lives, juxtaposing the carefree seaside trippers with the more careworn workers who must remain at home in London. The electricity that powers the train to Portsmouth also helps 'those who cannot get away just now', enabling them to entertain friends and feed husbands. Shots of hands ironing, cooking and washing are dissolved onto images of dingy urban houses, contrasting with the freedom and glamour of the train. Once the 'more fortunate' have departed, class divisions can be forgotten as 'All kinds of people' come together in the freedom of the new surroundings.

In his 1932 account of leisure in Britain, the philosopher and academic Delisle Burns lauded the government for spending more on subsidised leisure activities, stating that 'the expenditure of public funds on facilities for recreation may be a first sign of returning civilisation, after the barbaric concentration on wealth-getting in the earlier industrial period.'[4] In this, the British government could be seen as taking its lead from communists in Russia. More stridently than the British, the Soviet government had devoted itself to funding and supporting working-class leisure from the time that Lenin proclaimed the eight-hour day in 1917. From 1928 to 1940 Stalin promoted fitness and leisure through official sponsorship, holding the first Physical Culture Day parade in Red Square in 1931. The apparently happy, healthy working-class seaside in Russia was joyfully documented by Dziga Vertov in his 1929 film *The Man with a Movie Camera*, which provided inspiration for the GPO filmmakers. Vertov presents a group of energetic swimmers and gymnasts who seem to be the forerunners of the sunbathers and divers in Rotha's film.

At the same time as they were granted more free time, the ever-expanding train network enabled London workers to reach the seaside at Brighton or Southend in a day. *The Way to the Sea* documents the improvement in the train line between London and Portsmouth, showing that between 1935 and 1937 the entire line was electrified. It is this electrification that is celebrated in Auden's poem. At the opening the train drivers linger, 'Waiting for Power', and the crowds are only able 'to escape' their cares because they are powered by electricity.

The crowds at the seaside prompted anxiety about mass culture that had its roots in the nineteenth century. Friedrich Nietzsche announced in Germany that 'a declaration of war on the masses by higher men is needed' and his ideas quickly migrated into Britain where W.B. Yeats recommended the German philosopher as 'a counteractive to the spread of democratic vulgarity'.[5] Raymond Williams writes that the word 'masses' as it emerged in the early twentieth century was a new word for 'mob', which came to be used interchangeably to describe the separate mobs in industrial towns and factories, as well as the newly developing self-organised working class. In Germany in the late 1930s, Walter Benjamin contrasted this new class of empowered workers – the 'newly created proletarian masses' – with the nineteenth-century working classes.[6] For Benjamin, the German working class had been 'corrupted' by the notion that it was moving with the current, but the 'masses' were the hopeful inheritors of a decaying civilisation, whose mass-produced art could provide a redemptive political force.[7]

Although the scornful hostility John Carey has described as characterising the intellectual attitude towards the working classes in 1920s Britain was no longer pervasive in the 1930s, British writers were often warier than Benjamin in embracing the mob.[8] Even the new band of left-leaning writers was fearful and dismissive of the working classes as soon as they saw them metamorphosing into the masses. In the late 1930s, as fear of fascism intensified, many British writers worried that the mass identity of the working classes would make them gullible victims of totalitarian regimes. In her postwar novel *The Heat of the Day* (1949), Elizabeth Bowen presents the working-class Louie as eagerly believing everything the papers choose to tell her about wartime Britain and suggests that if this is the intellectual position of the masses, democracy has dubious value. The artist describing the popular seaside resort had to confront the workers at play as a mass phenomenon.

Glittering Trash: Artistic Depictions of Blackpool

If British intellectuals were ever going to come to terms with the masses, the seaside was a good place to start. The seaside mob had the advantage of being on holiday and was more relaxed and less threatening than the crowd in the town and factory. *The Way to the Sea* and *Hindle Wakes* both present the seaside crowd as congenial company. In Rotha's film, the camera focuses first on a series of individual families playing and laughing, before drawing back to show a faceless mass of holidaymakers. The way to the sea leads to liberty; the seaside is a charmed and dreamy land where even the lonely can '[dare] to look for an amazing romance'. Here and only here can people 'eat out of doors', 'exchange confidences with strangers' or just 'be' and not 'think at all'. Auden exhorts the audience to

> Be extravagant,
> Be lucky,
> Be clairvoyant,
> Be amazing,
> Be a sport or an angel,
> Imagine yourself as a courtier, or as a queen.
> Accept your freedom

and with each line of verse Holmes flashes an image of seaside freedom and happiness onto the screen in a montage of good-natured play. Bathing costumes flutter airily on a washing line, puppets wave their enormous monkey-like heads surreally in the air and a girl dresses up triumphantly as a queen. The image of the teenage girl, regally facing the camera, illustrates the lure of the popular seaside resort in 1930s Britain. She is a garish queen and does not fool anyone for a second, but in her ecstatic smile she demonstrates that by revelling in the excesses of the seaside she has accepted its freedom.

With its pleasure domes and Illuminations, it was Blackpool that typified the 1930s seaside, and *Hindle Wakes* is a more triumphantly joyous celebration of the 'ecstasy of freedom' possible beside the sea. In adapting Stanley Houghton's successful 1912 play for the screen, Maurice Elvey brought together all the techniques of avant-garde cinema to celebrate the popular coastal resort. The original play told the tale of the heroine Fanny's return from Blackpool, where she had spent a week in sin with the factory owner's son Allan. Fanny had shocked the Edwardian audience by refusing to marry Allan, even though she would regain social respectability through the marriage. Instead, she insisted that women too were entitled to a bit of fun – that Allan was her 'fancy' just as she was his. Elvey's version provides the back story that was impossible to show on stage, opening in the Lancashire town of Hindle before the annual 'wakes week' holiday and portraying the mass exodus to Blackpool and then the seaside holiday itself. He reinforces the message of the original play by endorsing the licentiousness of Blackpool. Fanny and Allan's encounters on the rollercoaster, the dance floor and the promenade are seen as romantic rather than seedy, and Blackpool is portrayed as a land of dream-like happiness and possibilities.

By opening at Hindle, Elvey is able to contrast the routine of the factory with the freedom of the seaside. We see Fanny and her friend Mary at work on the morning the holiday begins and see a montage of abstract, monotonous factory work as cotton reels are produced and set to work. The contrast between the two settings is highlighted by the synecdochic calves that punctuate the film. As the girls stream excitedly out of the factory, the camera focuses on a row of quickly moving calves, which we see freeing themselves of work shoes and easing into the heeled shoes of leisure. Later in Blackpool there is a close-up of the same calves and shoes dancing rhythmically on the dance floor, which reminds us of the distance they have come from the work shoes and the factory. The leg imagery is reinforced by another close-up of the carefully choreographed calves of the Blackpool chorus girls (see Figure 2).

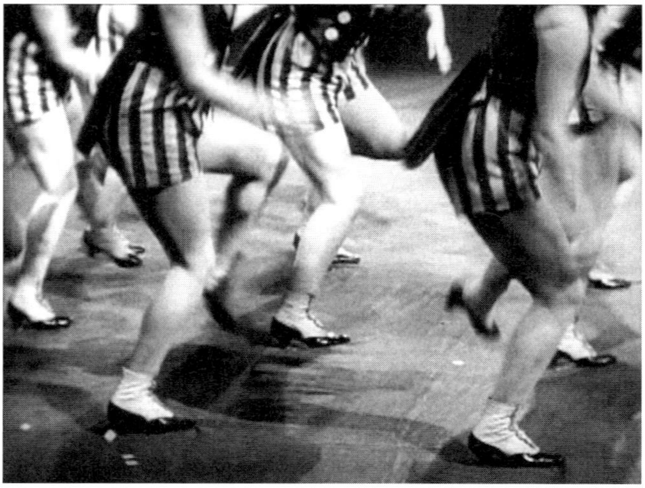

Figure 2
Working calves; Dancing calves; The chorus girls

The calves that run gleefully from the factory are joined by other signs of the mass movement of the crowd in a film that enthusiastically endorses the mass behaviour of the Hindle workers. As calf after calf leaves the factory, hand after hand cashes in pay-cheques so that they have enough money to spend at the seaside. The seaside mob in Elvey's film is never frightening and rarely de-individualising. We can always make out Fanny and Mary amongst the other holidaymakers. The biggest crowd is the one on the dance floor, where Fanny and Allan gaze longingly into each other's eyes. Elvey slows down and darkens the film so that each shot looks like a painting, and the roving dance lights seem like rose petals, floating over the dancers. The mass of people, collectively swooning, seems to add their collective pleasure to the dreamy and romantic quality of Fanny's own experience (see Figure 3).

Tom Gunning has described early silent cinema as an exhibitionist 'cinema of attractions' that openly solicits the attention of the spectator by 'supplying pleasure through an exciting spectacle'.[9] Elvey offers the viewer something akin to the experience of actually being in Blackpool. This is most evident in the extended sequence on the rollercoaster. Most of the time the camera is positioned with Fanny and Allan so that the audience rises and plummets with them, faced at one minute with the ground rising towards us, at the next with the sky. At strategic points Elvey reverses the camera so that we see the couple, giggling or leaning towards each other, and seem to have our own reactions mirrored or elicited by theirs. When the couple goes to look at the Blackpool Illuminations the audience is given its own spectacle. The black screen is lit up by lights and the camera passes along the display, so that a brightly dotted boat seems to move across the screen (see Figure 4). Blackpool is as appealing

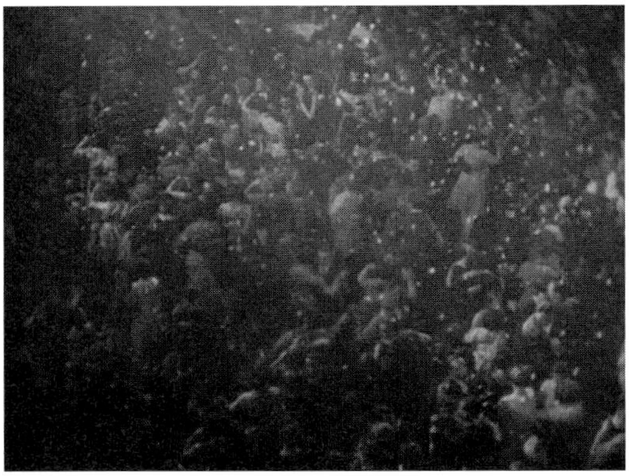

Figure 3 Collective swooning on the dance floor

for the audience as it is for Fanny, and we too are seduced into an acceptance of Allan's caresses and of the glitter of the seaside.

Blackpool comes in for a less favourable treatment from J.B. Priestley in his 1934 account of his travels, *English Journey.* In the 1930s, Blackpool was the most overabundant and the most crowded of seaside resorts, and therefore the most prone to the charge of vulgarity. Priestley divides British seaside resorts into two types, the picturesque and the vulgar, and splits the holidaymakers along the same lines. He visits Blackpool and finds that it is graced with only one sort of holidaymaker, whom he describes as 'passive' and 'listless' and lacking intelligence or enterprise.[10] These are the working classes who follow their neighbours to the most obvious destination, seeking the same polluted crush on holiday that they leave behind at home. In the planned, book-long version of the reports, edited by Tom Harrisson, Mass-Observation found that the majority of 'Worktowners' chose to go to Blackpool because they went 'to the places where the crowds are, where the rhythm is as fast and the noise almost as great as that of the mill'.[11]

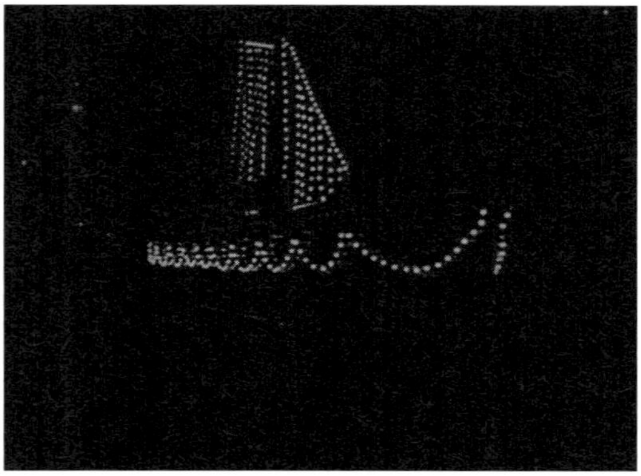

Figure 4
The Blackpool Illuminations

Priestley portrays the other section of working-class holidaymakers as more original and more demanding: 'it does not care for mass entertainment and prefers to spend its leisure in quieter places, cycling and walking and playing games in the sun.'[12] This group is prevalent throughout 1930s literature and the more intelligent and enterprising worker is often presented as a refined form of noble savage, more in touch with the beauty of the nature he visits than his upper-class counterparts. In *Major Operation* (1936) the communist Scottish writer James Barke portrays his upper-class hero George Anderson as gaining peace and solace from his hikes in the country with his former secretary, Sophie: 'My God, Sophie! I never believed I could know such happiness.'[13] Similarly, in *Love on the Dole* Walter Greenwood demonstrates the nobility of the socialist Larry Meath by making him as committed to hiking as to socialism.

For Priestley, and three years later for Mass-Observation, the failure of the Blackpool holidaymakers is partly a failure to enjoy the sea itself: they go to the seaside only for the 'side'. The middle-class Mass-Observers were disparaging about the lack of interest in the actual water evinced by many of the holidaymakers at Blackpool. They noted that not one of the twenty visitors they followed from the railway station went straight to the sea and found that only twenty-eight out of sixty holidaymakers surveyed were even favourable to the idea of the sea.[14] They complained that although 'the sea gave Blackpool its start in life' its position was 'seldom acknowledged on its posters nowadays'.[15] With disingenuous humility, the middle-class observers contrasted themselves with the Worktowners, who grew bored with looking at the sea after two minutes: 'we, who go in for the obvious, step out of the door and look to the west, to the sea, which phrases the seaside.'[16]

The Mass-Observers were worried by the crowds at Blackpool. When they were not timing the length of kisses or attempting to blend in on the dance floor, the Mass-Observers were counting the sheer numbers of people at the resort. On a fine day in September they found ten thousand people on the sand. On bank holidays they estimated forty thousand (see Figure 5). They were bothered by these numbers, and by the reported seven million people who came to Blackpool each year; the working classes in Blackpool were clearly 'the masses'. 'No other place in England can show a comparable scene,' said Tom Harrisson. And he found it all the more disturbing that the crowds were an attraction rather than a deterrent for potential visitors. Blackpool even used its 'crush photos for publicity'.[17] Observers found that the crowd was less friendly and less joyful than it should be. Apart from in the 'Social Mixer', where strangers were hurled together in a frenetic ride as they struggled to stay on a spinning circular disc, people tended to stay in their original groups. The 'middle-class observers' were surprised by 'how little laughter there was in Blackpool crowds'. One watched a strip of pavement in the main amusement zone for fifteen minutes without recording a single

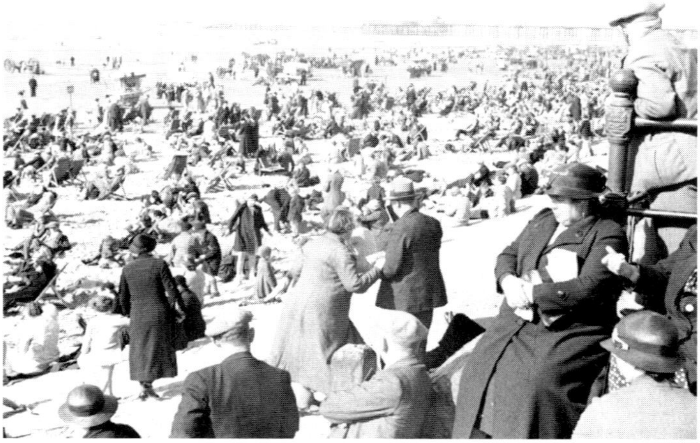

Figure 5 Humphrey Spender's Mass-Observation photograph of the crowds on the sands

laugh. Holidaymakers were 'too engrossed in pennies, resting, reading, gazing, and gaping' to have time to enjoy themselves spontaneously.[18]

The tone of these particular reports is unusually harsh. Other observers describe strangers meeting easily on the Blackpool dance floor and telling bawdy stories with much hilarity (though not on the observers' own part). Perhaps Harrisson disapproved of the Blackpool crowds because, in their contented acceptance of their mass identity, they went against the whole ethos of Mass-Observation, which was to restore individuality to the masses. Stuart Laing has written that 'Mass Observation's concern was with collective experience and behaviour as observed by and within *individuals*'; the word 'mass' in their name did not imply an acceptance of the homogeneity and passivity of a manipulated majority.[19]

The mass activities that Harrisson and Madge did endorse were quirky and spontaneous pursuits like the Lambeth Walk. In their 1939 book *Britain* they see this Cockney dance as uniting the community in a manner far superior to any upper-class pursuit, and even as a possible source of resistance to fascism. They report that a group of anti-fascists broke up a Mosleyite demonstration in the East End by 'doing the Lambeth Walk'.[20] They compare the cockney cavorting favourably with the ballroom dancing of the upper classes on the grounds that:

> ballroom dancers sleep walk to [the music's] strains with the same surrender of personal decision as that of uniformed Nazis. These Lambeth Walkers are happy because they find they are free to express *themselves* without the hypnosis of a jazz-moon or a Führer.[21]

The authors imply that if people could keep dancing the Lambeth Walk, it might challenge the uniformity of the fascist goose-step.

The masses at Blackpool were rejecting the potential offered by their weekly holiday to be individuals. They were sleepwalking to dance music in the ballrooms and surrendering their power to make personal decisions by blindly following the crowd. The observers were therefore disappointed by the mass behaviour they witnessed at the seaside, both in its homogeneity and its gullibility. Long sections of the planned book are devoted to the popularity of witch doctors and fortune tellers. Blackpool even boasted a cheap 'telepathic robot'. For a penny, Worktowners could learn their destiny from a machine and, Mass-Observation tut-tutted, the fact that they relinquished their hard-earned pennies so easily suggested that they took the robot more seriously than they should do (see Figure 6).[22] For the Mass-Observers, the behaviour of the Blackpool masses made them a manipulative, credulous bunch. If they were this easily seduced by the Blackpool publicity and attractions, how would they resist the empty promises of their government or the indoctrination of a conquering power?

But for the writer or filmmaker, the lure of Blackpool was partly an artistic one. It was fun to represent just the cheap thrills that Mass-Observation condemned. Even Priestley seems to have succumbed to something akin to a 'literature of attractions' in his account of Blackpool. The energy of his prose belies his contempt as he describes the 'huge mad place, with its miles and miles of promenades [...] its switch-backs and helter-skelters, its array of wine bars and oyster saloons and cheap restaurants and tea houses and shops piled high and glittering with trash'.[23] And for the black-and-white filmmaker, the attraction of Blackpool was more obvious. At the end of their illicit holiday in *Hindle Wakes*, Fanny and Allan are filmed at just the sort of picturesque and rugged seaside that Priestley was keen on, and though the resulting image may be quietly beautiful, it has nothing like the allure of the earlier Blackpool scenes.

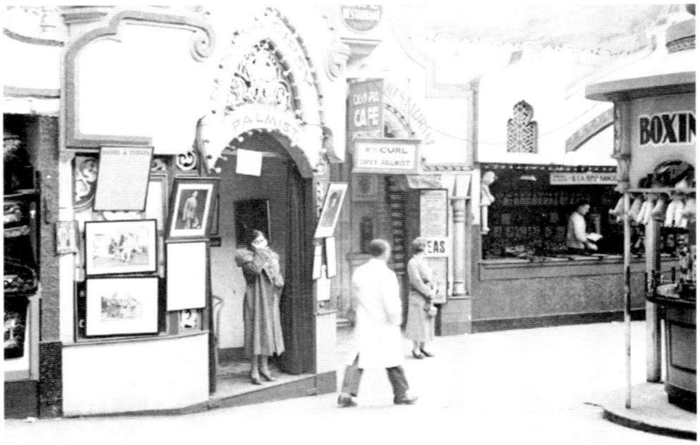

Figure 6
Cheap thrills for the credulous

Perhaps Walter Greenwood had *Hindle Wakes* in mind when he decided to transport his own lovers from a quiet seaside village to Blackpool when he helped adapt his novel *Love on the Dole* for the screen. In the 1933 book, Harry and Helen follow the advice of the hiking socialist Larry Meath in escaping to a remote seaside village, which Larry describes as a wholesome, isolated place with a 'rugged coast line' and 'glorious country walks'.[24] On arrival, Harry and Helen are struck above all by its purity, and they relish the chance to examine nature, carefully and slowly, in all its beauty. For the first time they can observe the day-to-day workings of their world. Caught in a rain shower they are 'fascinated by its quick evaporation' (p. 121). As a self-proclaimed working-class novelist, Greenwood was inclined to idealise his holidaymaking protagonists, and Harry and Helen prove their credentials as the better sort of visitor by enjoying the sea itself as much as its side – itself a rugged coastline rather than a resort. Looking at the sea and perceiving the 'purple patches' and the 'long weeds waving in the currents', Harry has 'a glimmer of the significance of the word "beautiful"' (p. 122).

But Greenwood realised that the sight of two lovers watching a rain shower would be less enticing for the viewer than the glittering Blackpool lights, and so the 1941 film saw Harry and Helen excitedly setting off for Blackpool, where they and the viewer are greeted with the jaunty music of the popular seaside and the sight of that metonym of pleasure, the Blackpool tower (see Figure 7). Director John Baxter treats the viewers to a typical seaside montage; images of people playing on the beach are dissolved onto fairground rides. In the tradition of *Hindle Wakes*, shots of Harry and Helen on the rollercoaster (see Figure 8) are cross-cut with dizzying views of the tracks, and we then see them dancing in a crowded ballroom and gazing at the Blackpool Illuminations. In the novel, they looked around the village and wondered if they could ever live there, considering whether it would be possible to buy a cottage and for Harry to earn his living as a fisherman. In the film they have the same conversation on the Blackpool promenade, and it strikes rather a false note in a resort where there are fewer cottages than hotels, fewer fishermen than fortune tellers. Greenwood sacrificed the original message of the seaside holiday to allow the filmmakers to dazzle the audience with a visual display of pleasure.

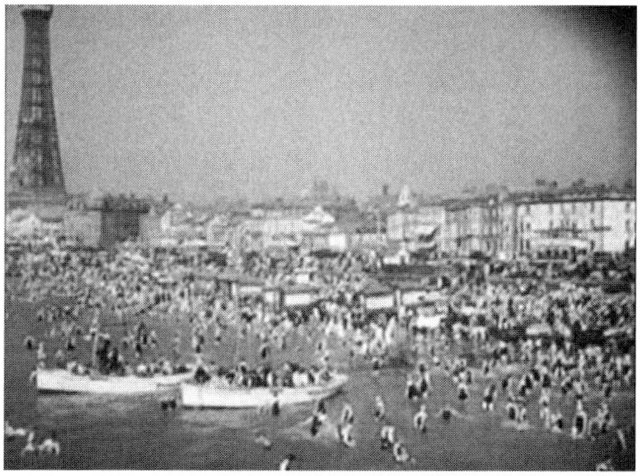

Figure 7
The arrival in Blackpool

Guinness, Oysters and Song: Graham Greene's Brighton

Graham Greene wrote in 1980 that 'no city before the war, not London or Oxford, had such a hold on my affection' as Brighton.[25] Unlike Hale, the doomed hero of the opening section of *Brighton Rock*, and unlike Pinkie, its Catholic anti-hero, Greene was neither frightened nor appalled by the delights of 'London-by-the-Sea'. The lively resort provided him with a suitably garish background for his potent moral fable of Catholic damnation but also provided him with the colour and texture of what is insistently a pleasurable book. To ignore the pleasure of the excess is to misread Greene.

Since its publication in 1938, *Brighton Rock* has been read (both approvingly and disapprovingly) as a moral fable. George Orwell complained in

1948 that Greene had presented Hell as 'a sort of high-class night club, entry to which is reserved for Catholics only' and forty years later John Carey echoed Orwell's sentiments, bemoaning that Greene had constructed his novel 'around the idea that by comparison with Catholics ordinary mass mankind does not truly exist at all'.[26] These readings rely on accepting Pinkie's point of view as the point of view of the novel. He is the saint who, as in Greene's description of the eccentric Catholic man of letters Baron Corvo, 'if he could not have Heaven [...] would have Hell'.[27] In Carey's view, his 'good and evil' is set against Ida's middle-class 'right and wrong'; his horror of the crowds and of the sexual licentiousness of Brighton is Greene's own horror. Indeed the crowds are so dangerous that the policeman suggests to Ida that they caused Hale's bruising, by pushing him 'here and there'.[28]

But in fact it was the crowds that protected Hale, as long as they could, and that protect Ida, Pinkie's joyful, big-breasted nemesis. 'Come off it,' she commands the policeman and then, tellingly, 'Be human.' Brighton, she insists, is 'big enough' to accommodate its crowds without bruising them. She has the humanity that Pinkie lacks – he in whom 'human feeling [...] died' long ago (p. 6). And every description of Brighton as a seaside resort is inflected at once through Pinkie's horror and through Ida's pleasure, a pleasure that is endorsed by Greene's writerly delight in describing it. The panning shot of Brighton on the day of the races provides a good example of this.

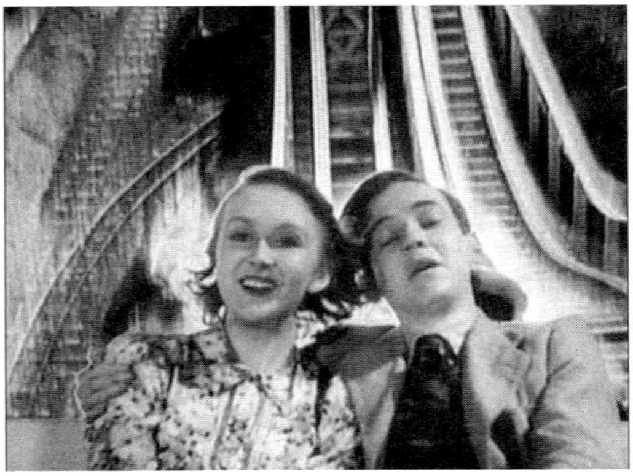

Figure 8
Harry and Helen whirl on the rollercoaster

The scene begins from an omniscient, bird's-eye point of view. The narrator observes the crowds 'surg[ing] like some natural and irrational migration of insects up and down the front', with the 'irrational' making the insects comic rather than frightening (p. 107). The humour continues as the narrative camera focuses on a 'negro', who calls out 'hilariously' to a group of children and who lends the scene colour with his 'bright striped tie', his dark skin setting off his 'great teeth' which '[gleam] like an advertisement' (p. 107). The simile is overloaded; teeth do not resemble advertisements, though they may feature in them, and rather than describing the teeth it seems to juxtapose them with a separate, gleaming advertisement, or even to turn the scene itself into a colourful seaside poster. The overwrought imagery continues throughout the scene. The crowd of taxicabs and old Morrises strains up the hill to the racecourse 'as if the whole road moved upwards like an Underground staircase in the dusty sunlight'; the junior Roedean girls playing hockey below jostle 'like ponies racing on the turf' (p. 108). Cars do not resemble a staircase any more than schoolgirls resemble ponies and the imagery serves to crowd the scene with fantastic detail that blends with the actual recorded details in a lurid montage.

Into this heady scene Greene introduces two set pieces. The first is a brass band that comes up the pavement through Old Steyne, mingling its joyful noise with the 'rumble of the crowd'. This could have been the band that parades round Portsmouth in *The Way to the Sea* but Greene renders it strange and disturbing; the musicians are blind and must walk in the gutter, 'feeling the kerb with the edge of their shoes'. The onlooker who raises his eyes in expectation of twirling drumsticks is faced with 'pale blind eyes, like those of pit ponies' (p. 107). The second is a scarlet racing car that carries about it the atmosphere of 'furtive encounters in by-lanes off the Great North Road', winks with the glow of the sun, and is crammed tight with a woman, sat on a man's knee, whose singing merges with the hooting of the car and the trumpeting of the band. The woman's song is Ida's leitmotif, a song about 'brides and bouquets', which goes with 'Guinness and oysters and the old Leicester Lounge' (p. 108). Although she is not named and her identity in this scene is confirmed only much later, she is identified operatically by the familiar seaside motifs.

In the next paragraph we become aware of the presence of Pinkie, observing the scene. The reference to weddings makes him think of Rose with 'sullen disgust' and as the point of view shifts we revisit the seaside pageant from his angle. But Pinkie's revulsion cannot undo the enjoyment of a scene that is addressed foremost to the reader. The narrator invites us to dwell on the attractions of the seaside, even addressing us in the second person – 'You heard the music a long way off' – eliding us with the onlookers. This is Greene's Brighton and ours, and Pinkie, introduced at the end of the scene, remains an outsider from its joy and from the narrative point of view.

Of course Ida's boisterously vivacious point of view is no less limited than Pinkie's. The narrative voice at its more authoritarianly Catholic looks down on her socially and morally. She belongs to the great 'middle law-abiding class' who obey the laws of England but transgress the laws of God. She is obsessed with fighting wrongs such as murder that contravene the law but she is happy to have a one-night stand without '[telling] tales to your wife' and in fact though she shares the 'amusements' and 'superstitions' (the salt over the shoulder) of her class, 'she [has] no more love for anyone than they had' (p. 84). Through Ida, Greene condemns the easy morality of a class who choose superstition and right and wrong over religion and the truer values of good and evil. But Ida's world remains joyful, and intersects with the narrator's own joyful vision of the seaside. She arrives at her hotel to find the sun shining and the passage outside her room 'gritty with sand'. While she is with him she is capable of saving Hale from death simply through her maternal yet carnal presence.

Ida is part of the seaside setting that powers the novel and makes it pleasurable. The narrow asceticism of Pinkie's world is made most vivid when he collides with the gaudy seaside that surrounds him. Hale is murdered with Brighton Rock; Pinkie and Rose spend their desultory wedding night on the pier, and it is because Rose persuades him to indulge in one of the cheap tourist gimmicks that he records the message of hate that provides the dark ending of the book. And at the same time, the reader is periodically removed from Pinkie's world and set free to stroll around Brighton in a book that was labelled as an 'entertainment' in its original American edition and only reclassified as a 'novel' on the eve of its publication in Britain. Entertainment or novel, it is a work that artistically endorses the seaside, gaily and energetically, and that creates a literature of attractions to rival the cinema of attractions in *Hindle Wakes*.

Rationing and Austerity: The Reining-in of Excess

The literature and cinema of attractions that had developed in 1930s depictions of the popular seaside were to be abruptly cut short by the onset of the Second World War. As fear of a precarious future took hold, and rationing and patriotism set the British on the course of wartime austerity, the hedonism of the seaside started to seem irresponsible. For strategic reasons much of the coast became inaccessible to the public in any case. It was now the sea and not its side that graced the cinema screens, as the GPO, rechristened the Crown Film Unit, produced film after film that opened with bleak images of the British coastline, defiantly asserting the nation's island status as its defence against the enemies across the Channel.

The new attitude towards the seaside is manifested clearly in Randall Swingler's wartime poem, 'August Bank Holiday, 1939', where the poet's invitation to 'sleep in the sun, forget, dream, pretend' and 'forget the weeks of worry and fret' is cross-cut with the insistent capitalised refrain 'BUT IF – '. Swingler suggests that it is impossible to forget contemporary events, personified by a 'man down there on the beach / Waving his arms and making a speech'; even the roundabout siren 'hoots like a cry of despair' that also evokes the inevitable hooting of the bombs.[29]

The scenes in Brighton in Patrick Hamilton's *Hangover Square* take place in the summer of 1939, only a little later than the action of *Brighton Rock*. But Hamilton's novel was published in 1941 and with wartime hindsight he condemns Brighton without allowing the intrusion of any of the joy of Greene's novel. Like Pinkie, George Harvey Bone, the weak and pernickety hero of *Hangover Square*, is repelled by the crowds and by the sexual licentiousness of Brighton. On arrival he is greeted by a 'huge outing of violent girls' (down for a day in 'London-by-the-Sea') who look at him 'boldly, nastily' and occupy every pub and street.[30] As an upper-middle-class tourist, possessed of a private income, Bone looks down on the girls and looks out to the sea. He walks along the glistening front and watches the sea 'rising and pounding against the beach in the freshening breeze' (p. 143). He is redeemed by the seaside air, enjoying his golf and constructing visions of an idyllic future. The idyll fades when he returns to the station to greet Netta, his contemptuous beloved, and is frightened by the mass of people and the 'rolling, echoing noise' (p. 149).

In his new, alienating surroundings, it seems appropriate that when Netta does arrive she is accompanied by two other men and all three are aggressively drunk. This seems symptomatic of the degraded morals of the city and it is fitting that he is eventually forced to listen to her having sex with another man through the thin walls of their one-night cheap hotel.

At the end of *Hangover Square*, war is announced, and dimly impinges on Bone's increasingly deranged consciousness. In abruptly introducing the war, Hamilton seems to be saying an anxious 'I told you so' to hedonists like Netta and her lover Peter, who ignored the threat of international conflict, with Peter espousing Hitler's views and even sporting a neat moustache. He later wrote that he was trying to present 'a "black" social history of my times. There were so many "white" portraits of the Twenties and Thirties that I wanted to show the other side of the picture.'[31] In Bone's eyes, Brighton starts to take on the same moral degradation as Hitler's Germany and when war does come it seems the inevitable consequence of the moral carelessness at home.

The declaration of war in September 1939 saw the end both of the popular seaside holiday and the art of excess that celebrated it. Nonetheless, while it lasted, the interwar seaside had spawned a group of novels and films that introduced a defiant note of pleasure to the 1930s literary scene, allowing the workers to lay down their tools – and their chroniclers to set aside their social consciences. Liberated by the pleasure beach and the rollercoaster, these writers and filmmakers created a cinema and literature of attractions that were as exuberant as the 1930s seaside itself.

Michael Bracewell

Michael Bracewell is the author of six novels and three works of non-fiction, including most recently, *Re-make / Re-model: Art, Pop, Fashion and the Making of Roxy Music, 1953–1972*. He has written catalogue essays for many contemporary artists, including Glenn Brown, Sam Taylor-Wood and Gilbert & George, and his writing has been anthologised in *The Faber Book of Pop* and *The Penguin Book of Twentieth-Century Fashion Writing*. He was co-curator of *The Secret Public: The Last Days of the British Underground, 1977–1988* at Kunstverein München and the I.C.A., London (2006/2007), and a Turner Prize judge in 2007. He is a regular contributor to *Frieze* magazine, and is currently researching the life and work of the artist and musician Stuart Sutcliffe.

Morecambe

The Sunset Coast

'Everything here is equally modern.'

—from a postcard written by a guest
at Morecambe's LMS Midland Hotel, 1943

A GRASSY EMBANKMENT flanks the length of the broad promenade between Heysham village and Morecambe – a remote, struggling resort on the northernmost coast of Lancashire, in the northwest of England. Crossed with an undulating maze of narrow paths, the steep escarpment falls away from a walled parade of neat suburban villas. Up until just a few years ago, the grass on the bank was long and unkempt, and along the promenade – with its spectacular view across Morecambe Bay towards Arnside and the Cumbrian hills – the old, ornate iron balustrade has been patched together with sheets of wire meshing.

Postcards from the 1920s and 1930s, however, show a very different scene. All those years ago, the grassy bank and its maze of little paths were a popular seaside attraction in their own right. They were called 'Sunny Slopes', with benches, gardens and a boating pond. At the Morecambe end stood the imposing bulk of the Grosvenor Hotel, a rust-coloured edifice of late Victorian (1898) *haute bourgeois* architecture. With the vast bay windows of its salons and breakfast room – crimson-papered, palm-lined, with heavily framed photographs of the King – overlooking the sea, the Grosvenor represented the last summer of nineteenth-century English imperialism.

With their decaying confections of fantastical architecture (rotting art deco, the dance-hall glitterball and the ornamental balustrade), English seaside towns have become like a melancholy but intoxicating Venice of the national vernacular. With faded grandeur abutting seafront dereliction, accompanied by the atonal electronics of unplayed arcade games, these are the places where popular culture, from Victorian gaiety to the accelerated fantasies of pop consumerism, have played out their imperial phases for much of the last one hundred years. They make eloquent a mass of contradictions, and in their every detail you can glimpse an earlier age – the more so in those run-down resorts which bespeak Graham Greene's pronouncement that 'Seediness has a very deep appeal [...] It seems to satisfy, temporarily, the sense of nostalgia for something lost; it seems to represent a stage further back.'[1]

Morecambe is, above all, a richly romantic location: against the backdrop of its legendary sunsets, the place is an accumulation of fantastical glamour. It is the ceremonial portal to the Lake District, so celebrated by Victorian cults of the sublime in nature; it is a playground for holidaymakers, dizzy with shows and amusements and distraction; and it is one of the first exuberant sites of modern popular culture – of pop groups and beauty queens, television stars and gauzy, gawdy souvenirs (a Tommy Steele charm bracelet; cuff links in the shape of electric guitars; George Formby presented with a ukelele made out of flowers by the mayor, for all the world like some surrealist sculpture).

To a particular kind of cultural tourist, the seaside towns of England have always articulated an extreme form of romanticism, first in a literary idiom which would then be updated by pop. From T.S. Eliot's apostatical reference to Margate Sands, through Paul Nash's essay on 'Seaside Surrealism' to the 'sopping esplanade' from which W.H. Auden predicted England's decline, the seers of British modernism set out a particular – and enduring – relationship with the ritual landscape of the English coastal holiday.[2] In the protracted twilight of Edwardian gentility, what they found there was the quality Frank Kermode once described as 'the sense of an ending'.[3]

Morecambe's Grosvenor Hotel was demolished in 2002, despite attempts to have the building preserved. But still, when you walk this promenade today, recreating in your imagination how it would have appeared a century ago, the defining sense is that of formality and grandeur, of a rigid code, informing every aspect of the scene. This would have been a social landscape, above all, richly eloquent of the minute gradations of the English class system. And thus hotel, promenade and boating pool would all have held their place within the broader pattern of the seaside resort.

Two great piers (one swept out to sea in a storm, the other burned down) were the focal point of Morecambe proper, with the Winter Gardens and the Alhambra theatre completing the grid of their exuberance. Then the high terrace of smaller, 'family' hotels for the less well off, and the oyster restaurants, and the tearooms. And lastly, at the promenade's furthest end – the coast road heading off around the bay towards Carnforth and the Lake District – you would find the ceremonial landscaping of Happy Mount Park, with its 'Japanese garden' and its beds of bright flowers, and its sun-facing benches 'reserved for the blind'.

Such pronounced romanticism is fundamental to the cultural identity of the English seaside and has been since the British modernists of the inter-war years looked back on the ruins of an older order. As described by John Betjeman – the architectural historian and great poet of English suburbia and provincialism – writing about Margate during the Second World War, the seaside landscape had become eloquent of an earlier epoch: of an innocence and order remembered, in the face of uncertainty and fear. Thus the principal imagery of his poem 'Margate, 1940' is that of sunlight, dusk and darkness:

> As soft over Cliftonville, languished the light
> Down Harold Road, Norfolk Road, into the night.[4]

The remembered Margate is bathed in the soft dusk tones at the end of a summer's day, to which is compared the town during wartime, where the terrace is now 'dark', and the poet's memories are of 'fairy-lit sights'.[5] In terms of a psychological imprint, it is as though the seaside towns have absorbed generations of summer days, and now acknowledge that accumulated history with a kind of autumnal melancholy.

The English resorts took their place throughout the greater part of the twentieth century as articulations of pleasure and repose, health and holidays. When the Miss Great Britain bathing beauty competition began in 1945, Morecambe was poised to resume its role, subsequent to the Second World War, as one of the most popular and up-to-date of British seaside resorts. Since Victorian times, the town had been known for the rich romance of its spectacular sunsets and dramatic views across Morecambe Bay towards the Cumbrian hills. At the turn of the last century, the resort was billed as 'the Naples of the North', and the elegant curve of its promenade boasted grand terraces of five-storey houses, extravagant Winter Gardens, and the marble-staircased Alhambra dance hall. In the 1920s, the town enjoyed renewed fame as the home for the audaciously modern LMS Midland Hotel (see Figure 9), designed in the height of the art deco style by Oliver Hill, and opened amidst great fanfare in 1933.

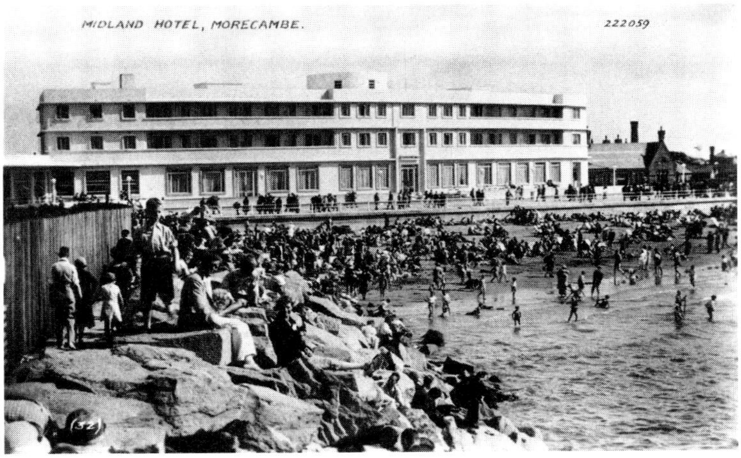

Figure 9
The iconic Midland Hotel at Morecambe

Unsurprisingly, at the turn of the twentieth century, Morecambe prospered as a popular holiday resort. Postcards show parades and lights and novelties – including the somewhat formal cutting of the biggest Christmas pudding in the British Empire. And a Midland Hotel had existed since 1848 – grey, Georgian in style, utterly respectable. This was replaced in the most spectacular fashion, however, by a new hotel commissioned by the London, Midland and Scottish Railway Company in 1931, to be designed by the smart young architect Oliver Hill, whose interest in buildings was holistic and multi-allusive. The most important word in the (continuing) history of Oliver Hill's Midland Hotel is singularly and emphatically 'modern'. The Midland Hotel is one of the great statements, internationally, about the nature of both modernism (a pan-cultural movement across the arts, from verse to ceramics) and modernity – as an attitude to living and lifestyle.

A century earlier, Turner and Ruskin had made artistic responses to the high romanticism of this coastal gateway to the Cumbrian hills and lakes; and so in 1932, Oliver Hill and the artists and designers with whom he worked to make the environment of the Midland a total modern experience, were likewise evolving a new conception of Morecambe's stunning location. Hill and his colleagues were engaging not with the sublime but with a cult of youth and coastal ozone, chic and gloss and acceleration. Theirs was a world of cocktails, dark glasses, high dives and dinner suits, new fashions for sunbathing and callisthenics imported from the South of France. The Midland Hotel was a temple to all of these new ideals for living.

The railway company had requested of Hill 'A building of international quality in the modern style' and Hill himself wrote that 'you have here a unique opportunity of building the first really modern hotel in the country'. Later, a guest staying at the hotel would remark that 'everything here is equally modern'. Within the hotel, all the equipment of living – from chairs to bathplugs to carpets – was designed as modern art. With its famous carved reliefs by Eric Gill and Eric Ravilious, furnishings by Duncan Grant and rugs by Marion Dorn, this was a hotel as a statement of modern aesthetics, a sun-drenched cult of newness on the northwest coast, in which the latest in fabrics, materials, design and colour was brilliantly conflated with modernist ideals in art and craft. Its surface treated with crushed blue glass, the underside of the windows glazed green, the outside of the hotel was electrically polished – a modern mirror for the ageless sunsets.

During the 1930s, the Midland Hotel was famously proclaimed to be 'an extravagant gesture of hope at a time of great Depression'. And in many ways this uplifting, muscular phrase has proved prophetic of the hotel's triumphant survival: reinvented for new generations in its relaunch of 2008, the 'first really modern hotel in the country' has been rekindled as a beacon of slick, exuberant and coolly romantic modernity.

The seaside architecture, amenities and gardens were built to suggest a fantastical, exotic environment – dedicated to a carnival by the sea (however chilly) and to a world distinct from the daily routine of work and family.

From the aristocratic mansions of Brighton, to the gentility of Broadstairs or Worthing, to the working-class exuberance of Blackpool, the seaside resorts of England were concerned with both social codes and displays of exotica. In Blackpool's Tower Ballroom, for example, with its extravagant rococo interior, a fantasy of the Neapolitan Riviera is painted on the backdrop of the stage, while a line from Shakespeare's 'Venus and Adonis', running across the proscenium arch, completes the sense of romance: 'Bid me discourse, I will enchant thine ear.'

In the historically 'working-class' northern English resorts such as Blackpool or Southport, the extravagance of the architecture is, if anything, more pronounced than in regal Brighton or genteel Weston-super-Mare. In Blackpool, where the mill and factory workers of Lancashire, Yorkshire, Glasgow and the Midlands would take their yearly holidays (thus leaving their home towns more or less deserted, as the work places closed down for a week), the circus at the Blackpool Tower was advertised at its opening in 1894 as 'a palace of pleasure in itself'. Similarly, the gaudy and often brash (tasteless, even) amusements along Blackpool's promenade earned its frontage the title 'The Golden Mile'. To this day, the holiday season ends each year with the famous Illuminations – six miles of electric light displays, running almost from St Anne's to Fleetwood.

As with Nigel Henderson's photographs of London's East End in the 1940s, Alfred Gregory's intoxicating photographs of Blackpool in the 1960s seem to enter the very consciousness of their subject. In terms of a broader cultural history, Gregory's images describe the impact of mass media and mass consumerism on the English seaside town: how the first generations of the pop age enjoyed (or endured) a heady conflation of traditional amusements (the piers, donkey rides, ice creams, side shows) and the new populism of rock and roll, television variety shows and burgeoning permissiveness. Seen now, of course, these photographs of girls wearing novelty cowboy hats and boys with quiffs, strolling down wet side streets, past the lurid doorways to strip clubs, fortune tellers and steam-filled cafes, have all the romantic appeal of a lost English glamour – the terrain of a social realist film from the early 1960s, as it might be reclaimed in a song by Morrissey.

A little further south from Heysham village, the coastal flatlands known as Middleton Sands still house the ruins of the old Pontins holiday camp, its ranks of derelict guest chalets grouped around a main building which was designed to resemble, and included original fittings from, an ocean liner. With the slogan 'Cruising on Dry Land', this Pontins camp was typical of its era – the postwar, early pop epoch of British holiday camps, the dawn of bottled colas, teenagers and the Twist.

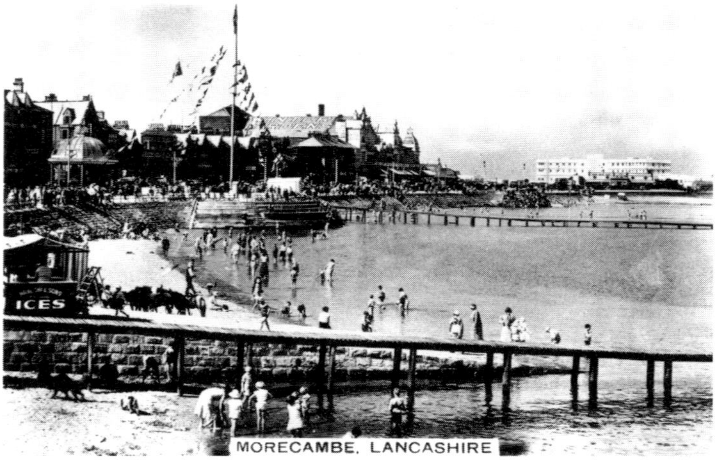

Figure 10
The beach at Morecambe in the 1930s

Visited now, the place has all the bewitching, elegiac charm of any Gothic ruin; the paint is peeling on the dry-docked liner with its scarlet and black funnels, the BMX cycle track is cracked with weeds. What remains is a ghost of the first pop age and the golden years of the coastal holiday camps. Prior to their decline in the face of cheap holidays to Spain, these camps were encoded with an erotic pop glamour of dance crazes, novelty competitions and glittering red guitars, cutting across an England of National Service and meat teas.

This is the landscape which we see in a film such as *The Leather Boys* (1963), on the ill-fated honeymoon of Reg (a biker with his heart in the right place) and Dot, his teenage bride, played by Rita Tushingham. Typical of its genre, *The Leather Boys* now takes its place as a classic example of the British social realist cinema known as 'kitchen sink' dramas, a label reflecting the concentration of such films on primarily working-class, frequently dour and industrial settings. Within these films, Rita Tushingham – best known for her performance as an unmarried teenage mother in *A Taste of Honey* (1961) – comes across as the embodiment of dreamy teenage angst. In *The Leather Boys*, she plays the role of a young woman whose premature marriage has curdled her youth, the decline of her hopes being framed in the setting of a damp seaside resort. Like Sir Laurence Olivier's performance as a fading seaside comedian in the film of John Osborne's misanthropic seaside drama *The Entertainer*, the gradual dereliction of happiness in *The Leather Boys* becomes almost too in love with its own sense of hopelessness. With regard to the identity of the English seaside resorts, however, these films exemplify their relationship to a sense of requiem and elegy.

As the seaside towns developed in step with the history of popular culture, so in their dance halls, winter gardens and ballrooms you can feel pop's ghosts around you – even as the seaside's first duty to commerce will be busy with the latest pop craze. Morrissey's epic hymn to the melancholy of the English seaside, 'Every Day Is Like Sunday', was both a celebration and a lament. David Bowie's appearance as Pierrot, walking down the beach at Hastings in his video for 'Ashes to Ashes' was like a prose poem on the whole abstraction of remembered youth.

When the Rolling Stones played at Morecambe's 'Floral Hall' in the autumn of 1964, the group were just approaching the zenith of their stroppy Mod cool – prior to the beginnings of their acid dandyism. Speaking with local people who went to such concerts – seeing Brian Jones on the promenade, Andrew Loog Oldham on one side looking unapproachable – what emerges is the recollection of Britain's first pop landscape, in which the seaside venues, holiday camps and fun fairs were a vital feature.

As seaside gentility has remained in our consciousness of the English resorts, so too have the slick, vulgar, exuberant and sexy manifestations of pop. It is to this conflation – the imprint of pop's innocence and the faded grandeur of Edwardian formality – that the seaside towns of England owe the potency of their current identities. And it is this that explains their increasing popularity and increasing gentrification, in the south of England, as homes of choice for the formerly urban young middle classes.

In the lobby of the twenty-first century, the state and status of England's coastal towns have become a persuasive statement about larger changes not just in British society, but in our deeper, allegorical, sense of ourselves. More than any other aspect of the English landscape, these seaside towns have come to represent an intense, endlessly renewing contract with nostalgia. It is rather as though their original purpose – for holidays, retirement and convalescence – has been subsumed by the heady way in which they seem to describe their past within their present.

Andrew Kötting

Andrew Kötting studied at Ravensbourne College of Art and Design and the Slade School of Art, London. In 1989, he collaborated with Leila McMillan in setting up BadBLoOd & siBYL studios in the French Pyrenees. In 1996, his first feature film, *Gallivant*, was premiered to great acclaim at the Edinburgh Film Festival, where it won the Channel 4 Best New Director Prize. Subsequently he made *This Filthy Earth* (2001), loosely adapted from Zola's *La Terre*, and *Mapping Perception* (2002), a short science, film and art project. Most recently he took an inflatable effigy of his dead father to the Faroe Islands and to Mexico for the 'Day of the Dead' celebrations, and the resulting *In the Wake of a Deadad* premiered at Dilston Grove in London as a 65-monitor installation; a single screen version of the project was also presented at the Barbican Centre in 2008. His work has been shown extensively throughout Europe and America as installations and films. Awards and commissions include FilmFour, Channel 4, The British Film Institute, the Wellcome Trust and the AHRB research board. He is a professor at the University for Creative Arts, Maidstone.

A DVD of the film Gallivant along with 12 other short films is available through the BFI and Amazon. Kötting's most recent work can be seen at www.deadad.info.

Beside the Seaside, Beside the Sea

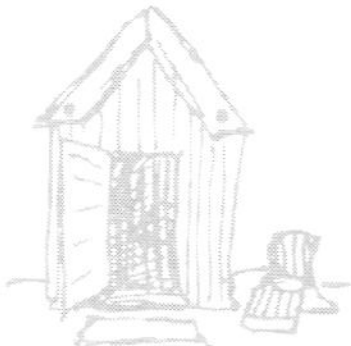

THE PULL OF THE SEA ALWAYS HAD ME.
It wanted me.
And
It was my grandparents Gladys and Albert who took me on my first trips to the seaside.
Caravanning or camping but always with a carload of bickering siblings.
Most summer holidays we would head for the south coast, Seaton, Beer or Bexhill-on-Sea.
Knickerbockerglories, 99s, deck chairs and the funny ha-ha of a Punch and Judy.
Dada.
The De La Warr Pavilion.
The building had an effect on me.
And as a famous modernist landmark it stood out in stark contrast to the wooden beach huts, esplanades, bandstands and colonnades.
Old people shuffling around with cups of tea, Rod Hull and his Emu, Brass Bands, Toby Jugs and winceyette tights.
A paradox and anachronism.
Not modern.
But it belonged to my seaside memories and I wanted to do something with it. **As traveller and inveterate confabulator** I had hatched a plan to circumnavigate the whole coastline of Britain, never venturing inland and sticking wherever possible to the coastal roads. I wanted to immerse myself in the idiosyncrasies and iconographies that littered the shoreline of these islands and what better place to start.

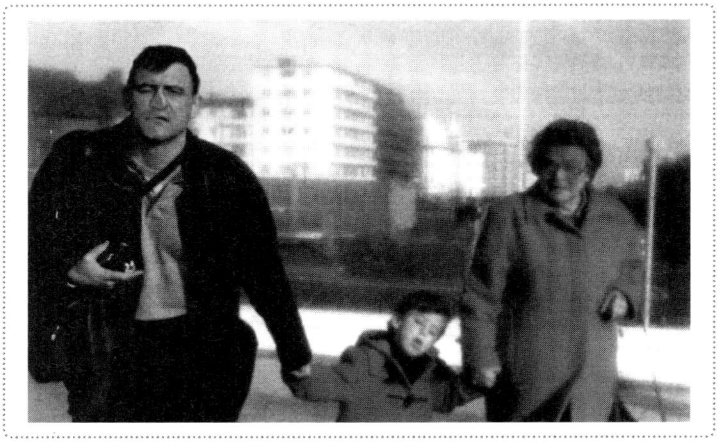

Figure 11
Nose

My featurelengthhomeroadmovie and odyssey, *Gallivant*, came about from a desire to document a trip along the beaches of England, Wales and Scotland with a Super 8 camera and a simple DAT recorder. There was to be no sound-sync and a minimal crew, just myself and a photographer.

Ultimately despite having made some research trips north, south, east and west of this country that film was never made. However it resurfaced and was presented to the BFI with my grandmother **Gladys** and my daughter **Eden** attached. The idea of taking the two of them with me was in no small part determined by the fact that my grandmother had just lost her husband Albert and was overwhelmed by grief. We began to visit her more often than usual and I noticed a strong relationship growing between her and her great grand-daughter.

Eden has a very rare neurological disorder in the form of Joubert Syndrome, which proved intimidating and upsetting for Gladys when she was first born. She found it difficult to communicate with her and would often turn to ask '*What's she saying of?*' or worse still '*It's such a shame, it shouldn't be allowed*'. But the familial bonds that hold a great grandmother and a great grand-daughter together overrode the anxieties she felt about her disability and they grew closer.

I started filming these encounters on Hi8 video and as a minor revelation one Sunday afternoon realised that the two of them might be placed at the film's very centre. They were to become its heartbeat and motor.

This is what I proposed in collaboration with the producer Ben Woolford at Tall Stories:

Gallivant. *Simply, this film is a record of an actual trip to be made around the coast of Britain. But of course it's not that simple: the convolutions of the coastline are matched by the eccentricities of the people and places encountered, not to mention the idiosyncrasies of the camera operator and the lure of the apparently irrelevant. We will be alert to the deep heritage of the land, while our ears will be opened to the zeitgeist, the bombardment of sounds from a multicultural society set against relics from the past, surviving through the oral tradition. Folklore, festivals, customs, traditions and mysteries, as well as places of outstanding natural beauty and sites of historical interest will serve to feed our voracious appetite and rampant curiosity. The filming (on super 8 and 35mm) will be over a period of some months. The full gamut of post-production edit techniques will be used to produce an intense, visceral and absorbing odyssey and multi-layered narrative.*

The idea is to document the coast, through the eyes of real people (Gladys, Eden and Andrew), through meetings with genuine coastal residents (the interviewees), and through the places visited (coast towns and paths, ports, estuaries, and marshes). The film technique will allow the documentary nature of the project to be subverted by a strong editorial input from the filmmaker. This will be achieved by the use of post-production techniques (transposition of voices, additional voice-over, sound effects etc) but also by cultivating the strangeness of the 'real' people encountered, so that the authenticity of interview statements may be called into question (are they genuine, set up, scripted or improvised around a theme?). Thus the viewers will have

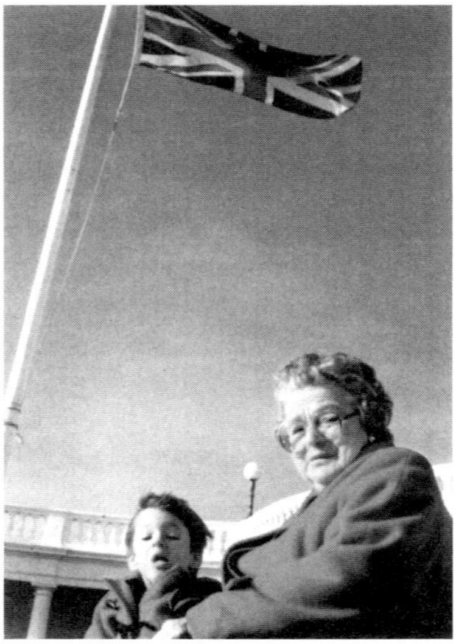

Figure 12
Flag

to confront their own assumptions about the way things are, rather than simply take on board the point of view of the film.

The film is therefore a snapshot of Britain today (1996), complete with its past, which is part of today, and like a snapshot it may contain apparently irrelevant or unstructured elements; the background figure who wanders into the frame of a family group on the beach may not be deliberately included, but their puzzled stare into the lens may transform and enhance the overall result. (Film unlike factory-processed Snappy Snaps has a post-production period that allows subsequent manipulation of both sound and image.)

The social and political perspective offered by Gladys and others in the film will be included but not melded into a consistent point of view. In this sense the film aims to be pre-political, to offer an undigested (if well-constructed) view that can be seen and interpreted in different ways. Its strength will lie in the vividness and humour of outlook, careful thematic development, and the power of the basic device of seeing things through the eyes of two such different family members as Gladys and Eden.

This will be an idiosyncratic view, a view (literally) from the margins which will welcome the marginal; and it will be an affectionate view, with little room for sneering and as much self-mockery as mockery. The picture that emerges will be as much about the three main characters as about the country itself; memory and hope, pleasure and fear, tradition and prediction – discovery, self-discovery and revelation.

Several structures run through the film. Ostensibly (and actually) it is a 'gallivant' around the coast of Britain. This will be signposted in the pre-title sequence in which a TV weatherman (1950s or 60s television archive, and not the hi-tech nonlinear world of the 1990s) will mark out the coastline with a pointer while a know-it-all voice-over academic will expound on the nature of the woad-covered island race and things historically British. Throughout the film, and to accentuate where we might be, we will return to this image of the Man and his Pointy Stick.

It was this 'Master of Ceremonies' with his *pointy stick* that enabled me to weave into the fabric of the film the voices of *timesgone*, the voices of the hoi polloi and the voices of the hoity toity. It was meant as an homage to the old black-and-white public information films that were projected into the classroom for me as a child and films that to this day act as a mnemonic and catalyst. They are at odds with a lot of the modern technologies and yet through their powerful pull towards the nostalgic they work as transporters and signifiers. They become a sonic or visual glue for some of the disparities of filming techniques and help to hold together the 'gleaned' or 'bricollagic' effects common throughout my work.

The film as flotsam and jetsam is also held together by Gladys and Eden and their evolving relationship. They are testament to my own home movie as *timewellspent*.
We travelled wide-eared, wide-eyed, far and wide.

The littoral truths of this island were everywhere.
From the Piers and the Pubs to the Milkmen and the Morris Dancers, the Lollipop Ladies and the Lidos, the Pickled Eggs and the Paper Boys, from the Seaside Chalets to the Cairns and from the fibreglass Guide-dogs-for-the-Blind and the concrete Garden Gnomes.
The coastline was awash with a very particular paraphernalia and the ebbing and flowing of the oceanic horizons worked its magic on the retina.
Respite for the city dwellers gaze.
A calm came over us and after almost four months we returned to the *journeysbegin*.
The De La Warr Pavilion.
Bexhill-on-Sea.
East Sussex.

Iain Sinclair (poet and filmmaker), writing for *Sight and Sound* in 1997 when the film was first released had things to say about it:

What Kötting does, it's so simple a notion, is to go the whole way, clockwise around Britain. To return to his point of departure. The journey takes about three months, out of summer and into autumn .... If that was all, it would still be a voyage well worth our attention. A mingling of personal vision with a highly evolved documentary impulse. A multiple-focus trek made within modest limits, cinema returned to its infancy. And without top heavy production clutter, without budgetary excess. (See the crew picnic on condensed milk.) This is a homage to that archetypal home-movie, the seaside excursion. The day out, remission from mundane routine. Time for putting together oldest and youngest members of the family for that hell of British togetherness .... But Gallivant has something more – a notable cast, Kötting's trump cards: Gladys Morris (85) and Eden Kötting (7) ... and to gallivant according to the Random House Dictionary, 'to wander about, seeking pleasure or diversion; to go about with members of the opposite sex'. And this is what – full throttle – Kötting does .... This new British cinema (born of the polytechnics and art schools) – promoting psychogeography, the journey, the quest, a close examination of random particulars – is a vitalising alternative to the once-lively, now largely inert, documentary programme-fillers of mainstream television. Hi-8 cameras, 8mm film blown up, creative sound-tracks ('cut-ups' that owe something to William Burroughs, something to sampled rave-bunker noise) have liberated filmmakers in a way that harks back to the co-operatives of the 1960s, to the American underground of Stan Brakhage, Jack Smith, and the chamber cinema of Robert Frank and early John Cassavetes .... Gallivant is blitzed with found texts, hints, signifiers. The yellow lettering of a Spastics charity shop, swastikas on walls, the madcap calligraphy of fairgrounds and piers. Eden, the child, strokes an empty belly, or signs her desires for home, with soft quick fingers. Gladys learns to 'read' her. Kötting mimes through the window of the camper van, before falling off and shattering his ankle. The various camera-eyes are hungry for guidance. The furry sound-stick is an unsatisfied predator. 'Tell me a story, sing me a song.' When the anarchic crew arrive in South Wales at the old steel dock of Port Talbot, they find a notice in the mud, in front of all the apocalyptic industrial squalor; a message that seems precisely to define their case. DO NOT ANCHOR BETWEEN SIGNS. *Keep moving, get out of town. The road's end is its beginning.*

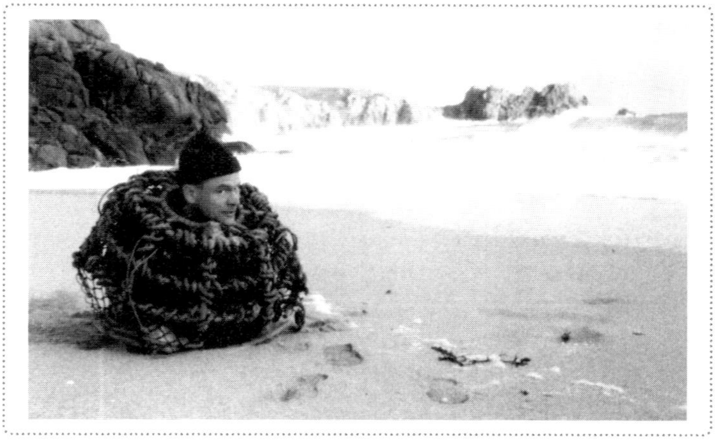

Figure 13 Self-Portrait

These edgelands still have a pull on me and a few years ago I moved to St Leonard's-on-Sea. I'm always in the sea and more recently I found myself swimming the English Channel with two of the bickering siblings for company. We were supported by the crew of a small boat called the *Gallivant* and the wisdom and strength of Iain Sinclair. Eden, now twenty, sat at the water's edge on Shakespeare's Beach waiting for us to return 'home' and in a short film called *Offshore* she plays the part of 'Mistress of Ceremonies'.
Alone, waiting for the return to the place from which we began.
Time moving on and time changing. Always the same.

PS: The De La Warr Pavilion has been reconfigured, revamped and rediscovered.
Its magnetic-pull recharged, the *culturalists* from all over come to bear witness to its newly painted splendour.
A bastion of Lottery donation.
And once inside they stand wide-eyed-bewildered by the new art inventions-pretensions interventions-presentations-installations and ongoing shenanigans.
A post postmodern make-over
And
Anachronistic no longer?

Part II

SAND AND STUCCO

Nicola Moorby

Nicola Moorby works in the Curatorial Department at Tate Britain where she specialises in British art of the nineteenth and early twentieth centuries. She has published a number of essays on J.M.W. Turner and Walter Richard Sickert and is co-author of the Tate's online catalogue of works by the Camden Town Group. She is currently involved in research for the Tate's new online catalogue of the Turner Bequest.

London to Brighton

The Indian Summer of the Camden Town Group

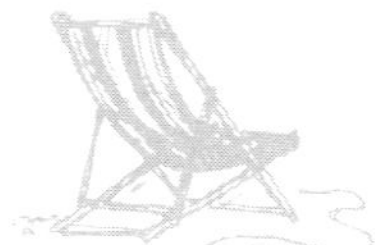

IN THE YEARS LEADING UP to the First World War, modern artistic activity in Britain was largely a London-based affair. Ever the professional, commercial and academic heart of the visual arts, the capital at the beginning of the twentieth century had also become inextricably associated with the very essence of progressive British art. Alongside a cultural framework of art schools, galleries and other institutions, an interconnected network of social cliques and circles evolved which gave rise to an artistic vanguard actively promoting work of a modern character. The metropolitan make-up of these groups was often central to their existence. Cross-fertilisation amidst the London intelligentsia flourished within sociable environments and was as much reliant on personal connections as commonality of purpose. Two such alliances, the Fitzroy Street Group, and its more famous offshoot, the Camden Town Group, wore their urban-centricity firmly on their sleeves. Their city identities were embedded within their titles, meeting places and even their subject matter, and in the third and final reincarnation of the two societies, the 'London Group', they finally adopted the name of the breeding-ground which had nurtured their existence thus far.

The last hurrah of the Camden Town Group, and the maiden voyage of the London Group, however, was an exhibition entitled *English Post-Impressionists, Cubists and Others*, held not within the eponymous city, but in an unlikely alternative, the Sussex coastal town of Brighton. This essay examines the relationship of the Camden Town Group with Britain's most cosmopolitan resort over a short but significant time when the seaside town became an outpost of the British avant-garde. It will conclude with a discussion of Walter Richard Sickert's painting *Brighton Pierrots*, an image which consciously heralds the end of British post-impressionism and is an indirect homage to that brief moment when Brighton became the new London.

The Evolution of the Camden Town Group

The Camden Town Group, and ultimately the London Group, evolved out of an earlier enterprise, the Fitzroy Street Group, described by its founder, Walter Richard Sickert, as an agency 'interested in painting and in the things of the intelligence' designed 'to accustom people to mine and other painters' works of a modern character'.[1] Inaugurated in 1907 it was essentially a commercial enterprise where invited participants shared the rent and overheads for a Fitzroy Street studio in exchange for the opportunity to tout their work to a sympathetic audience. Its meetings adopted the form of quaintly domestic 'at homes' where modestly priced paintings and drawings were exhibited to a like-minded milieu of friends and colleagues in the convivial atmosphere of an afternoon tea party. Within the conservative art market of Edwardian Britain, Fitzroy Street was a financial and professional life-line for struggling modern artists such as Spencer Gore, Charles Ginner, Harold Gilman and Robert Bevan. The group was a perfect illustration of strength in numbers and proof of its success lay in the spirited progress of its individuals. In 1911, the most ambitious and talented core went on with Sickert to form the Camden Town Group, a more high-profile exhibiting society of sixteen artists who showed together three times between 1911 and 1912.[2] Although their lifespan as an association was short, the paintings produced under the aegis of the group represented some of the most successful marriages of modern idiom and subject matter in British art of the period.

The key to the Camden Town connection with Brighton was Walter Taylor (1860–1943), one of the regular customers who made participation at Fitzroy Street worthwhile. Taylor was an amateur artist and friend of Sickert's whose considerable private fortune had been inherited from his father, a successful tobacco manufacturer.[3] Although he trained as an architect his private income meant that he never had to practise, and instead he went to art school, first in Paris and then to the Royal College of Art. Henceforth he divided his time between travelling and painting for pleasure. Affectionately known amongst his contemporaries as 'Old Taylor', he was an unlikely enthusiast for all things modern. Osbert Sitwell described him as a man who, with his 'red face and white imperial, his prominent nose, slow movements, leisurely gait, and with a little the air of a seaside dandy, appeared always to be elderly. Everything about him seemed to be leisurely, not least so his voice, with something of an inescapable boredom in its slow, single-toned unemphatic flow.'[4] Yet Taylor's old-fashioned nature belied an intelligent and genial disposition, and a love of 'the rage for the day after tomorrow'.[5] The liberality of both his wallet and his artistic tastes made him a valuable sponsor for emerging talent. Up-and-coming artists to benefit from his purchases included Gilman, Sickert and Gore, the last of whom made him godfather to his son, Freddy (later the painter Frederick Gore, C.B.E., R.A.). As Jan Gordon, art critic of the *Observer*, later recalled, the rumour of Taylor's attendance would apparently 'make the hearts of the younger progressives living about Fitzroy-square or Charlotte street beat a little faster [...] To be bought by Mr. Taylor was almost equivalent to receiving a mention in the despatches of contemporary painting.'[6]

Although Taylor kept a London house, which enabled him to maintain his links with the capital's art scene, his permanent address was Brighton, a place which continued to be his home for over a decade. The town also featured in his own work, principally landscape or townscape watercolours of the seafront and local architecture, in a competent but rather unexciting style characterised by bold charcoal lines and clean, flat washes of colour.[7] Taylor operated in a modest way on the periphery of the Camden Town Group. In 1911 he shared an exhibition at the Carfax Gallery with his friend and fellow Brighton inhabitant, Douglas Fox Pitt (1864–1922). Like Taylor, Fox Pitt was a regular patron of the Fitzroy Street circle and bought works by Sickert, Gilman and Ginner.[8] The importance of both men to the Camden Town Group, therefore, was as collectors and supporters. Their location in Brighton attracted other more experimental painters to the town who turned their attention to the seaside as a potential site of modernity.[9]

Spencer Gore in Brighton

In 1913, Taylor's seafront house in Brunswick Square played host to Spencer Frederick Gore and his family. Since the eighteenth century Brighton had represented an alternative experience for Londoners, an accessible resort within easy reach of the capital which offered public entertainments coupled with the healthy benefits of the seaside. Once the playground of the privileged aristocracy, by the Edwardian era its pleasures were well established and geared towards a wide social diversity. As an urban development it was symbolic of many benefits of the modern world, such as improved transport links and increased leisure time. Gore, a painter who sought to distil modernity from naturalistic observation of the world, found it an imaginative stimulus for his work. From the first-floor balcony of Taylor's house, he completed two pictures which married his advanced stylistic vision with the picturesque contemporaneity of the subject: *The West Pier, Brighton*, 1913 (Mellon Bank, Pittsburgh) and *Brighton Pier*, 1913 (Southampton City Art Gallery).

The experimental and formalist elements of Gore's artistic vision crystallised in certain locations. He found in Brighton (as in Camden Town, Letchworth and later Richmond) a certain quality of spirit of place combined with spirit of age. His two paintings of 1913 depict the view looking east towards the cultivated lawns and beach huts of the seafront, and the large pavilion theatre of the famous West Pier. Both focus on the civilised geometric ordering of the landscape. For example, the foreground of *The West Pier, Brighton*, is dominated by a triangular corner of garden. Vibrant patches of red and yellow dance amongst the herbaceous border which manages to be modern, traditional and quintessentially English at the same time. Wide bands of colour dominate the sea in the background whilst along the front, rows of bathing machines are grouped like strange cubist sheds on wheels. Gore's aesthetic delight in their blocky forms recalls his paintings of the red and white Arts and Crafts houses of Letchworth of the previous year and anticipates his treatment of Richmond's suburban streets in 1914. The second painting, *Brighton Pier*, 1913, shows a similar but more populated scene. The sunlit promenade is as densely crowded with pedestrians and traffic as a London street but a sense of civilised calm and cheerful optimism prevails. Through a pictorial objectivity, Gore transforms the space into a carefully balanced arrangement of bright colours and simplified, almost child-like forms. This is a quiet, idealised urbanity where aesthetic order equates with social order. In a similar manner to his pictures of the Alhambra theatre in London, the bold intervention of the diagonal balcony rail across the foreground asserts the immediacy of the scene, artfully poised between the real and the imagined.[10] Modernity is not necessarily all that is new, but all that is contemporary, familiar, recognisable and accessible to the man or woman on the street. It is in everyday environments such as Brighton's seafront, Gore is saying, where the experience of modern life is best visualised.

The Brighton Exhibition

Gore recognised that Brighton was not only a place where the modern could be painted, but also somewhere where art could be seen to be modern. It was no coincidence that the winter after his stay a large exhibition opened at the Public Art Gallery called *English Post-Impressionists, Cubists and Others*. Subtitled in the catalogue as the work of the 'Camden Town Group and Others', the group had been invited to form the show by the Fine Arts Committee of the Public Art Gallery, although in reality it was Gore as president who was largely responsible for its inception and organisation.[11] Described by local newspapers as 'far and away the most challenging thing of the kind that Brighton has ever seen', the exhibition was held from 16 December 1913 to 14 January 1914 and represented one of the first opportunities for modern British art to be seen outside London.[12] With typical energy and efficiency Gore had seized the opportunity as a platform from which to launch the next stage of Camden Town development, the embryonic London Group, probably seeing Brighton as perfect neutral territory from which to embark upon the transitional phase of expanding the membership of the group.[13] Consequently the exhibition featured many radical and experimental young artists, a fact which brought nationwide attention to the host venue. Brighton was widely praised in the newspapers for its aesthetic courage and enlightened receptiveness to art.[14] In a speech opening the exhibition, meanwhile, Sickert described the town's heritage as making it a welcoming place for modern artists, reflecting that impressionism had first found a home there in the collection of Captain Henry

Hill, and he praised Brighton's 'sporting spirit' for 'giving a hearing to many things with which they might agree and many with which they might not'.[15] As the *Sussex Daily News* maintained, 'London has recently been made to open its eyes very wide in the same way, and one need not conclude that the universal nerve in Brighton is less robust.'[16]

The theme of the exhibition was artistic freedom of speech. Participants were chosen from amongst the ranks of potential London Group constituents.[17] Members of the original Camden Town Group made up eleven of the thirty-six exhibitors, whilst associated Fitzroy Street artists represented a further eleven.[18] Walter Taylor and Douglas Fox Pitt were both amongst those admitted, probably partly in recognition of their roles in bringing the event to Brighton. The remainder was comprised of artists shortly to be elected to the London Group, or angling for election, and a couple of other virtual unknowns. This resulted in an extraordinarily catholic mixture of artistic styles and it became clear that the hang of the show would have to be segregated. Consequently a curatorial division was enforced. The first two rooms contained works by the Fitzroy Street and Camden Town circles, chiefly oils and watercolours of landscapes, portraits and figures in interiors, but the third room, described as 'Cubist', displayed paintings and sculptures by more experimental and avant-garde representatives such as Wyndham Lewis, Jacob Epstein, David Bomberg, Edward Wadsworth and C.R.W. Nevinson. Even the catalogue required separate introductions, a peculiarity which was indicative of the counter-intuitive aims of the London Group at this stage of its existence. Camden Town stalwart James Bolivar Manson outlined in his text a utopian aesthetic fraternity where all modern methods could be at home. According to him, the new society, and by extension the Brighton exhibition, was a place where 'Cubism meets Impressionism, Futurism and Sickertism join hands and are not ashamed, the motto of the Group being that sincerity of conviction has a right of expression'.[19] Conversely, in the same publication, the radical Camden Town cuckoo, Wyndham Lewis, asserted that he and his cubist colleagues formed an isolated faction, 'a vertiginous, but not exotic island in the placid and respectable archipelago of English art'.[20]

Unsurprisingly, the local coverage of the exhibition was dominated by reactions to the Cubist Room and the consensus of opinion was very much in line with that of the general British public at the time. In a manner reminiscent of the reviews of Roger Fry's first Post-Impressionist Exhibition of 1910, the Brighton press threw up their collective hands in bewilderment at the geometric abstractions of Lewis and his circle, employing popular adjectives such as 'ugly', 'meritless', 'weird', 'crude' and 'incomprehensible' to describe the cubist elements. 'Some of these comic horrors would make a cat laugh' exclaimed the *Sussex Daily News*, 'Brighton people may call this the "Mad Room".'[21] The *Brighton Gazette* reflected that the 'person of average intelligence can only gaze at these apparently aimless splashes of colour and vague geometric designs with stupefaction',[22] and the *Brighton and Hove Society* advised its readers: '"Don't go to this exhibition after a bad night" [...] for the glare, the piling on of opaque, the reckless splashing of colour, the extraordinary attempts at design, the crude liberties taken with all freely conceived notions of art may reasonably lead many people to ask after seeing some of the pictures, "Do they drink very hard in Camden Town?"'[23] Some attempts were made at explanation and understanding. The *Brighton Herald*, for example, recognised that it needed 'a new set of words, a new scale of values'. In reference to the angular figures in a painting by Wyndham Lewis, the critic admitted: 'They seem at first the mere bogeys of childish nightmare imagination. Yet it is possible to study them and find in them a growing sense of strong, ghastly fascination. At first ludicrous they evolve uncanny suggestion.'[24] By contrast, the rest of the exhibition was accepted with equanimity and, on the whole, praise was apportioned to the more realistic and classically conservative offerings by artists such as Walter Bayes, Lucien Pissarro, Harald Sund and Walter Taylor. Ironically, the works which merited the least discussion were those by the original Camden Town Group members such as Gilman, Bevan, Ginner and, the organiser of the show, Gore.

Despite the general rejection of the more extreme and revolutionary elements of the exhibition, the critics of the Brighton newspapers were determined to prove themselves equal to the task of reporting upon an art event of this nature and to represent the town in an intellectual light. In one thing at least all were agreed: regardless of what was thought of them, it was an excellent thing to have the opportunity to see modern artists in the town. Most of the newspapers followed the example of the mayor, who was reported as being 'a little staggered' when he passed into the third room but believed that 'in spite of all that the pictures were deeply interesting'.[25] The *Sussex Daily News* averred that 'no one who cares for the development of art, even when it takes such strange forms, will regret that this exhibition has been arranged in Brighton. When a ferment is going on it is never wise to sit on the safety valve',[26] and the mood was best summed up by the *Brighton Herald* which wrote: 'Taken all round, the exhibition is a most instructive lesson in the value of the open mind. One cannot but congratulate the Fine Arts Committee on their courage and catholicity, and hope that whenever they find artists with anything to say they let them say it in Brighton.'[27]

In keeping with the original principles of Fitzroy Street, visitors had the opportunity to buy the art on display at prices affordable to people of moderate means.[28] The records of sales made, however, reflects the general reception of the exhibition.[29] Works purchased by Brighton and Hove locals were the least obviously modern examples, and included landscapes and other accessible naturalistic subjects by Walter Taylor, Renée Finch, James Bolivar Manson, Paul Nash and Harald Sund. Brighton Art Gallery bought Robert Bevan's painting, *A Cab-Yard, Night*, the first and only work by the artist to enter a public collection during his lifetime, whilst Taylor himself bought a drawing by Sickert. The only other purchasers were a Frenchman, André Germain, and Arthur Clifton of the Carfax Gallery, the London dealer who had sponsored the Camden Town Group exhibitions.[30] No sales at all were made from the Cubist Room.

Sickert's *Brighton Pierrots*

Despite Manson's promise in the catalogue that the London Group would offer 'hospitality to all manner of artistic expression', in reality certain individuals struggled to practise the open-minded approach to stylistic experimentation that such an ideal demanded.[31] In particular it was Sickert who, like the citizens of Brighton, found himself unable to stomach the radical abstractions of his cubist and futurist colleagues. Despite being the guest of honour at the opening of the show he publicly dissociated himself from the more revolutionary artists in his speech. Dismayed by the linking of his name with what he described as Epstein's and Lewis's 'pornometrics', in early 1914 he resigned from both the Fitzroy Street and the London Groups. He explained his decision in a letter to his friends Nan Hudson and Ethel Sands:

> I'm afraid you will think me more 'swing of the pendulum' than ever. But like the lady in bridal attire who bolts at the church door the Epstein Lewis marriage is too much for me & I have bolted. I have resigned both Fitzroy Street and the London Group [...] At Brighton the Epstein Lewis Etchells room made me sick & I publicly disengaged my responsibility. On Saturday Epstein's so-called drawings were put up on easels & Lewis's big Brighton picture. The Epsteins are pure pornography – of the most joyless kind *suit-dit* & the Lewis's pure impudence. Then I felt, once for all, *that never again for an hour* would I be responsible or associated in any way with showing such things. I don't believe in them, and, further, I think they render any consideration of serious painting impossible.[32]

Sickert's resignation and complete dissociation from the pioneering societies he had helped to establish left him temporarily bereft of an artistic identity. Since his involvement with the Fitzroy Street and Camden Town groups, public perception of him had centred on his role as the serious leader and star turn of a group of younger disciples. Despite the evident differences of his dark, shadowy Camden Town interiors from the highly keyed post-impressionism of many of the other core members he was (and still is) popularly believed to have been the central figurehead of the Camden Town genre. A canny self-publicist, Sickert was happy to play along with this misconception for a while – until Brighton, when the group he was seen to be heading became something he really could not endorse. His reluctance was compounded in March 1914 by the untimely death of Spencer Gore, and an acrimonious breakdown in relations with Ginner and Gilman.[33] By the end of 1914 he had entirely extricated himself from all collaborative activity and was left isolated from the continuing advancement of a modernist push which he had been instrumental in instigating. This unusual junction in his career found full expression in a painting of 1915, *Brighton Pierrots*.

In 1915, following in the footsteps of Spencer Gore and in search of an alternative to his usual French vacation, Sickert too stayed with Walter Taylor in Brighton.[34] The town offered a wide range of entertainments, even for someone used to the diversions of the capital, and Sickert frequented Brill's municipal baths and swam in a 'roughish & somewhat sooty sea at the door before breakfast'.[35] He also relished the Aquarium where he considered making drawings of the 'theatrical light & shade of the tanks'.[36] His favourite spectacle, however, was the 'delightful and interesting' pierrot theatre to be found performing daily on the seafront, which he patronised every night for five weeks. The resulting painting was *Brighton Pierrots* (Ashmolean Museum, Oxford), a creation which Sickert considered to be such a 'bit of all right', that he painted it twice, revisiting the subject in a second version commissioned from the studio by William Jowitt, the eminent barrister (see Plate 2).[37] Apart from small details in composition and colouring the two pictures are identical and are mutually referred to here throughout.

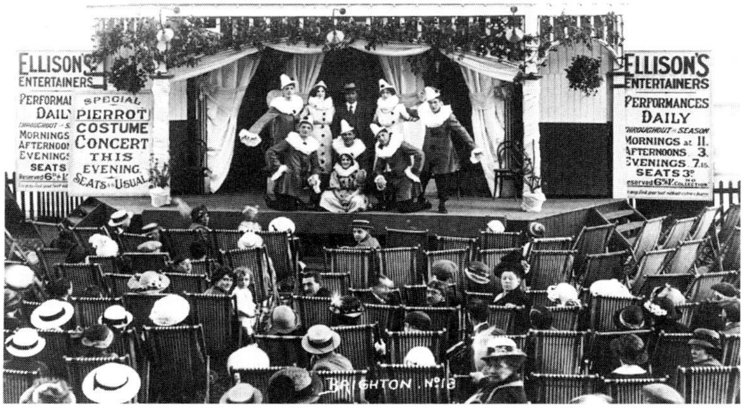

Figure 14
A pierrot troupe on the seafront at Brighton in about 1912

Seaside pierrots are a peculiarly British tradition. The first group appeared during the 1890s as the inspiration of Clifford Essex, a banjo-maker and performer who was struck during a visit to France by the appearance of the silent pantomime character *pierrot*.[38] Perhaps inspired by the play on words of 'pier' and 'pierrot', he combined pantaloons, pom-poms and conical hats with the hearty family entertainment of seaside song and dance. The formula quickly caught on and pierrot troupes became an established feature of beach resorts up until the Second World War. Each troupe occupied its own pitch and performed on a portable wooden stage, usually erected directly on the beach (see Figure 14). Members of the audience seated in deckchairs were asked to pay a nominal fee to watch whilst a 'bottler' circulated amongst everyone else collecting tips. Richard Shone has suggested that the Brighton pierrots depicted by Sickert could have been a company known as the 'Highwaymen', a group run by a local entertainer, Jack Sheppard.[39] The troupe had an established alfresco pitch on the beach opposite the Brighton Metropole Hotel, within very easy walking distance from the West Pier and Walter Taylor's house.[40] Half-way through their act, the performers often swapped their traditional costumes for more contemporary outfits such as top hats and tails or, like the men foremost on the stage in Sickert's painting, blazers and straw boaters.[41]

Despite the association of seaside pierrots with carefree holiday fun, the pervasive mood of Sickert's painting is one of tension and melancholy. The contrived atmosphere of a stilted performance is suggested by the stiffness of the figures on the stage, particularly the disjointed body and dislocated, kicking legs of the man behind the central pole, whilst the acidic colours and artificial lighting undermine the perceived joviality of the act. This disquieting quality was recognised by contemporary viewers. After seeing one of the versions exhibited at the Carfax Gallery in 1916, the critic of the *Daily Telegraph* wrote:

> Here we have a company of players in more or less Italian comedy (*commedia dell'arte*) costumes, performing on a stage set up in the open, with a background of Brighton houses of the more old-fashioned type. The charm of the picture is in the conflict between the luminous air of evening and the artificial lights, under which these poor abraded butterflies of the stage appear half-immaterialised, and with a glamour that is theirs but for this short moment.[42]

Previous readings of *Brighton Pierrots* have frequently focused on the background context of the First World War. This is certainly a valid consideration. Sickert's original title for the painting, *Brighton 1915*, placed greater emphasis on the specifics of time and place, and the ongoing conflict had an unavoidable presence in Brighton, perhaps more so than in many other English towns.[43] The *Brighton Gazette* gamely reported an upbeat mood in the town but also printed the weekly casualty lists recording heavy losses from the front. The summer of 1915 in Brighton was literally an 'Indian' summer. The requisition of the Royal Pavilion, the Dome and the Corn Exchange as hospitals for wounded Indian soldiers afforded the locals the 'strange spectacle of Red Cross vans occupied by parties of wounded Indians in loose blue robes and white turbans, and here and there a badly wounded soldier from the East being wheeled along the promenades in a hospital chair by a British orderly'.[44] Lights were shaded early across the south coast for fear of nightly bombing raids and evening performances on the piers were suspended or commenced earlier than usual. On clear nights it was said that it was even possible to hear the sound of the guns in Flanders across the Channel. The pierrot troupe in Sickert's painting represents a poignantly brave, if rather pathetic effort to inspire laughter and recall happier days at a time when the general populace was experiencing fear and loss on an unprecedented scale. Comparison of the depleted deckchairs with the more crowded audience visible in a preliminary sketch (Walker Art Gallery, Liverpool) shows that the artist has deliberately exaggerated the lack of numbers as a tacit reminder of loss and absence.[45] The painting, however, is not simply a social-historical illustration of wartime England. Its theme is the transience of life in which the war is an agent of changing times. The wider context is the overtaking of an old order by events on a national and individually personal scale. As such, it reflects both the shared widespread anxieties of a nation under threat and Sickert's own situation at this time.

In addition to the changes brought about by war, *Brighton Pierrots* commemorates the passing of an era when Sickert was most fully in step with the artistic movements of the moment. With its heightened intense colouring, Degas-esque composition and references to urban popular culture, the painting is not so much modern, as a memorial to the visual languages of impressionism and post-impressionism, now old-fashioned and being overtaken by other movements. The Camden Town Group had been among the first artists in Britain to adopt such devices in their work but, as the Brighton exhibition had demonstrated, in relation to more recent developments of cubism and futurism their work was already outmoded and rather passé. Sickert had rejected the new radical styles of Wyndham Lewis and others, but had also cut himself off from English post-impressionist artists such as Gilman and Ginner and was temporarily caught, like the pierrots, in a shifting world. The painting may even represent a subtle tribute to the late Spencer Gore, an artist whom Sickert greatly admired and described in his 1914 obituary as the 'perfect modern'.[46] The decorative, vibrant colouring and theatrical references recall Gore's series of paintings of London's Alhambra theatre, particularly, *'The Mad Pierrot Ballet' at the Alhambra*, 1911 (private collection).[47] Gore's death affected Sickert deeply and memories of his friend seem to have surfaced in Brighton. A drawing by him, *West Pier, Brighton*, 1915, repeats almost exactly the view painted by Gore of the promenade a couple of years earlier.[48] According to the electoral roll, Taylor had moved house in 1914 from Brunswick Square to nearby Bedford Square, an address slightly further east along the front towards the pier. Sickert seems therefore to have deliberately recreated Gore's viewpoint from Brunswick Square gardens, even including the same lamp-post and garden bench visible in Gore's *Brighton Pier*. Gore's tragic demise had followed hard on the heels of Sickert's resignation from the Fitzroy Street and London groups, and irrevocably signalled the end of an era for the older artist.

The painting also marks the beginning of the next stage of Sickert's career, eliding post-impressionist subject matter and style with a significant change in his technical practice. For years he had been struggling to refine the perfect painting technique, and in 1914–15, his theories began to take definite shape. The pigment in *Brighton Pierrots* has been applied with a method which he increasingly eulogised as the ideal way to paint in oil, a technique he called the 'camaïeu' [cameo] preparation.[49] The lights and shadows of the composition were first coarsely blocked in on the primed canvas with two contrasting pale colours, in this case light blue and pink.[50] When this layer was bone dry, it was almost entirely covered by thin layers of opaque paint scrubbed hard across the surface. Small areas of the lighter camaïeu would remain visible beneath the overlayers, intensifying the depth and contrast of the colours. This preparation gave him an unmistakable style and dominated his later work of the 1920s and 1930s. In its early adoption of this method, *Brighton Pierrots* represents a significant watershed in his career.

The painting is loaded with references which revolve around the figure of the pierrot as a complex cipher for modernity. Despite being annexed by the British entertainment circuit, the pierrot was a European creation, evolving from Italian commedia dell'arte and the world of French 'Harlequinade' pantomime.[51] By the nineteenth century 'Pierrot' was established as a dramatic type, a lovelorn, silent clown in baggy black and white garb, simultaneously inciting pity and laughter. In the late nineteenth and early twentieth centuries this dual role of the tragic comedian assumed a new visibility and intellectual resonance in modernist culture. The vulgar, improvisational world of the commedia dell'arte became extremely influential for a number of modernist artists, writers and composers who were drawn to its subversive nature and irreverent spirit.[52] Themes and symbols drawn from its colourful stock of stories and characters were taken up and absorbed into high culture: in the poetry of Charles Baudelaire and Jules Laforgue; in Arnold Schoenberg's opera *Pierrot Lunaire* of 1912; and in the work of visual artists such as Gustave Courbet, Gustave Doré, Honoré Daumier, Paul Cézanne, Edgar Degas and even Henri Rousseau, an artist who usually worked outside established cultural conventions. Most famously, the commedia inspired the magnificent costumes and quirky performers of Sergei Diaghilev's Ballets Russes, a company which brought its shows to Britain in 1911. Meanwhile, more recently in the work of the European avant-garde the pierrot had emerged as a symbolic hero of sensibility, emblematic of the role of the artist in society. Artists such as Picasso, Georges Roault, James Ensor and Emil Nolde adopted the persona in their images in order to identify themselves with a certain position: the ability to employ parody and humour in the face of tragedy and the struggle of the artist to both critique and remain complicit with the experience of modern life.[53]

Sickert's depiction of seaside pierrots engages with the power and pathos traditionally associated with the character. Whilst the performers in twentieth-century dress illustrate the contemporary social-historical relevance of the British seaside pierrot, the figures in stereotypical costumes recall the European heritage of the character. Despite the prominent position on the stage of the male duo in red suits, the principal focus for the viewer is actually the pierrette on the left playing the piano. She is the pivotal figure placed at the vanishing point of the painting's perspective and her presence is a conscious reminder of the European, and particularly French, cultural origins of the trope. The vibrant pink of her dress arrests the eye and she turns to stare at the viewer as if complicit in the artist's exposure of the theatrical and artistic deception.[54] Behind her, in the Tate's version of the painting, is a second figure, partially but not entirely rubbed out. This ghostly 'abraded' pierrot seems to be a visual reminder of the threat to French culture currently posed by the German invasion and a metaphor for vanishing traditions. Not only were pantomime figures such as the pierrot rather archaic by the twentieth century, they were symbolic of a nation now literally under attack in the present conflict overseas.

Cosmopolitan Sickert, who himself had a hybrid European background, was particularly sensitive to the desecration being wrought by the war in France.[55] In his mid-fifties he was too old to enlist but writhed 'like a worm on a pin with impotent fury and concern for France'.[56] His 'constant personal terror' was for the fate of Dieppe, caught up in fighting since 1914.[57] He had initially felt personally oppressed and stifled by the conflict, writing 'What a stupid year 1915 will have been. One goes on in a kind of constipated dream' and in another letter: 'This war constipates my heart & pen.'[58] His stay in Brighton, however, seems to have broken the creative deadlock and revitalised his artistic energies. His seaside pierrots are a mournful elegy for a beleaguered French nation, particularly relevant in Brighton, the English equivalent of Sickert's beloved Dieppe. His evocation of a dusky evening by the sea in late summer is a poignant and self-aware visualisation of the remnants of artistic and social prewar traditions caught in their final decline. It might therefore be described as his last 'Camden Town' picture, painted at a moment when he was at a junction in his career, in the twilight years of English post-impressionism.

Deborah Parsons

Deborah Parsons is a Senior Lecturer in Nineteenth- and Twentieth-Century English Literature at the University of Birmingham. She is the author of *Streetwalking the Metropolis* (2000), *Djuna Barnes* (2003), *A Cultural History of Madrid: Modernism and the Urban Spectacle* (2003) and *Thinkers of the Modernist Novel* (2007), and is currently writing a monograph critically reappraising the work of Edith, Osbert and Sacheverell Sitwell.

'Remember Scarborough'

The Sitwells on the Sands

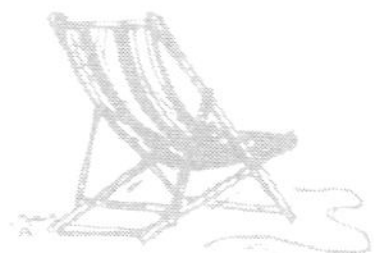

'IN THE LIVES OF ALL HUMAN BEINGS, there are certain times and places that remain haunted by the spirit', Sacheverell Sitwell writes in 'A Sketch of Scarborough Sands', 'scenes to which the mind familiarly recurs'.[1] The Scarborough of his infancy was one such place, where he, Edith and Osbert 'were for ever walking in the spring tide of our lives and scheming our escape into lands beyond the seas'.[2] If Edith would always remember her childhood as a time of much unhappiness, rarely returning to it in her later writing, both brothers by contrast recall the North Yorkshire spa town as the site of their awakening identity and aesthetic awareness, and it is to the genius loci of its immense bay and shifting sands that their imaginations continually return. Looking back in later life, Sacheverell would comment that of his many travels devoted to the study of artistic beauty, 'each and every one of them ha[d] started and had its end upon the Scarborough sands'.[3] In the first book of his five-volume autobiography *Left Hand, Right Hand!* (1945), Osbert too identifies Scarborough as one of the key sites of his childhood memories, and the place where he first began to be aware of the existence of both his own discrete self and the existence of things and others around him. 'It is places more than people,' he remarks, 'and words more than thoughts, that remain to me from my earliest days.'[4]

In this essay I examine the significance of Scarborough in the Sitwell brothers' memoirs, for both their self-narrated myths of artistic origin, and the location of those myths within a seemingly halcyon lost world. The late-Victorian scene of faded elegance that they evoke may have little in common with the interwar 'seaside avant-garde' of white, geometric architectural design that is the focus of many of the essays in this volume, but it epitomises that alternate face of English modernism, haunted by, at the same time as it critiques, its shattered past. For all the Sitwell siblings' group rhetoric of rebellion against the prewar cultured aristocracy spectacularly embodied by their eccentric parents, their very preoccupation with this past results in a narrative of estrangement that is saturated with the ambivalent nostalgia of Oedipal resistance and desire. The social landscape of Scarborough evoked by Osbert and Sacheverell in their writings is that of an Edwardian world prior to its destruction by the twin traumas of war and family crisis (their mother's conviction for fraud in early 1915). For Sacheverell, always the family favourite, the recollection of the pierrots and other itinerants who make their living upon the sands, along with the fascinating tales spun by the town's various octogenarian inhabitants, are revisited and recreated in the vision of an atemporal fantasia on sea. For Osbert by contrast, in whose writings such direct, involuntary memory of the past, untouched by the bitter knowledge of retrospect, is impossible, Scarborough is made the stylised, satiric portrait of an entropic Edwardianism, basking in the face of its impending destruction.

A Seaside Childhood

Scarborough had evolved from fishing village to fashionable spa following the discovery of its mineral waters in the early seventeenth century, and was soon drawing visitors as much for the social amusements of its 'spaw season' as the medicinal promise of its pump rooms and bracing climate. With the extension of the railway line from York in 1845, and such ambitious building projects as a new music hall designed by Joseph Paxton (architect of the Crystal Palace) and the Grand Hotel (the largest purpose-built hotel in Europe when it opened in 1867), Scarborough established itself as an exclusive summer resort, enjoying the patronage of the pleasure-loving Prince of Wales. Both sides of the Sitwell family were prominent figures amongst the wealthy social set living in the palatial limestone terraces and pavilions of its elegant South Cliff. Sir George Sitwell stood as Tory candidate for Scarborough from 1884 until 1900, both Edith and Sacheverell were born in the town and, following the onset of Sir George's nervous illness in 1902, the family moved there for much of the year.

Victorian and Edwardian resort culture was an elite affair, operating its own social rituals and etiquette. Over the summer season this followed a daily routine of walks along the Spa promenade and garden complex, a carriage drive on the Esplanade, attendance at the Assembly Rooms, Theatre Royal and Grand Opera House, and a calendar of gala nights and social events culminating in the end-of-season cricket festival in late September. The Sitwell siblings delighted in the huge conservatory at their grandmother's house Wood End, filled with exotic plants and birds. They were fascinated by the organ-grinders, pierrots and fish-sellers on the beach, the spectacle of the bay from the promenade and the constant sound of the 'German' sea. In the winter months, when the crowds abated, the town's ageing residents – the 'Monstrous Regiment' as Osbert would call them – came into their own, patrolling exclusive standards of attitude and behaviour. The intrigues of this world, performed behind twitching lace curtains, were reported to the young Osbert and Sacheverell by eccentric family friends (the seemingly ageless Miss Lloyd or the latter's occasional 'tutor' Major Viburne), and they would later become the butt of Osbert's acute if sympathetic satire.

Such social insularity, in which the turn of the twentieth century hardly seemed to register, continued until the morning of 16 December 1914, when German battlecruisers emerged out of the dawn mist, firing on the coast. The Grand Hotel alone received thirty-six shells and over two hundred buildings were hit, with more than eighty casualties and the loss of eighteen lives.[5] This attack on an undefended town shocked the entire country, not only in its contravention of the Geneva and Hague conventions, but also its demonstration that England could no longer arrogantly assume supremacy over the waves. None of the Sitwell siblings was living in Scarborough at the time of the raid. Edith had removed herself with hard-won independence to a flat in Bayswater; Osbert was with the Grenadier Guards, about to embark for the front; Sacheverell was at Eton. But the presence of their parents at Wood End, which was mildly hit, brought the attack close to home. Sir George took refuge in his cellar, writing to his eldest son with advice about how to deal with what would undoubtedly be less dangerous gunfire in the trenches. He recommended, in particular, a good diet of nourishing food and a regular afternoon nap. Osbert records in his autobiography that Lady Ida remained resolutely in bed, before catching a train to London to bestow as a good-luck token a piece of shrapnel that had broken into the house.[6]

In Osbert's satiric novella *Before the Bombardment* (1926), Scarborough is made a metaphor for the destruction of the Victorian age, and the social and political complacency that led up to it. Yet later, in his vast autobiography *Left Hand, Right Hand!*, it is inseparable from the nostalgic recollection of his Edwardian childhood. Sacheverell's writings draw upon the same landscape and figures, but are more empirical and impressionist in tenor and style, lacking the biting tone of the more cynical Osbert. Significantly, where Osbert's autobiography portrays the development of its writer, from the stirrings of an aesthetic temperament to the shaping of that temperament by wider historical circumstances, moving from images of timeless luminosity to caricatured portraits of a social scene, Sacheverell's *All Summer in a Day* (1926) takes the form of what he himself would call an 'autobiographical fantasia', a medley of impressionistic scenes and reflection in which empirical sensation yields to imaginative fancy.

Remembering

Characteristic of both Sitwells' representation of their memories of Scarborough is an emphasis on its role in the formation of their self-identity, and as the ground of their earliest sensory apprehension. Scarborough is not simply, or even primarily, a geographical or social locality in these recollections, but rather the very ground of experience and, gradually, the glimmerings of a burgeoning creative imagination.

In his discussion of the 'aesthetics of affect', Charles Altieri has explored the relationship of the artistic imagination to affective states, or what he describes as the 'immediate modes of sensual responsiveness to the world characterised by an accompanying imaginative dimension'.[7] Such imaginative affect, Altieri suggests, can be distinguished into four kinds: *feelings*, raw 'elemental affective states' linked to 'immediate processes of sensation'; *moods*, modes of feeling in which the agent's subjectivity seems diffuse and 'sensation merges into something close to atmosphere [...] to pervade an entire scene or situation; *emotions*, which construct certain attitudes in relation to sensations, 'and so situate the agent within a narrative'; and *passions*, modes of emotion in which the agent projects 'significant stakes for the identity they make possible'.[8]

The Sitwells articulate just such an aesthetics of affect, preoccupied with a self-reflexive exploration of consciousness, the imagination and identity, and both brothers appeal to the raw feelings of primary childhood sensation for the development of their later writings. Yet where Osbert's imaginative satire sets Scarborough within the broader narrative context of Edwardian and personal history, corresponding to the workings of emplotment characteristic of emotion and passion in Altieri's sense, Sacheverell's fantasia is more appropriately aligned with the concept of imaginative mood. In direct contrast to *Left Hand, Right Hand!*, written with the hindsight of half a century of past time, Sacheverell had published his own autobiography *All Summer in a Day* in 1926, staunchly defending what may have seemed to his readers a precipitate undertaking. 'It is surely of more value to set forth your memories when you are twenty-five than after you have reached seventy-five', he declares in the Preface, to record 'the little flashes and flickers of light [that] are one's own property and visible to no one else', and that as we age 'get further and further away'.[9]

The difference between Sacheverell's 'little flashes and flickers of light', and Osbert's mature recreation of such experiences in his own later memoirs, is that the former really are conveyed as the unprocessed material of involuntary memory. *All Summer in a Day* offers little narrative of self, setting down instead the fleeting impressions of the mind as it begins to register the distinctions of subject and object, past and present, sensation and intentionality. The first chapter sets out Sacheverell's Proustian approach, in an involuntary memory of blackberrying at Renishaw: 'I was filled, of a sudden, with this double-consciousness, both realising the moment and wondering how long I should be able to remember it' (p. 13). The second chapter shifts to Scarborough, and a second memory, this time of a walk with 'Colonel Fantock' (Major Viburne) through the Spa gardens and down to the sands. It is a composite scene, the single 'memory' bringing together in snapshot form what Sacheverell knows to have been many such instances. The result is a luminous impression, removed from any causal chain of events. At first it is saturated with the rich colour and scent of the flower beds. Then, reaching the edge of the cliff, Sacheverell sees the 'huge surging bay' spread before him: 'a kind of immense amphitheatre, in which I occupied the highest seat' (p. 54). In contrast to Osbert's winter town, with its rough seas and blackened skies, Sachaverell's Scarborough is remembered in the 'drowsy heat' of high summer (p. 45). 'Nobody that I remembered had then died,' he notes, 'and this remote contingency, seemingly but an alternative to life, lay too far ahead to be considered in its effect' (p. 67). And so he does not consider it. He turns back instead to the rockpools, 'bright sunlight', and the fascination of Colonel Fantock's 'Utopias of the fancy' (p. 69).

Later in the book, while looking at Cruickshank watercolours in a northern art gallery, an adolescent Sacheverell is led back again in his imagination to the rockpools and the pierrots. Much of this later reminiscence repeats word for word the earlier scene – the 'huge surging bay, a kind of immense amphitheatre' – a narrative device in which again the Proustian methodology is at work (p. 217). But for this older Sacheverell the troupe of pierrots, performing the last minutes of their show hurriedly against the incoming tide, have come to hold a greater significance as part of his own 'private and personal legend'. They are now placed within a narrative of Sitwell's own artistic identity. He recognises that the pierrot theatre on Scarborough sands first prompted his fascination with the commedia dell'arte. From these early spectacles came his later personal identification with the harlequin, a figure to whom he devoted his early collection of poems *The Hundred and One Harlequins* (1922).

The atmosphere of the magical and the phantasmagoric in Sacheverell's fantasia-on-sea is distinctly absent from Osbert's typical memories, but there is one episode in *Left Hand, Right Hand!* which is identifiable with the imaginative experience of this fantasy landscape. During a three-month period of severe pleuritic illness Osbert was removed from Eton to convalesce at Wood End. He described this period as 'the most important of my whole childhood', affording 'apparently endless time – in which to think and still more to feel'.[10] In his fevered state, the Scarborough seaside was exotically transfigured:

> I gazed at the shifting and melting castles, the fulgent towers and palaces, shapes that in their turn revealed processions from times past [...] I visited countries

> and kingdoms I was never going to see again, equatorial vistas of sand, and snow landscapes with an organisation of their own, more wild in architecture than the forms to which even limestone can lend itself, floating alpine heights built up in a golden flame that was like a lion's steadfast glare, vast cities washed by huge seas, that undulated in answer to the moon's call, through a mist of prismatic spume [...].[11]

This passage again registers the affective relationship of place and subjectivity, but here sensory experience is transformed through hallucination. Osbert admits in *Laughter in the Next Room*, however, that such imaginative activity was for him rare, writing that 'as a rule I am rationed in this other life, and usually given distorted variations of the scenes most familiar to me.' Of these, he notes, there were three: Renishaw on a 'vast, flawless summer day or night [...] always beautiful'; a London street, 'very neat and orderly'; and the winter sea at Scarborough, 'dashing gigantic wings to batter falling cliffs, under the pounce and glitter of bitter-beaked sea gulls materializing out of a nothingness of white foam, and yellow sky, while a voice cries slyly in the hollows under the lull, "*Rags and bones; rags and bones!*"' (pp. 91–2).

In Osbert's early auditory memory the cry of the rag-and-bone man was a disembodied Scarborough sound, an association of words and place, rather than people and place. 'At the time of which I write, people still scarcely existed for me', he observes in *Left Hand, Right Hand!*, 'the cry, the song, the tune on the barrel-organ, but not those who uttered or produced them' (p. 83). As his perception begins to form, however, his interest extends first to the ragman himself, and then to 'the beggars, the tramps, the pedlars, the clowns, the organ-grinders, the contortionists, the company of the crazy and of the street-singers', of which, he recalls, 'Scarborough in those days offered an inexhaustible supply' (p. 82). Shortly afterwards he remarks his growing cognisance from initial sensations to an awareness of the externality of place, things and people:

> As the light grows stronger, it reveals this strange population against the background of a world, stippled and very pale in tone, with the glitter of the sea about it on the fronts and the roofs of the houses and in the sky itself. Even the ordinary people – the men in their bowlers, boaters, close-fitting caps and with their

> carefully trained or trailing moustaches, the women with their narrow-waisted bodies, like continents, their huge hats feathered and contaminated with milliners' flowers, decaying in purple and deep pink – walking, riding horses, riding bicycles, driving in varnished shells of wood, were strange enough, looked back upon; but how do justice to these other capering figures at the world's edge, on the faces of whom the light plays with the same trembling power of emphasis as the mirror flashed in the sun upon the features of an unsuspecting person by some small child? (p. 165)

A landscape of sea and sky starts to form, along with the buildings and houses of the town, providing the background against which both the feathered and moustachioed nobility and the shabby poor, indistinguishable to the child's eyes, are set. This recapturing of raw apprehension is then drawn into the wider narrative of Osbert's literary autobiography: 'how do justice?' he muses, as he identifies the scenes, figures and motifs that would be the basic material of his fiction.

Osbert noted that in the trenches of the First World War the content and aspect of his dreams shifted significantly. He became 'concerned with people more than places', the auratic landscapes of his prewar imagination now being exchanged for 'a degree of psychological observation [which] gave a peculiar sharpness to their doings and sayings: they behaved in this sharp, swift world reflected from their own behaviour, in a fashion that was more essentially typical of themselves than they themselves were, in everyday life' (p. 92). These are the words of the satirist rather than the impressionist, Osbert himself noting in this new imaginative activity the 'chrysalis' of the future novelist. The pieces he would write after the war, the short stories of *Triple Fugue* (1924) and the novella *Before the Bombardment* (1926), articulate just this sharp, caricatured observation of type and behaviour. '[J]ust *how* innocent is the eye of childhood?', Osbert asks in the introduction to *Left Hand, Right Hand!*, in reference to a comment by Edith that after reading *Before the Bombardment*, she had 'never been able to look a child between three and twelve straight in the eye again' (p. ix). Yet my point here is that neither Osbert's satire, nor his later autobiography, record the perceptions of the child of three or ten, but rather the recollections of a man returned from the traumas of the trenches, for whom involuntary memory of the past cannot be recovered. As the narrator declares in *Before the Bombardment*, 'our story must be told to the monotonous accompaniment of waves beating like the drums of gathering armies'.[12]

Satire and Critique

Newborough, as it appears in Osbert's short story 'Low Tide' (*Triple Fugue*) and *Before the Bombardment*, is a thinly veiled portrait of the Scarborough of his boyhood. Into 'this wind-bound, sea-pounded town', he writes in the Preface to *Before the Bombardment*, 'the nineteenth century has been allowed to project its heavy shadow across the opening years of the young era' (p. vi). The Grand Hotel is renamed the Superb, the Spa has become the Winter Gardens, and the names of the more memorable caricatured residents have been changed, but all are easily identifiable. Its residents exist in 'long settled comfort and confident respectability', marking social status by the possession of a sea view (p. v).

Warmed by the rays of 'the golden sun of Edwardian prosperity', Newborough enjoys a comfortable existence: '[e]very day the arm-chairs could almost be seen growing, like the Empire, larger and softer', while the public gardens are submerged beneath an 'avalanche of Dorothy Perkins roses', 'fallacious sub-tropical exoticism' and an 'absolute epidemic of Japanese rock-gardens' (pp. 98–101). Yet, as the narrator of *Before the Bombardment* observes, it was essentially 'the crowds that gave life to the town', and 'Newborough depended, in fact, for its characteristic air of vitality as much upon the fluttering mobs that in the season decked it, as an old tree counts for its adornment upon the yearly birth and unfolding of its buds' (pp. 62–3).

Significantly, both 'Low Tide' and *Before the Bombardment* are set during the winter months, when the fashionable grandees who frequent the town in the summer season have departed, and the minor, local noblesse 'crept out from their several retreats, gradually inflating themselves to a due degree of importance, and at the same time aping in their manner, with much accuracy, the great who had just gone away' (p. 68). This is the 'Monstrous Regiment', the host of octogenarian spinsters who rule social opinion in the town. Located far from London, at the terminus of the railway line from York, Newborough in the winter is a world upon which the new century has yet to make its mark. Osbert's scathing eye observes how the local doctors perpetuate this state of affairs. Dependent for their existence on the year-round patronage of their patients, they aim to hasten neither cure nor death but instead 'a subtle state of suspended animation, which corroded the will and transformed the visitor, as if by magic, into a resident' (p. 65).

'Low Tide' is an anecdotal tale about the Misses Cantrell-Cooksey, who have embraced in middle age the frills, trinkets and cosmetics they had never had the chance to enjoy in their youth. Bedecked with 'little pieces of lace, numerous ribbons and a thousand other joyous trifles', their cheeks 'a blaze of Babylonish colour', they appear 'a pair of music-hall sisters, some popular variety turn of the late "seventies", left over from that age but defiant of time'. They are looked upon with ridicule by Newborough's smart visitors, and stern disapproval by its established residents.[13] Their eccentric appearance ('I can't bear people who aren't like anybody else', declares the doctor's wife, Mrs Sibmarsh) and their bright eyes ('drugged!' she pronounces) are enough to bring them disfavour, despite their mild manners and morally and socially irreproachable routine of church-going, music and afternoon tea. For 'the vision of the town', Osbert writes, 'a vision sharp and narrow, could not pierce through this extraordinary outward aspect to the essential goodness and kindness within' (p. 22).

What ultimately sets Miss Frederica and Miss Fanny apart, however, and is the cause of the fantastic dress and glowing eyes, is their 'Romantic Temperament', in contrast to the sturdy provincialism of Newborough opinion. This is what leads them down to the beach after stormy weather to watch the beach-combers raking their 'alternately romantic and prosaic treasury': 'silver pennies of the Plantagenets, old biscuit tins full of sea-biscuits, gold coins from Spain, a piece of rusty armour that had been gnawed by the waves for centuries, coppers that had been thrown to the pierrots in the summer [...] all the trifles that time and the cruel tides had left over' (p. 46). Unfortunately the Romantic Temperament also leads to a passion for speculative investment on the part of Miss Frederica, which, combined with her credulous embrace of the urge to 'Think Imperially' in her reading of Kipling, eventually brings the sisters to financial ruin. Clinging to the courage of appearances, they desperately maintain their increasingly tattered apparel and rouged cheeks in an 'agonising pretence that all was as it should be', until Miss Frederica finally makes a suicidal leap from the window of their boarding-house room, leaving Miss Fanny to visit the sands alone to watch the strange treasure washed up upon the shore (p. 64).

Both plot and characterisation are relatively thin, neither humane nor satiric enough to evoke in the reader either pity or laughter, and Newborough is not quite the concentrated microcosm of the Edwardian age that it will become in *Before the Bombardment*. But the constituent landscape, themes and characters that would be extended in the subsequent novella are all in place: the town's 'monstrous regiment', the strange human detritus of the Victorian age, washed up at this terminus of life, and the eternal tides, depositing history on the ever-shifting sands.

The greater part of *Before the Bombardment* takes place during the same period as 'Low Tide' – the Misses Cantrell-Cooksey appear briefly as two of its eccentric corps de ballet – although its epilogue moves the narrative forward to the surprise attack by the German battlecruisers in December 1914. Sitwell's primary aim here is not just the 'imaginative reconstruction of an epoch', as he states in his Preface, but also a critique of its 'Credo', its 'belief in the inherent rightness and righteousness of the prevailing system', that leaves it blindly unaware that 'something was being prepared far away behind the curtaining of the grey foam, the black rolling waves, something sudden and disastrous' (p. 64). The supreme manifestation of this Newborough credo is the Superb Hotel in all its Victorian grandeur:

> It stands there, its two vast façades capable of holding out against the four winds, a rock composed of yellow brick in an undeniably rare tint, decorated with surface patterns in other bricks of equally unusual red and purple, crowned with a high slate roof and four barrel-like domes, the colour of cinders. [...] When it was built no other social system was deemed possible, and so it was intended like the Great Pyramid to stand through all eternity, but an eternity that was to differ in no respect from the present. [...] Upon this monstrous hub the entire system of the town's summer life revolves. Bath chairs, cabs, funiculars, tramways, shops, public gardens, promenades, crescents, terraces, the sands, the sea even, flutter round it as coloured ribbons whirl round an electric fan. In the winter, the prospect, while it lacks such gaiety, gains a compensating air of proud desolation, and of

> great forces temporarily held in check; it compels such respect as all men must feel before some mighty machinery, mill or furnace, at rest. (pp. 110–11)

In its very architectural design, the Superb upholds a myth of eternal order: four corner towers represent the seasons, there are twelve floors for the months of the year, fifty-two chimneys for the weeks and 365 rooms for the days. Its seemingly impregnable façade looks out to the sea over which it presumes to rule, oblivious to the warning of the ruined keep of a previous glorious age overlooking it from Castle Hill. If the town has seen its share of raids and slaughters in barbarous times past, it is now confident in the natural and eternal existence of its established social system and beliefs. 'To the people of Newborough, History had seemed dead', Osbert writes in the Epilogue, and yet very soon 'the old harridan was to rush out of her prim, neatly-kept grave, and sweep down without reason on this unoffending place' (pp. 296–7).

When the Great War begins, Newborough remains unaffected and unconcerned. It seems a regular and rather dull morning in December when Hester Waddington props herself against her pillows with the morning newspaper and a tray of toast and marmalade: 'It was chilly, the old lady observed, distinctly chilly in spite of the fire, and she was just asking for an extra shawl ... when, quite without warning, death darted at her from the sea, and Miss Waddington, and her bedroom with her, was pulverized, fading with a swift, raucous whistling and crashing into the murky air.' Seconds later the Superb has become 'a gigantic honeycombed rock, full of gaping caves formerly the dwelling, it was obvious, of some race of splendour-loving troglodytes' (pp. 300–1).

The subsequent destiny of Miss Waddington, metamorphosing from elderly invalid to muscular, marble giantess as she is taken up by the shrewdness of the war propagandists and from thence to the hearts of the public, is the sparkling set piece of the Epilogue. 'For some reason or other the fate of this particular old woman was seized on as an aid to recruiting', the narrator recalls, her name blazoned on placards reading 'REMEMBER NEWBOROUGH AND HESTER WADDINGTON' (p. 302). If the satire of 'Low Tide' had been vague in its object, here it is incisively directed at the concerted propaganda campaign that followed the Scarborough raid, Osbert offering a fictional parallel of the 'Remember Scarborough: Enlist Now' poster depicting a strapping

Boudicca, pointing young men forward with her sword, against the background of a burning coastline. 'Thus at the moment of her cruelly sudden atomization', Osbert writes, 'Miss Waddington entered the sphere of History, and remained as she had always been, a leader', her doom 'not confined to herself' but instead extended to the thousands of young men who rushed to recruiting-stations in her name (p. 306).

Shifting Sands

Both Osbert and Sacheverell Sitwell identify their memories of Scarborough with their aesthetic identity. But of course the corollary of the interdependence of place and identity is that the loss or destruction of place also brings about a rupture of self. As Jeff Malpas writes in *Place and Experience*, 'the fragility and mortality of human life must be seen as nothing other than the same fragility and mortality that attaches to the places and spaces of human dwelling and just as inevitable'.[14] It is just this fragility of memory and identity that Sacheverell tries to avoid in setting down involuntary memory in *All Summer in a Day*, and this knowledge of mortality that so pervades Osbert's satires and later autobiography, as the chasm of the war years proves too deep for the recovery of that original place and self to be possible.

Ultimately, however, perhaps the genius loci of Scarborough's physical landscape – the eternally shifting sands upon which human beings play for only a short period – is its ability to symbolise at once the transitory and the eternal in the topographical imagination. The Scarborough landscape is 'immutable', Sacheverell writes in 'Sketch of Scarborough Sands', exactly because it is, 'in itself, impermanent and transitory': 'The tides sweep in and, when they ebb, new sands are discovered with no marks upon them.' The image of the sands, the surface of which is continually wiped clean of the traces of the day before, while their depths throw up relics and curios from the past, offers a metaphor for both the passage of time and the workings of memory. The sands, he states in summary, 'stand in symbol for all that has been written. The shaking quicksands are here and there, and everywhere. It is treacherous soil that is water half the day. And there are long nights when no one walks the stormy shore. Long days and years when our lives are forgotten.'[15]

William May

William May has taught at Bath Spa, Roehampton and Oxford, and now lectures in English at Southampton University. He has co-edited a collection of interdisciplinary essays, *From Self to Shelf: The Artist Under Construction* (Cambridge Scholars Publishing, 2007), with Sally Bayley. He has published widely on British twentieth-century poetry and fiction, and is currently working on a monograph on Stevie Smith.

‘A Good Time Was Had By All’?

Stevie Smith Beside the Seaside

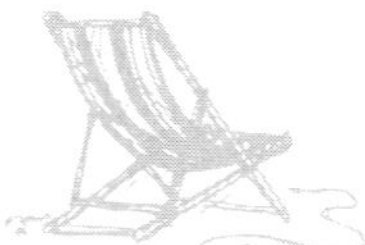

SOMEWHERE BETWEEN the compulsive nostalgia of John Masefield’s poem ‘Sea Fever’ (1902) and the desolate modernism of B.S. Johnson’s ocean voyage novel *Trawl* (1966) lies the work of the British novelist, poet and illustrator Stevie Smith (1902–71). Hers is a voice which captures with shabby, often desperate, humour both Masefield’s sense of the seaside as escape and Johnson’s feel for the relentless pull of the ocean and the precipitous edges of the crumbling cliffs above. In her most famous poem, ‘Not Waving but Drowning’, Smith’s dead subject hovers far out on the coastline’s horizon, and by the final stanza the poem’s speaker seems to have joined him:

> Oh, no no no, it was too cold always
> (Still the dead one lay moaning)
> I was much too far out all my life
> And not waving but drowning.[1]

Yet the difficulty of separating these two submerged speakers signifies the double-edged representation of the coast. Its promise of departure means it appears in Smith’s work as both a haven and a threat. The coast is a memorial to the past and a confrontation with an uncertain future. It is this central contrast that I want to explore here, drawing on Smith’s novels, short stories, poems and illustrations.

The Suburban Holiday?

Smith's lifelong commitment to her London suburb, Palmers Green, and her hymns of praise for it in various essays, poems and novels, have perhaps obscured her similarly acute descriptions of the British coast. Literary critics and general readers alike have tended to situate her geographically on London's branch lines: a post-industrial oddity, an eccentric. Yet her childhood beach holidays and in particular her 1911 trip to Saltfleet, Norfolk, formed founding memories for her, and ones to which she returned throughout her quasi-autobiographical work.[2] A passage from her second novel *Over the Frontier* (1938) suggests the symbolic significance of these memories, recreating Saltfleet through the voice of the narrative protagonist, Pompey Casmilus:

> I can in my imagination see the beachbaskets, the sandwalls surrounding them, the striped umbrellas and the notices stuck along the sand dunes: Beyond the waves is danger to life. Lebensgefahr. [...] And there at Saltfleet are the most grand and enormous sand dunes and vast cavities behind, ramparts and bastions of sand, grass tufted to stand against the open-sea winds [...] the first thing Pompey and Mary did was to go running running away from mama and Auntie Lion away out and across the salt marshes and sand dunes to get completely lost beyond the wide and treacherous river that flowed between our hired cottage and the seaboard [...].[3]

This passage seems typical of Smith's seaside excursions throughout her oeuvre. It sets the reader up for nostalgia, a vividly remembered image from childhood, only to undermine the innocent horizons of the past with the threat of death. The 'grand' sand dunes rest on 'vast cavities'; the holidaymakers' 'striped umbrellas' jostle with the painted warning sign. Tellingly, Pompey and her sister Mary are drawn to the 'treacherous' river rather than the contents of the beach-baskets, suggesting a vision which forgoes leisure for the temptations of death.

The insertion of the German 'Lebensgefahr' into the memory raises further political associations; throughout Smith's work, as we will see, the coast is the jumping-off point for a consideration of nationhood and culture. This is a landscape full of signs which, as famously in 'Not Waving but Drowning', go unread, ignored or misinterpreted. This is also a passage rooted firmly in the imagination, suggesting not only a coastal portrait that draws on personal memories but one that might make links between images of the coast and the creative process itself. This is, then, a highly personalised and sentimentalised response to the British coast but also one which gestures with inscrutable signs to a more allegorical and symbolic reading of this space.

Much of Smith's work depicting the seaside is humorous, associating the coast with hedonism or a return to childhood. In *Over the Frontier*, Pompey is prescribed a rest cure 'far from towns [...] near the sea' (p. 117). Yet, more often than not, Smith seeks to subvert the terms of the genre. Her short story 'Beside the Seaside: A Holiday with Children' was first published in *Holidays and Happy Days* (1949), where it took its place alongside more escapist vignettes of bucket and spade edited by Oswell Blakeston.

In the story, Helen accompanies her friend Margaret and her family for a day at the seaside near Dungeness. Their conversation ranges from Cold War politics and poetry to the merits of various brands of sun-tan lotion. Yet Margaret's children here are far from carefree emblems of youth: Hughie, her oldest, and Helen become engaged in a petulant power struggle which ends with her hitting him with a rolled-up copy of *Life* magazine. The title makes it an oddly appropriate weapon; Helen's anger comes half from Hughie's immaturity and half from a resentment that her own friendship with Margaret is threatened by the competing demands of her children. Here, Smith attempts to mine the material for jaunty seaside humour, as in Helen's closing insistence that 'what a pleasant holiday this was, how much she had enjoyed today for instance; hitting Hughie had also been quite agreeable' (p. 25).

Yet elsewhere, the comedy of the narrative stalls and breaks down into regretful nostalgia. Helen at one point confesses to 'her favourite Brobdingnagian dream ... if she were so high (say three inches) and the rest of the world was unchanged, how very exciting and daring would be this afternoon excursion; each puddle a solitary lake'.[4] Helen's desire to return to the diminutive here suggests a nostalgia not for the certainty of childhood but for the danger of it. As it is, the only promise of escape for Helen comes in a fleeting thought of death at the story's conclusion:

> If only the beach were really as empty as the moon, and she could stay here and lie out all night, and nobody pass by and no person pass again ever. But that no doubt was what it would be like when one was dead (this was always what Helen thought death was like), and then of course the poor soul would weep for its loneliness and try to comfort itself with the memory of past company [...]. (p. 25)

The double-sided motion which pulls Helen at once out to the desolate emptiness of the coast and back to the comfort of memory situates the coast as a perpetual in-between, promising but finally denying access either to the finality of death or a return to the past.

The story also includes one of Smith's poems, 'Advice to Young Children', ventriloquised here through her poet-protagonist Helen:

> Children who paddle where the ocean bed shelves steeply
> Must take care that they do not,
> Paddle too deeply. (*CP*, p. 174)

Helen introduces it here as a 'moral poem', but its apparently forbidding Victorian homily seems shifting and unsettled. When Smith first published the poem as part of her collection *Mother, What is Man?* (1942) the stanza appeared in speech marks, the poem concluding with:

> Thus spake the awful aging couple
> Whose heart the years had turned to rubble.
>
> But the little children, to save any bother,
> Let it in at one ear and out the other.[5]

The about-turn enacted in these two versions suggests Smith's unease about whether she returns to the coast as a child or adult, hovering between playful whimsy and philosophical struggle.

Smith's memories of Saltfleet, first worked out in *Over the Frontier*, were revisited in her poem 'Archie and Tina' from her final collection *Scorpion* (1971). Although again the subject is here the imagined coast of the past, the poem explores the processes of memory and escape itself. The poem begins with a recollection of holidays with her childhood playmates where they would 'paddle the samphire beds', and 'fish / Crabs from the sea-pool'. Yet after repeated invocations of 'oh if only' and 'Oh what pleasure', the speaker's attempts at sentimental reflection seem to give way to rational dissection:

> There never were so many poppies as there were then,
> So much yellow corn, so many fine days,
> Such sharp bright air, such seas.
>
> Was it necessary that
> Archie and Tina, Bam and Boy,
> Should have been there too?
> Yes, then it was. But to say now:
>
> Where are you today
> Archie and Tina,
> Playmates of my childhood,
> Brother and sister? Is no more than to say:
>
> I remember
> Such pleasure, so much pleasure. (*CP*, p. 549)

Here Smith interrogates the genre of the *ubi est* and finds it wanting. Her staunch common sense disrupts the appeal of the past. Beyond their deep place in the speaker's memory, the subjects of this poem are figures of indifference. If the coast is a staging point for the past then, its theatre is one that captivates Smith but leaves her suspicious and nervously alert, always prying behind the curtain of nostalgia.

Departure and Death

Smith's repeated prods at this curtain are particularly evident in her poetry. Here, the coast and water more generally provide an escape route from a socially restrictive English suburbia. Whilst her subjects are always seeking the coast – in 'Freddy', the speaker longs to get her strait-laced lover 'alone on the sea saltings / Where the sea licks up to the fen' (*CP*, p. 65) – any stretch of water which might lead us there will suffice if necessary. For Smith's poetic subjects, estuaries ('A Dream of Comparison'), wells ('Cool as a Cucumber'), rivers ('The Occasional Yarrow'), lakes ('The Frozen Lake'), canals ('The Ride') and forest pools ('Fafnir and the Knights') all provide possible means of escape, enchantment or imaginative potential. In 'Deeply Morbid' (*CP*, p. 296), a lonely secretary escapes through the frame of a Turner painting in the National Gallery, captured by the 'burning coasts of fancy'. By the poem's conclusion,

> There was no more of London Town
> She went upon the painted shore
> And there she walks for ever more.

Yet if this sense of the coast as not just a temporary holiday but rather a permanent point of departure emphasises the imaginative potential of the shore space, it also moves us from Smith's whimsy to her stoicism – or from Edward Lear to King Lear.

Whilst 'Not Waving but Drowning' provides Smith's most famous example of the shoreline as an emissary for death, her poem 'Harold's Leap' from her 1951 collection of the same name provides a telling parallel. Again, the seaside observer gets something more than they bargained for:

> Harold, are you asleep?
> Harold, I remember your leap.
> It may have killed you
> But it was a brave thing to do.
> Two promontories ran high into the sky,
> He leapt from one rock to the other

And fell to the sea's smother.
Harold was always afraid to climb high,
But something urged him on,
He felt he should try.
I would not say that he was wrong,
Although he succeeded in doing nothing but die.
Would you?
Ever after that steep
Place was called Harold's Leap
It was a brave thing to do. (*CP*, p. 233)

As with 'Not Waving but Drowning', the speaker approaches death with apparent Senecan stoicism but a formal inability to comprehend it; like Smith's more famous poem, 'Harold's Leap' suggests the possibility of the dead man's speaking voice or an implied response from the memorialised subject. Harold's shift into the third person in line 5 perhaps signals the end of this posthumous dialogue, but the continued presence of the 'I' voice casts our speaker dangerously close to Helen from 'Beside the Seaside': the childlike explorer now captivated by the possibility of oblivion.

The poem's title which, by the end of the poem, might refer to Harold's suicide or to the cliff edge from which he jumped, blurs the line between topography and action.[6] The coast becomes a perilous theatre for human desolation. There are other textual prompts which expand this cliff edge still further: the mention of promontories together with the subject's name suggest Hamlet and perhaps, by association, King Lear, whilst the image of them running 'high into the sky' creates a landscape of infinite horizons. The space becomes psychic imagination.

Yet the ventriloquised death acts of 'Harold's Leap' and 'Not Waving but Drowning' also suggest a necessary sacrifice for self-preservation. It is this sense of the coast as the place where the sea claims its martyrs that enables the speaker in 'Our Bog is Dood' (*CP*, p. 265) to remain unharmed by the poem's act of vengeful destruction. This much-anthologised poem explores the power of language as dogma. With a sceptical Blakean eye for the inculcation of children into religious orthodoxy, the poem imagines a cultish theology which bursts into vigilante violence:

Our Bog is Dood, our Bog is dood,
They lisped in accents mild,
But when I asked them to explain
They grew a little wild.

As the poem progresses, their lisping accents speak increasingly with the zeal of religious prophecy, threatening the poem's rationalist speaker with crucifixion 'if you do not think it so'. Yet the biblical 'flood', when it comes, threatens apocalypse for the converted rather than the sceptic:

And sweetest of all to walk alone
Beside the encroaching sea,
The sea that soon should drown them all,
That never yet drowned me.

Here the coast seems a site of survival, of facing and diverting the threat of oblivion. The sense of the shoreline as a place of imaginative fancy seems inseparable from its equally typical incarnation as a scene for death and destruction. Imaginative departure permits Smith to remain landlocked, suburban and inward.

Darling England

Strongly linked to the sense of the coast as a portal to memory and departure is Smith's use of the coast as way of framing England itself. It offers the promise of distance from suburbia's enclosure and, for the explorer going beyond its horizons, the opportunity to assess the nation at a safe remove. When *Over the Frontier*'s narrative departs from English shores, every subsequent sea voyage prompts a meditation on the first island it has left behind:

> Steaming slowly along the too familiar too boring coast of the Baltic Sea, the faces of my darling friends in their farewell group on the platform at Victoria are still before me [...] coldly sadly anxiously watching the coastline slipping slipping

> further and further to the westward of us how great a sense of foreboding I have and a nostalgie for their quiet home and darling England. (p. 120)

Here, in a passage that seems oddly prescient of the displaced coastal traveller in W.G. Sebald's *The Rings of Saturn* (1997), every shoreline mimics the speaker's homeland, although Smith's defamiliarised 'nostalgie' seems keen to keep sentimentality at bay.

Smith's attitude towards Englishness can in part be read through the shifting relationship to the shoreline cultivated by the protagonists of her three novels: Pompey Casmilus in *Novel on Yellow Paper* (1936) and *Over the Frontier* (1938), and Celia Phoze in *The Holiday* (1949). Pompey rages against Cornwall's 'diabolic coast' in *Novel on Yellow Paper*. Although her antipathy goes unexplained in the narrative beyond an aesthetic disgust at its cliffs and harbours, it is tellingly the only Celtic coast described in her work, perhaps reflecting Smith's own antipathy to Celtic culture (p. 184).[7]

Following Smith's autobiographical prompt, Pompey recounts how her father ran off to join the Navy. His journey from port to port elicits cryptic postcards home reading 'Off to Valparaiso love Daddy'.[8] The coast or port becomes a familial symbol for abandonment and treachery. Tellingly, while detailing her family lineage in *Over the Frontier*, Pompey informs us that her Lion Aunt avoids the coast altogether: 'My grandfather explored, his daughter, casting inimical and insular eyes upon the seaview of Riga, stayed aboard, preferring the accustomed discomfort of a marine existence to the unknown detestability of Muscovy' (p. 125). Smith's artist-protagonists are caught between these two conflicting responses to the coast. The shore is a contested place which announces familial loyalties and represents the possibility of a willed isolation.

In *Novel on Yellow Paper*, Pompey's numerous seaside holidays come to represent her reluctance to leave England behind. Reaching Felixstowe before boarding the boat to Germany early on in the novel, Pompey confesses that she cannot describe the point of departure:

> To the Ultima Thule of Felixstowe Beach, Reader, I have not penetrated, preferring to run along the esplanade and back in time for a good English dinner, that

> has got none of the Continental nonsense about it, like I said the Great Eastern Hotel has been debauched, stampeded and contaminated by trans-German-Ocean food fancies. (p. 84)

Here Pompey worries over a seaside hotel whose cuisine has been 'contaminated' by the country she is about to visit – Felixstowe has become a portal to another nation, rather than a defence from it. The arch observational humour masks a narrative voice that is unwilling to abandon its native shore.

If both *Novel on Yellow Paper* and *Over the Frontier* explore Englishness against the rise of the Nazi party through a series of German holidays (and, in the latter, a fantasy section of the novel finds Pompey transformed into a military spy), *The Holiday* concerns itself with a post-Empire Britain. Tellingly, thoughts of the Baltic give way here to memories of an 'Indian place by the sea' (p. 98), as the protagonist Celia navigates through her complex response to Indian independence. Celia here is still troubled by familial allegiance – her holiday takes her no further than the east coast of England – but she aligns herself with her absconding father to sign herself a 'sailor' in her holiday postcards home because 'I left them, I sailed away' (p. 150).[9] The shifting borders of a crumbling Empire seem echoed by Celia as she makes herself comfortable on the coast of her England: 'I shift myself, after a little while, to the edge of the cliff, and look down to where there are firm sands and a little staircase across the bay to the left of us' (p. 150). In this series of competing metaphors for England's future, perhaps the most confident expression of national identity comes from a passage that relies on a literary heritage rather than a political legacy:

> It is a wonderful smell of fish out here, I say, it is an especially English smell of an English washed coast, the *English* fine days are so much better than the others because of the wet days that go before and come after [...] all the dead sea fish came up from the deep bed of the ocean, and they floated in upon the steep single beach, as it is in those parts, and their stomachs were split quite open, and the smell of the dead fish girdled the coast from Dungeness to Shakespeare's Cliff, and may be right around the coast to Sandwich and Deal, and the smell of it came up inland for a matter of a mile or so [...]. (pp. 167–71)

Shakespeare's Cliff, jutting out amidst the smell of brine and the crunch of shingle, points up the possibility of landscape that might be reclaimed through literature. Might there be further possibilities for linking the shoreline with the literary text itself?

The Littoral Text?

Smith once wrote to her friend Denis Johnston about the 'parts round that Norfolk coast that look like nobody had ever been there before just dunes and sand and sea and nobody at all'.[10] Here is a suggestion of the coast as a *tabula rasa*, a blank space for creation and recreation. Yet this literary reading of the beach as the writer's muse or empty page ensures a continual process of erasure and reclamation as much as it offers privacy. A passage from her 1938 novel *Over the Frontier* presents the coast in an extended metaphor for the creative imagination itself:

> Well now, is it not sad? Why now certainly this Pompey is becoming very sad-case and dippy, for see now I am crying, yes the tears are coming out plop and rolling down my cheeks, to think of these thoughts that have so many behind them, coming rolling in with the long rolling surges of the Pacific Ocean up against the Australian coastline; with so many thoughts, crested and predatory, coming rolling up alongside, and behind them out to sea a whole ocean of thoughts to come rolling and slithering up the beach of consciousness. Oh there will perhaps not be time for all the thoughts, all that great wilderness of thought, coming rolling from the deep deep sea. (pp. 44–5)

Smith presents her protagonist's own consciousness as a coastline, a place continually buffeted by the 'long rolling surges' of thought. It is an image of the shore as a place of perpetual change rather than finitude. Tellingly, the 'wilderness of thought' here also expresses its own ineffability. It laps again and again, unending, unrecordable.[11] This is a defiantly modernist coastline with its interest in interiority and its scepticism about the possibility of representing itself in language, suggesting a literary lineage of Joseph Conrad and Virginia Woolf. As Conrad wrote in *Heart of Darkness*, 'watching the coast as it slips by the ship is like thinking about an enigma. There it is before you – smiling, frowning, inviting, grand, mean, insipid, or savage, and always mute with an air of whispering, Come and find out'.[12]

Yet, elsewhere, Smith's coasts aspire to literariness less through their interest in representation and more with their sense of Smith's texts as imperilled beachcombers, prowling the shore looking for the promise of permanence. The refracted self-portrait of 'Mrs. Arbuthnot' describes a 'lady poet' whose talent has left her, and who now lives alone by the sea crying:

> I should write a poem,
> Can I look a wave in the face
> If I do not write a poem about a sea-wave,
> Putting the words in place. (*CP*, p. 492)

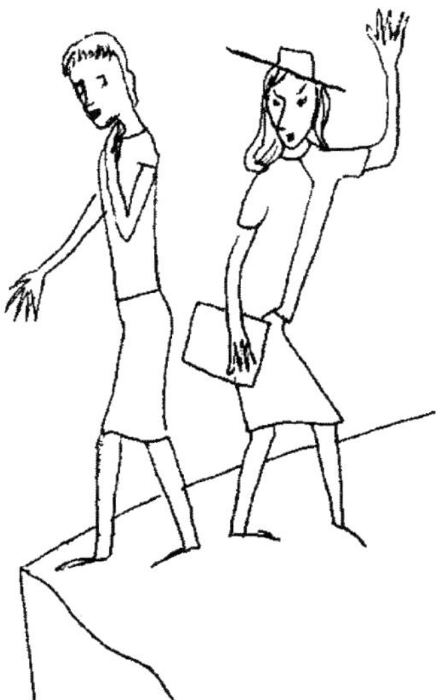

Figure 15

In this late poem, the coast becomes a metaphor for writer's block, the elemental promise of imaginative freedom only now recoverable as a shaming taunt.

The mechanics of writing and publishing are further literalised in Smith's illustrations of coast and cliff. This sketch (see Figure 15) was originally intended to accompany Smith's weekly book reviews in *Modern Woman* although it was never published.[13] As a depiction of a reviewer at work, both its sense of antagonism and its cliff-top setting are telling. Here, the book held by the reader on the right seems to be refracted by the precipitous book-as-cliff both the author and reader are standing on. The illustration finds them battling it out for supremacy, suggesting that the Romantic possibilities of the coast as a metaphor for artistic consciousness are soon disrupted by the reader as the jostling holidaymaker.

The illustration (see Figure 16) Smith includes in her publisher Hamish Miles's copy of *A Good Time Was Had By All* (1937), meanwhile, perfectly captures the jokey humour masking a deeper anxiety that characterises so much of Smith's writing about the coast.[14] Her three published books are represented by the three children (*Novel on Yellow Paper*, *Over the Frontier* and *A Good Time Was Had By All*) but here they make a dejected trio, scanning the shore for an author-mother they cannot see, and may even have had a hand in burying. They also seem to share a complicit acknowledgement that, having spent their day off in the sun, it may now be their own graves they are digging.[15] Smith's inclusion of lines from the poem 'Advice to Young Children' – 'Children who paddle where the ocean bed shelves steeply / Must take care that they do not paddle too deeply' – predates their first published context, where, as we have seen, Smith goes on to mock the kill-joy parents who would deny a child adventure in the interests of safety.[16] In this context, the 'shelves' of the ocean bed denote the precipitous drop from the library bookcase into obscurity. Smith adopts the role of the nervous guardian, hinting at a lingering regret about allowing her children-texts out in the first place. The accompanying inscription suggests a fear of not matching audience expectations, admitting to Hamish Miles that 'next time I may disappoint you'. She goes on to confess:

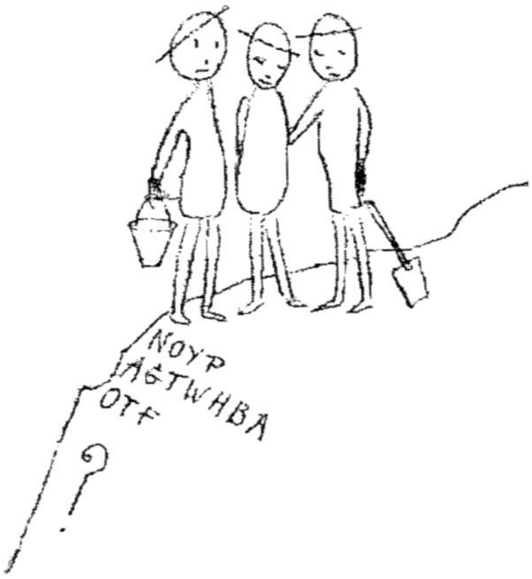

Figure 16

This thought turns my verse alas ends my rhyme for me
    Goodbye goodbye goodbye. Excuse
    Stevie.[17]

This coy but candid confession to her publisher suggests that the bucket-and-spade humour of her short story 'Beside the Seaside' veils anxiety under irreverence. The question mark tattooed into the sand undermines the bracing jollity of the title of her first poetry collection. Instead, the coast's relentless promise of unending horizons stutters into apology. Though the coast's possibility of escape and imaginative power creates and incites Smith's work, the interrogative here suggests that her own texts, and the creative consciousness that conceived them, will inevitability be washed over. The fear of impermanence is perhaps greater than the promise of escape.

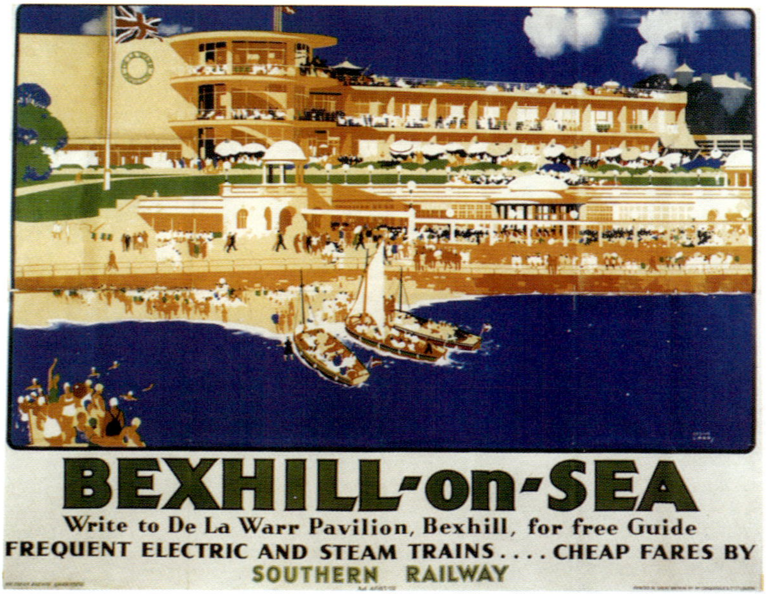

Plate 1

A 1930s railway poster promises sunshine and high style at Bexhill-on-Sea

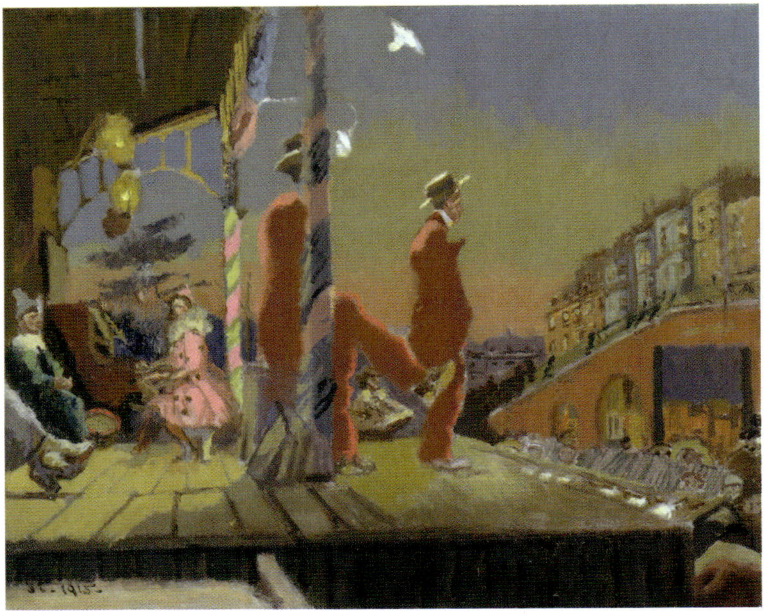

Plate 2

Sickert's melancholic painting of the Brighton pierrots playing to empty seats in 1915

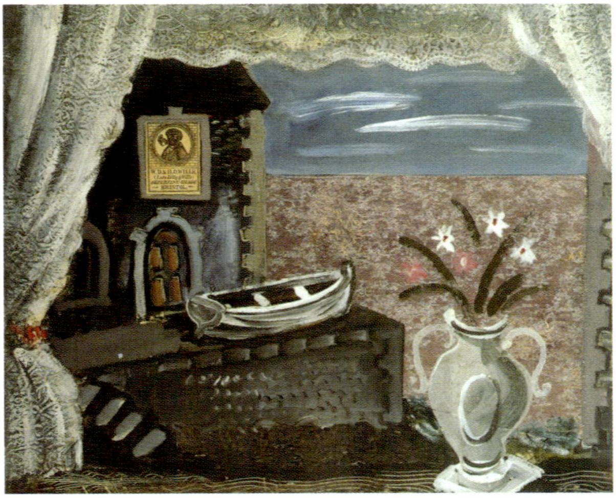

Plate 3

A coastal collage of foil and doilies:
John Piper's *The Harbour at Night*, 1933

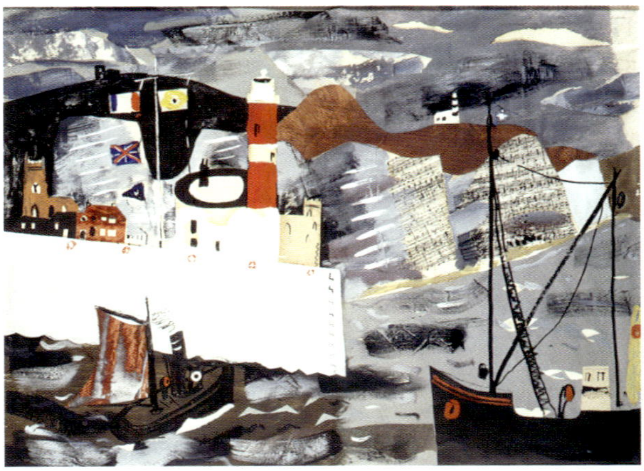

Plate 4

Harbour Scene, Newhaven, by John Piper, 1936–7

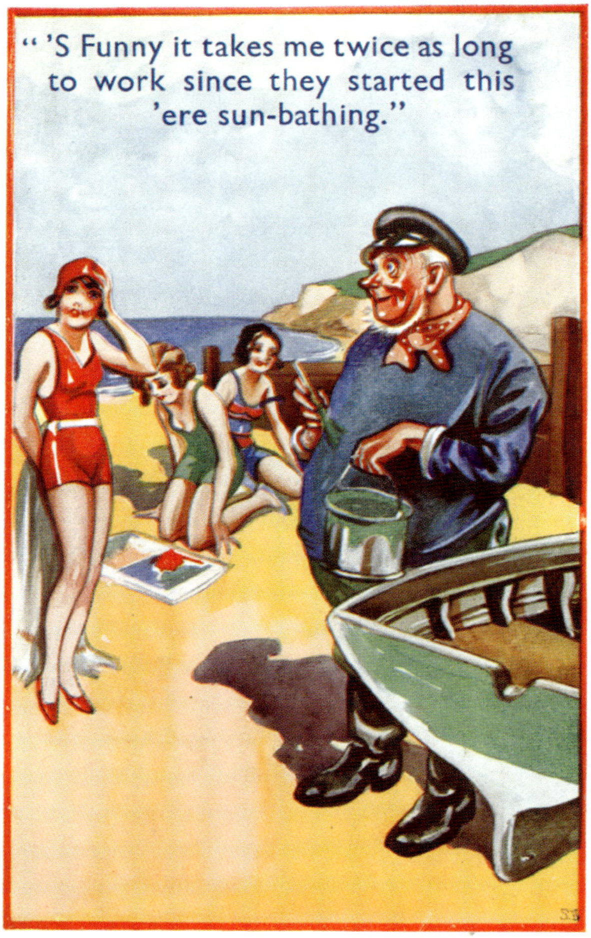

Plate 5

Cheeky and cheerful: the tradition of the seaside postcard

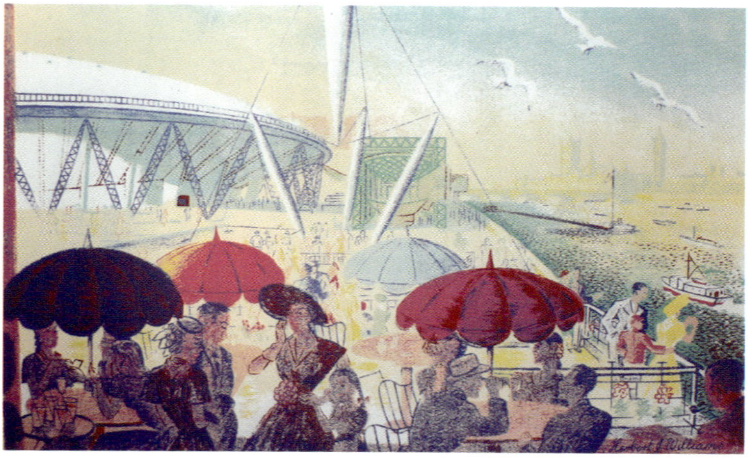

Plate 6

Parasols, promenades and seagulls at the Festival of Britain:
Festival Promenade, colour lithograph by Herbert Williams

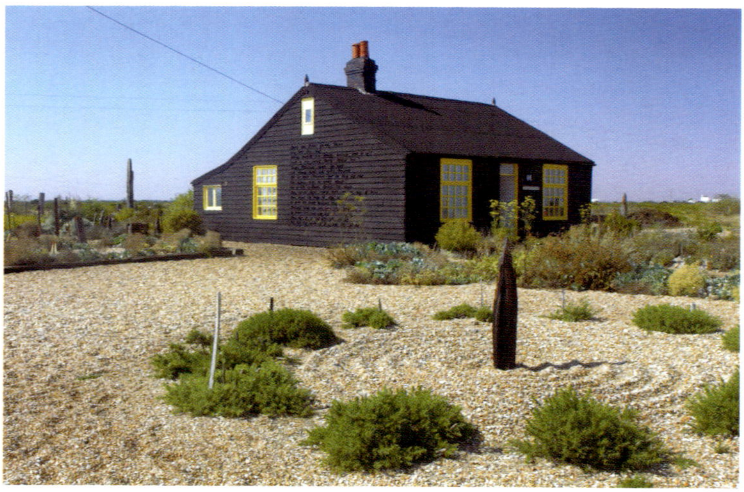

Plate 7

Magic Stones: Derek Jarman's garden at Prospect Cottage

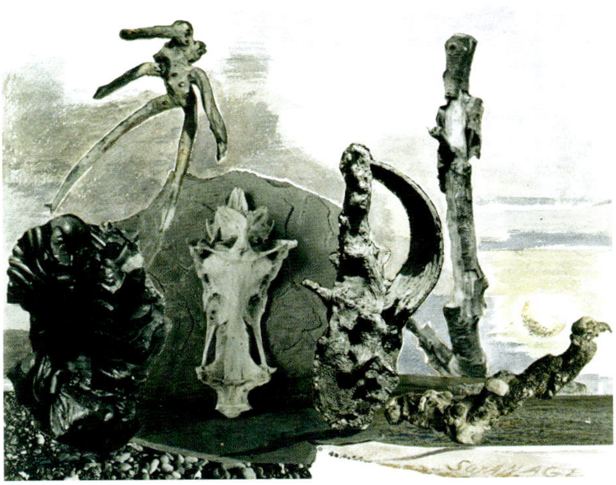

Plate 8

Paul Nash, *Swanage*, 1936

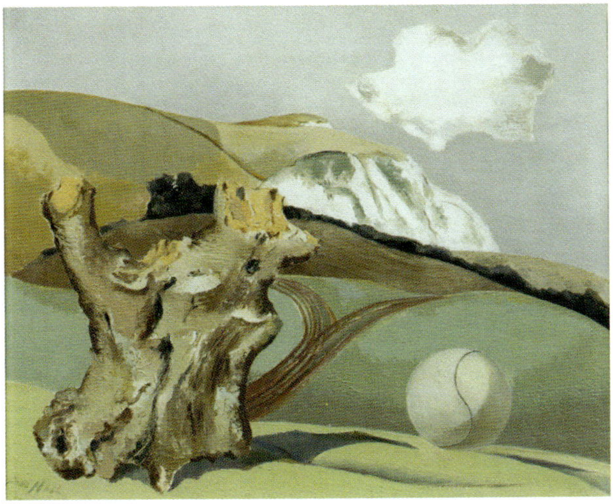

Plate 9

Paul Nash, *Event on the Downs*, 1934

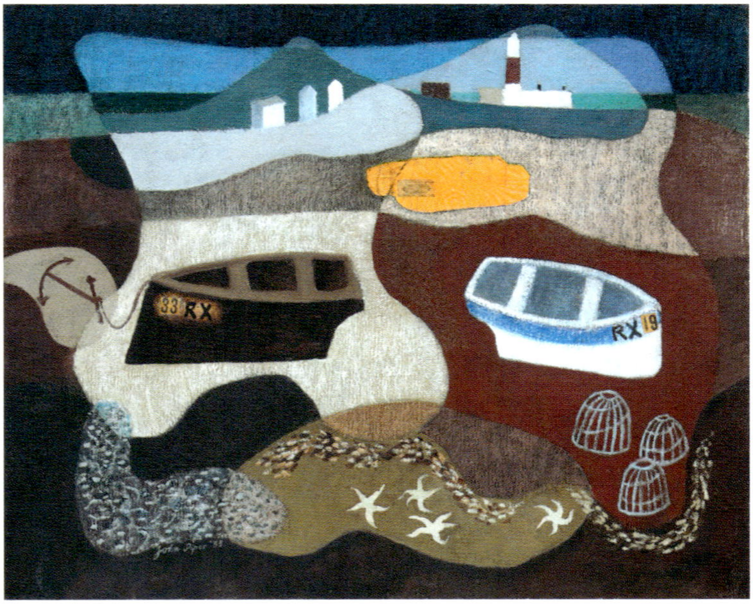

Plate 10

John Piper, *Foreshore with Boats, South Coast*, 1933

Part III

SEASIDE POETICS

David Bradshaw

David Bradshaw is Reader in English Literature at the University of Oxford and Hawthornden Fellow at Worcester College, Oxford. Among other volumes, he has edited *The Hidden Huxley*, *Decline and Fall*, *The Good Soldier*, *Brave New World*, *Women in Love*, *Mrs Dalloway*, *To the Lighthouse*, *A Concise Companion to Modernism*, *The Cambridge Companion to E.M. Forster* and, with Kevin J.H. Dettmar, *A Companion to Modernist Literature and Culture*. He is a Fellow of the English Association and the post-Romantic period editor of the *Review of English Studies*.

‘The Purest Ecstasy’

Virginia Woolf and the Sea

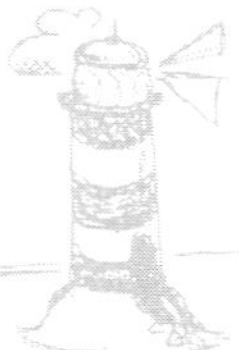

WHEN JOHN BOURKE ARGUED in his slender volume of 1954 that the sea has traditionally stood for three things in English poetry, freedom (both of movement and spiritual liberty), human life and eternity, he hardly whipped up a storm of dissent.[1] However, though the tweedy cut of his criticism is now as out of date as the clamour for dreadnoughts or Donald McGill’s fruity postcards, Bourke’s less than sensational reflections on the sea as a poetic symbol remain no less applicable to Virginia Woolf’s prose. No modernist writer, with the possible exceptions of Joseph Conrad and James Joyce, was so deeply inspired by the sea or spent so much of his or her imaginative life beside or beneath its figurative depths, and in the work of no other author from the modernist epoch is the sea invested with such rich symbolic value as it is in Woolf’s oeuvre.[2] And whilst the sea does function in her writings in the same broad ways that Bourke saw it functioning in English poetry at large, Woolf evokes it more frequently and profoundly as an emblem of the silenced and marginalised position of women. Similarly, although the submarine is occasionally represented as a place of security and peace in Woolf’s work, it is more commonly associated with isolation and annihilation. Above all, it seems likely that Woolf connected the beach, ambiguously positioned between land and sea, for ever shifting, always becoming more or less beachy, now terra firma, now washed away, with the first thirteen years of her life, a period of intense bliss before the sudden death of her mother in 1895 left her bereft not only of maternal affection and familial completeness, but also, no less suddenly, of St Ives, Cornwall, where

Woolf and her family had previously spent every summer vacation. Certainly, the beach symbolises a deep emotional fault-line in Woolf's fiction, a charged locus of joy, yearning, loss and grief. And if the littoral enchantment of her

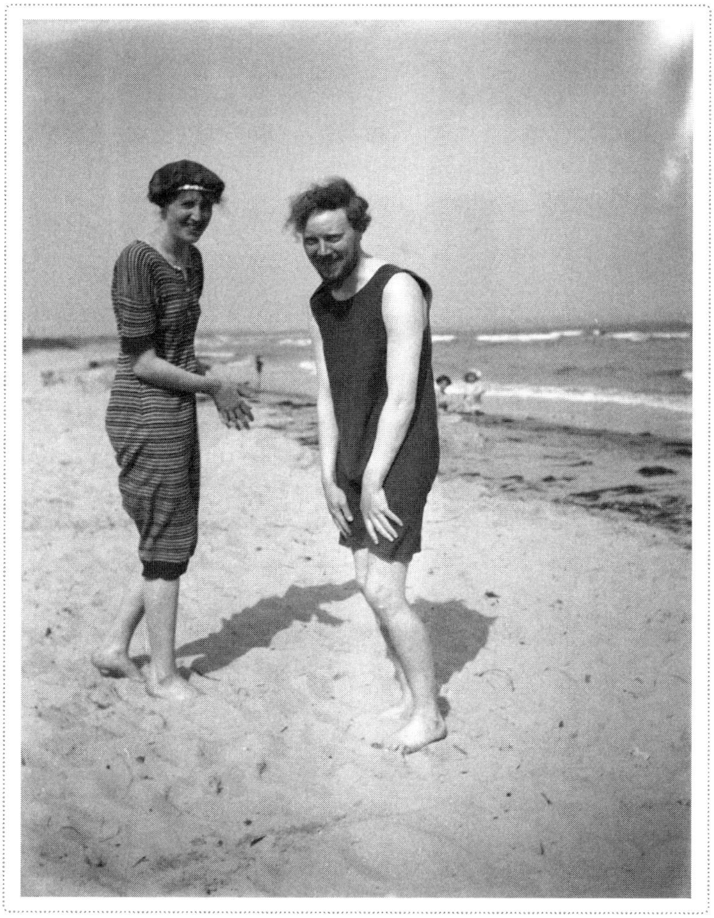

Figure 17 Bloomsbury on the beach: Virginia Woolf and Clive Bell at Studland Bay, 1910

childhood summers in Cornwall most obviously inspired parts of *Jacob's Room* (1922) and the whole of *To the Lighthouse* (1927), it oozes up as inexorably as sea water through the sand from the beginning of her canon to the end: indeed, it is the source from which flowed the whole wistful, lyrical, backward-looking, sea-salted, ghost-haunted cast of her genius. 'Why am I so incredibly & incurably romantic about Cornwall?', Woolf asked herself on the eve of a later visit to the county. 'One's past, I suppose: I see children running in the garden. A spring day. Life so new. People so enchanting. The sound of the sea at night.'[3]

In her late 'Sketch of the Past', Woolf reveals that her 'first memory, and in fact [...] the most important of all my memories' was of lying in bed and listening to the sea at Talland House, the summer home at St Ives which her father leased annually from 1882 to 1894. 'If life has a base that it stands upon', she writes,

> if it is a bowl that one fills and fills and fills – then my bowl without a doubt stands upon this memory. It is of lying half asleep, half awake, in bed in the nursery at St. Ives. It is of hearing the waves breaking, one, two, one, two, and sending a splash of water over the beach; and then breaking, one, two, one, two, behind a yellow blind. It is of hearing the blind draw its little acorn across the floor as the wind blew the blind out. It is of lying and hearing this splash and seeing this light, and feeling, it is almost impossible that I should be here; of feeling the purest ecstasy I can conceive.[4]

In August 1905, Woolf and her siblings, now orphaned (her father, Leslie Stephen, had died the previous year) and living together in London, returned to Cornwall. She wrote in her journal:

> It was with some feeling of enchantment that we took our places yesterday in the Great Western train. This was the wizard who was to transport us into another world, almost into another age. We would fain have believed that this little corner of England had slept under some enchanters [*sic*] spell since we last set eyes on it [...] we should find our past preserved, as though through all this time it had been guarded & treasured for us to come back to one day [...] Ah, how strange it was, then, to watch the familiar shapes of land & sea unroll themselves once more, as though a magicians [*sic*] hand had raised the curtain that hung between us, & to see once more the silent but palpable forms, which for more than ten years we had only seen in dreams, or in the visions of waking hours.[5]

Cornwall's 'silent but palpable forms', both natural and human, would haunt Woolf's fiction as powerfully as her mind, and the mingled sense of anticipation, trepidation, longing and curiosity which the four Stephen children carried with them on this 1905 journey back to the county seems to have been barely containable as they made their way at dusk towards Talland House:

> We could fancy that we were but coming home along the high road after some long day's outing, & that when we reached the gate ... we should thrust it open, & find ourselves among the familiar sights again. In the dark, indeed, we made bold to humour this fancy of ours further than we had a right to; we passed through the gate, groped stealthily but with sure feet up the carriage drive, mounted the little flight of rough steps, & peered through a chink in the escallonia hedge. There was the house, with its two lighted windows; there on the terrace were the stone urns, against the bank of tall flowers; all, so far as we could see was as though we had but left it in the morning. But yet, as we knew well, we could go no further; if we advanced the spell was broken. The lights were not our lights; the voices were the voices of strangers ... We hung there like ghosts in the shade of the hedge, & at the sound of footsteps we turned away.[6]

This powerful, painful account of the breaking of a spell, this bitter-sweet cameo of a fanciful homecoming, of hungering eyes and a lighted house, of belonging and severance commingled, is not, strictly speaking, a source for either *Jacob's Room* or *To the Lighthouse*, but the latter's setting in a summer home by the sea and its poignant fusion of mournfulness and rapture, nostalgia and deliverance, is drawn from the same deep well. Without her Cornish past Woolf's future career as a novelist would quite likely have taken a quite different shape and it is debatable whether her status as one of the great modernist writers would have been as assured as it is today.

Latent Inarticulate Passion

Jacob's Room rolls in on a high tide of elegy and eidetic topography. It opens with Betty Flanders, in tears, on a Cornish beach in September (just as the Stephens' summer vacations would typically stretch into that month) and immediately brings into focus a mother writing a letter, a bay and a lighthouse, all three being drawn directly from Woolf's own childhood: St Ives' Porthminster beach below Talland House; the view across St Ives Bay from the beach and Talland House to the Godrevy Lighthouse; and Julia Stephen's generation of relentless correspondence. Moreover, no sooner has the novel started than the reader is hand in hand with a distraught and fatherless child, Jacob Flanders, who has lost sight of his mother. In search of her, Jacob almost jumps from a rock onto a man and woman 'stretched entirely rigid, side by side', as if the corpses of his parents have been drawn up on the beach rather than it being an unknown couple taking a nap.[7] Reunited with his mother, Jacob leaves the beach carrying a sheep's skull, a *memento mori* that reappears throughout *Jacob's Room* and resurfaces as the boar's skull nailed to the nursery wall in *To the Lighthouse*. The narrator remarks early on that Mrs Flanders carries in 'the depths of her mind [...] some buried discomfort' (p. 8) and something very similar, it may be assumed, drove Woolf's pen forward as she wrote the opening chapter of *Jacob's Room*.

In her 1917 review of a new edition of Conrad's *Lord Jim* (1900), Woolf argued that '[t]he sea and the tropical forests dominate us and almost overpower us' in the novel and she goes on to speak of 'their largeness, their latent inarticulate passion'.[8] These observations shed interesting light on Woolf's own fiction from the same period. For example, they help us make sense of a striking paragraph in the second chapter of *The Voyage Out* (1915). The *Euphrosyne* has sailed down the Thames and into the English Channel on its journey to South America. The French coast is barely visible in the pale light of early morning as the passengers experience a remarkable sense of almost John Bourkian liberation: 'They were free of roads, free of mankind, and the same exhilaration at their freedom ran through them all.'[9] Up to this point in the novel the narrative has been completely realistic in mode, but when Rachel Vinrace suddenly observes Helen and Ridley Ambrose exchange a few intimate words and kiss, both she and the reader are plunged to the bottom of a rather more imaginary English Channel:

> Down she looked into the depth of the sea. While it was slightly disturbed on the surface by the passage of the Euphrosyne, beneath it was green and dim, and it grew dimmer and dimmer until the sand at the bottom was only a pale blur. One could scarcely see the black ribs of wrecked ships, or the spiral towers made by the burrowings of great eels, or the smooth green-sided monsters who came flickering this way and that. (p. 20)

Rachel is dredged up from her make-believe seabed by her father's 'smart blow upon the shoulder' (p. 20), but the reader lingers beneath the waves and begins to make connections between what Rachel has 'seen' on the floor of the sea and her predicament as an uneducated and unworldly young woman. The wrecked ship is a portent of Rachel's watery and untimely death, while the burrowing eels and 'green-sided monsters' may be read as manifestations of the sexual oppression of women in general (there are a number of references to prostitution and a prostitute in the novel) and Richard Dalloway's impending molestation of Rachel in particular. But it is also worth noting that in Woolf's first fictional evocation of the submarine, the world beneath the waves is not necessarily a sphere of isolation, estrangement or even death. In Rachel's eyes, it is almost a zone of comfort, sanctuary and security, of 'latent inarticulate passion' as opposed to the dogmatic and authoritarian world of patriarchal discourse. The 'great eels' and 'smooth green-sided monsters' also have a companionable appeal for her.

Significantly, when Rachel is first introduced to Hirst and Hewet in Chapter 10 she holds out her hand and then immediately withdraws it: '"It's all wet," she said', while towards the end of Chapter 12 she tells Hewet and Helen Ambrose that she 'feel[s] like a fish at the bottom of the sea' (pp. 117, 155). Hewet later recalls that when he first set eyes on Rachel he thought she was 'like a creature who'd lived all its life among pearls and old bones. Your hands were wet, d'you remember …' (p. 277). Rachel peers over the edge of a cliff to the bottom of the clear sea at the beginning of Chapter 16 – 'So it had been at the birth of the world, and so it had remained ever since' (p. 194) – and her observation is recalled further on in the chapter when Hewet reveals to her his curiosity about the domestic confinement of women, how 'until a few years ago no woman had ever come out by herself and said things at all. There it was going on in the background, for all those thousands of years, this curious silent unrepresented life' (p. 200). As Rachel and Hewet move off into 'the depths of the forest' in Chapter 20 it is as if they are submerging themselves under the waves and descending ever closer towards 'this curious silent [...] life' of women: 'the light grew dimmer, and the noises of the ordinary world were replaced by those creaking and sighing sounds which suggest to the traveller in a forest that he is walking at the bottom of the sea' (p. 256). By Chapter 25, Rachel, now terminally ill and bed-bound, has become identified with the goddess Sabrina, from Milton's *Comus*, who spends her life 'Under the glassy, cool, translucent wave' of the River Severn: 'The glassy, cool, translucent wave was almost visible before her, curling up at the end of the bed, and as it was refreshingly cool she tried to keep her mind fixed upon it [...] She was completely cut off, and unable to communicate with the rest of the world, isolated alone with her body' (pp. 311–12).[10] As she sinks out of life Rachel enters

> a deep pool of sticky water, which eventually closed over her head. She saw nothing and heard nothing but a faint booming sound, which was the sound of the sea rolling over her head. While all her tormenters thought that she was dead, she was not dead, but curled up at the bottom of the sea. There she lay, sometimes seeing darkness, sometimes light, while every now and then some one turned her over at the bottom of the sea. (p. 322)

In no time at all she has passed away, yet her symbolic submersion and especially Hewet's earlier sense of Rachel being 'like a creature who'd lived all its life among pearls and old bones' is brought to mind in the third part of *To the Lighthouse* when Cam is described in the fishing boat with her father and brother:

> Her hand cut a trail in the sea, as her mind made the green swirls and streaks into patterns and, numbed and shrouded, wandered in imagination in that underworld of waters where the pearls stuck in clusters to white sprays, where

> in the green light a change came over one's entire mind and one's body shone half transparent enveloped in a green cloak.[11]

Cam's submarine imaginings transform her into a kind of caped wraith shrouded by the sea, and for both her and Rachel the undersea is connected with the hazardous transition from adolescence to womanhood as well as acting as a place of escape from that process.

This alone may explain why Jacob Flanders and Timmy Durrant, in their yacht off the Cornish coast in *Jacob's Room*, are solely preoccupied with surface matters. Jacob is 'trying to read Shakespeare' (p. 60) when we first encounter the two young men at sea, while Timmy is priding himself on possessing navigational skills that have brought them within sight of the Scilly Isles. The two men have quarrelled about 'the right way to open a tin of beef' and have regressed to 'sulky schoolboys', more irritated than enchanted by the fact that 'the waves tumble and lollop much the same hour after hour – tumble and lollop all across the horizon' (p. 60). Both men are conscious in a sensible, matter-of-fact way that '[s]hips have been wrecked here' (p. 61), but, unlike Rachel and Cam, they show no inclination at all to look out for them or even to try to imagine them below the waves. Timmy, on the contrary, knows all about the ships that 'go past, keeping their own side of the road. [He] knew where they were bound, what their cargoes were, and, by looking through his glass, could tell the name of the line, and even guess what dividends it paid its shareholders.' Both men resort to their pipes and Timmy writes up 'some scientific observations' (p. 61), enquiring of Jacob either 'the exact time or day of the month?' (the narrator is not sure which). Jacob then takes a quick, frisky dip in the sea, his volume of Shakespeare topples overboard, and it is the narrator, not one of the two men, who speculates about the sorrows that the Cornish hillsides have witnessed, especially when the tin mines were operating. Jacob and Timmy then have another 'tremendous argument' (p. 63) before going on to discuss, among other things, dress codes, their friend Marsham and the Duke of Wellington. Finally they sing hymns, but they may as well be hugging the Cornish coast in a touring car, a train or an aeroplane, so indifferent have they been to the ever-changing colours of the sea around and beneath them.

'Solid Objects' (1920) also opens on a beach and also involves a 'violent argument' between two pipe-smoking young men, Charles and John, as they approach the water's edge from a distance:

> 'Politics be damned!' issued clearly from the body on the left-hand side [John], and, as these words were uttered, the mouths, noses, chins, little moustaches, tweed caps, rough boots, shooting coats, and check stockings of the two speakers became clearer and clearer; the smoke of their pipes went up into the air; nothing was so solid, so living, so hard, red, hirsute and virile as these two bodies for miles and miles of sea and sandhill.[12]

As with Jacob and Timmy, the immensity of the sea is something Charles and John take no interest in at all: Charles has been 'slashing the beach for half a mile or so' (p. 54) before reaching the shoreline and begins skimming pieces of slate over the waves once he is there, whereas John, though fascinated by the oozy suction of the beach when he burrows his hand and arm into it, is even more keen on solid objects. Having encountered a lump of green sea glass, he holds it out in front of him. 'It pleased him; it puzzled him; it was so hard, so concentrated, so definite an object compared with the vague sea and the hazy shore' (p. 55).

That Woolf attributed 'vague[ness]' or uncertainty to the sea and solidity to men and the masculine fabric of things is noteworthy. For if the undersea lies beyond the pale of patriarchy, beyond the control of fathers, the masculine focus on solidity and tangibility, both in 'Solid Objects' and *Jacob's Room*, shows the outdatedness of such a view of the world: by the 1920s, the whole notion of solidity had been exposed as illusory. Indeed, it had become increasingly clear that even the most solid objects were really as vague as the sea. 'When we compare the universe as it is now supposed to be with the universe as we had ordinarily preconceived it', A.S. Eddington wrote in *The Nature of the Physical World* (1928), 'the most arresting change is not the rearrangement of space and time by Einstein, but the dissolution of all that we regard as most solid into tiny specks floating in a void'.[13] Eddington begins his 'Introduction' by contrasting the apparently substantial table on which he is writing with the table revealed by modern science, a table which is 'mostly emptiness' (p. 6), and in *To the Lighthouse*, published in the same year that Eddington gave the Gifford Lectures in Cambridge on which he based his book, Woolf, too, introduces 'a phantom kitchen table' (p. 22). When Lily thinks of Mr Ramsay's philosophical work she always brings to mind 'a scrubbed kitchen table' (p. 22), and there are further reflections on the porous nature of solidity in *The Years* (1937) and *Between the Acts* (1941).[14] To become obsessed with solid objects, like John does in the story of that title, is to show ignorance of the latest developments in epistemology, and to show no interest in the sea is equally obtuse, revealing a dire limitation of the masculine outlook.

The All-absorbing Blue of the Sea

Just as Woolf condemned the materialism of Galsworthy, Wells and Bennett, so her alternative approach to fiction accorded with the latest discoveries about the porosity of the atom, and all the tensions that *To the Lighthouse* explores between the real and the phantom, the vague and the material, Victorians and moderns are embodied in the lighthouse itself.[15] At one level it is a mere solid object, substantial and immovable, and its solidity is reinforced as the novel progresses. For example, as seen by Mrs Ramsay in 'The Window', it is 'the hoary Lighthouse, distant, austere' (p. 19) and it is remembered by James as 'a silvery, misty-looking tower with a yellow eye that opened suddenly and softly in the evening' (p. 251). In other words, it is a deeply romanticised and beguiling structure befitting Woolf's critique of Victorian and Edwardian ideals. But when the reader approaches it with James, his sister and his father in the final section of the novel, James suddenly realises it is no more than a 'tower, stark and straight [...] barred with black and white [... and with] washing spread on the rocks to dry. So that was the Lighthouse, was it?' (p. 251; see also pp. 273 and 274). By reaching the lighthouse with Mr Ramsay, James and Cam, the reader is able to see that it is just another place of work, a thing of utility, a solid object, not romantic at all. However, like the substantiality of a kitchen table, the solidity of the lighthouse is deceptive. Seen from the lawn of the Ramsays' summer home, the lighthouse is 'almost invisible, had melted away into a blue haze' (p. 280), just as, seen from the fishing boat, the Isle of Skye becomes merely a 'frail blue shape' (p. 279), and between them lies the vague and all-absorbing blue of the sea. In the same spirit, as Lily dips her brush 'into the blue paint, she dipped too into the past there' (p. 232): what has been, what is and what will be are reconciled as one, and it is the sea that acts as the agent of reconciliation in this novel, bringing together island and lighthouse, wealth and poverty, feminine and masculine, vagueness and solidity.

It could not be more appropriate, therefore, that Minta Doyle loses her grandmother's brooch on the beach. Although she is mortified by its loss, it is in reality yet another hopeful sign that the younger generation is gradually being released from the world of Victorian things, the hold of Victorian matriarchs and patriarchs. That 'the brooch which her grandmother had fastened her cap with till the last day of her life' (p. 63) must soon be washed over by the incoming tide to be eventually absorbed by the sand of the beach, provides a fitting counterpart to John's disastrous discovery of the sea glass in 'Solid Objects', after which his career and life decline into obsessive disorder and oblivion. 'One can hardly tell which is the sea and which is the land' (p. 103), says Prue at the beginning of 'Time Passes', and this symbolic shift into vagueness anticipates the bringing together of island, lighthouse and sea at the end of the novel. It is as if the 'swollen sea-moistened woodwork' (p. 103) of the house becomes part of the sea before being dried out and made habitable again by Mrs McNab and Mrs Bast. Earlier in the novel the dampness of the house has stood for the social and sexual inequalities it has accommodated, but during the war years the house becomes more and more dilapidated until it is eventually abandoned, 'left like a shell on a sand-hill to fill with dry salt grains now that life had left it' (p. 112). Things become so precarious that if a feather had shifted its position, 'the whole house would have plunged to the depths to lie upon the sands of oblivion' (p. 114). But when the guests return to the house at the end of 'Time Passes' it has been brought back to life, to a better life, and '[t]he sigh of all the seas breaking in measure round the isles soothed them' (p. 116), just as it had soothed Woolf as she envisaged the novel: 'I am making up "To the Lighthouse"', she wrote in her diary on 27 June 1925, ' – the sea is to be heard all through it'.[16]

Woolf hoped the sea would also be 'heard all through' *The Waves* (1931), and it does resound through its 'interludes', yet in this novel the beach is more associated with conquest and violence than with loss.[17] Even in the first interlude the waves are described as '*pursuing* each other, perpetually' rather than following each other. In the second interlude, the waves descend 'with muffled thuds, like logs falling, on the shore', but just as readily suggesting some kind of bombardment, while in the third the waves 'drummed on the shore, like turbaned warriors, like turbaned men with pointed assegais'.[18] By the fourth interlude the waves fall 'with the concussion of horses' hooves on the turf. Their spray rose like the tossing of lances and assegais over the riders' heads [...] They drew in and out with the energy, the muscularity, of an engine which sweeps its force out and in again' (p. 68). Further on in this interlude we read that the sea now beats 'like a drum that raises a regiment of plumed and turbaned soldiers' (p. 69). By the fifth interlude, when the sun has reached 'its full height', the beach lies exposed as the site of a battle or resisted invasion: a 'rusty cartwheel', 'white bone' and a 'boot without laces' are all exposed, 'stuck, black as iron, in the sand' (p. 93). At the end of this interlude and in the sixth the waves have acquired a destructive energy (p. 106), while by the eighth, as the sun sinks, their power has diminished. Even so, the image Woolf deploys continues to be linked to destruction: 'the waves, as they neared the shore [...] fell in one long concussion, like a wall falling, a wall of grey stone, unpierced by any chink of light' (p. 134).

As Woolf planned *The Waves* she realised that she wanted 'to saturate every atom. I mean to eliminate all waste, deadness, superfluity: to give the moment whole; whatever it includes. Say that the moment is a combination of thought; sensation; the voice of the sea.'[19] 'Autobiography it might be called', she wrote a few months later.[20] With this comment in mind it is significant that at one point during the novel's emergence Woolf envisaged the beach not as a place of conflict but as a kind of vast maternity suite, teeming with babies. 'It is a vision of life emerging from the sea', Julia Briggs remarks of this draft passage in the holograph, 'of individual lives endlessly begetting others, like waves, and of the endlessly repeated throes of childhood, through which each self must enter the world – a vision of maternal genesis challenging the patriarchal narrative of scripture'.[21] At another point in the holograph the beach is again described as inundated with babies: 'Soon they were staggering across the sand, & leaving foot prints, the toe of one touching the heal of another ... There were innumerable footprints ... innumerable children ... pullulating, bubbling walking everywhere. The beach was black with them.'[22] But by the time the novel was published the waves and beach in the interludes are specifically connected with male conquest and violence. There is not a baby to be seen.

It is not just in the novels with a littoral aspect that the sea is audible. Even in Woolf's most emphatically metropolitan works, with the notable exception of *The Years*, sea imagery occasionally washes into the text in surprising ways. For example, when Katharine Hilbery shows Ralph Denham the family pictures in the first chapter of *Night and Day* (1919), the inner room in which they are displayed is described as being 'something like a chapel in a cathedral, or a grotto in a cave, for the booming sound of the traffic in the distance suggested the soft surge of waters, and the oval mirrors, with their silver surface, were like deep pools trembling beneath starlight'.[23] And in *Mrs Dalloway* (1925), Septimus Warren Smith figuratively drowns, feeling himself 'falling through the sea', before he flings himself to his death. Prior to this fatal act he has heard 'the sound of water' in his sitting-room and birds calling to him 'through the waves'.[24]

Sir Henry Newbolt begins his 'Introduction' to his compilation of *Sea-Life in English Literature from the Fourteenth to the Nineteenth Centuries*, published in the same year as *Mrs Dalloway*, as follows:

> A nation living in an island, and especially in an island so small as Great Britain, could not possibly escape the influence of the sea. Many millions of Russians or of Chinese pass their lives in communities so far inland that neither physically nor intellectually have they ever realised the existence of coasts or sundering oceans. An English child may not yet have seen the sea, but he cannot long have attained the power to read before becoming aware that the sea is his boundary, his safeguard, the only highroad of his food supply and his foreign travel. Whether or not it is an influence in his own personal life, it comes to him unavoidably as an element in the national life, a fact of practical and historical importance. And if he reads our English literature he will soon find out that it has given experience, tradition, and impulse to the imaginative wishes of his country for many generations. In short, whether we are landsmen or seamen ourselves, sea life is

> essentially a part of national life, part of its daily course, part of its record, part of its imaginative experience.[25]

Newbolt's patriotic tone helps us to appreciate why neither the sea nor the seaside figure prominently in modernist literature beyond the writings of Conrad, Joyce and Woolf. By the end of the First World War, the sea had become associated with a conception of character which was being debunked, a view of history that was being repudiated, a hallowed version of England which had lost its appeal and a hearty communality that many modernists reviled. The briny had by then as little attraction as the bosky. Newbolt, on the other hand, was so taken with the glamour of the sea that he seems to have overlooked Blériot's dashing Channel crossing of 1909 and the German air-raids on London during the First World War, both of which showed categorically that the sea was no longer England's 'safeguard'. It is this misplaced sense of national security, of England as an island fortress, that Woolf critiques in *Between the Acts*. Miss La Trobe's pageant may have been '*Drawn from our island history*', but Woolf and many other intellectuals in the late 1930s were all too aware that this was a comforting narrative that could easily come to an abrupt end with Hitler's forces gearing up for invasion; the planes that shred the Revd Streatfield's leisurely interpretation of the pageant bring this home all too forcefully: 'The word was cut in two. A zoom severed it'.[26] No area of the British Isles was beyond the range of Hitler's bombers and the sea would prove to be no obstacle at all to their menace.

The 'silent but palpable forms' which accompanied Woolf and her siblings on their visit to St Ives in 1905 remained with her throughout her life, despite her feeling that with *To the Lighthouse* she laid to rest the ghosts of her parents.[27] 'Often now I have to control my excitement – as if I were pushing through a screen ; or as if something beat fiercely close to me', Woolf had written in a diary entry of 13 June 1923. 'What this portends I don't know. It is a general sense of the poetry of existence that overcomes me. Often it is connected with the sea and St Ives.'[28] That these comments were written as the land-locked *Mrs Dalloway* flowed from her imagination and not one of her more obviously Cornwall-inspired fictions, provides the most telling testimony of all, perhaps, to the importance of the sea in and to Woolf's work and her life-long tendency to fly southwestwards in her mind to the landscape of her lost content. And, finally, perhaps it also helps explain why Woolf chose to drown herself in March 1941 rather than take her life in any other way – to dispatch herself to the 'sands of oblivion', to curl up, Rachel Vinrace-like, at the bottom of the River Ouse.

Ben Morgan

Ben Morgan is Williams Fellow and Tutor in English at Exeter College, Oxford. His research specialism is Shakespeare – his PhD thesis at Oxford traced the evolution of Shakespeare's dramaturgical theory and practice through his use of metatheatre. Since master's level he has also sustained a parallel interest in twentieth-century literature, particularly postcolonial and American writing, and has published on both Sylvia Plath and J.M. Coetzee. His poetry has been widely published in magazines from *Oxford Poetry* to *The Liberal*. As a graduate student he published prose in *The May Anthologies* 2006, a publication which led to the completion of his first novel. He is now beginning work on a longer project about Shakespeare and the limits of representation.

Survivals of Ariel

Sea and Form in Sylvia Plath's Poetry

Full fathom five thy father lies;
Of his bones are coral made;
Those are pearls that were his eyes;
Nothing of him that does fade,
But doth suffer a sea-change
Into something rich and strange.[1]

IMAGES OF THE SEA focused Sylvia Plath's anxieties about how to write poetry. The sea was a particularly charged image for a woman who crossed the Atlantic, and who wrote and married on its other side. Sylvia Plath looks at the sea with the eye of a culturally sensitive reader on her way to becoming a writer, paying attention to the sea's history as a literary image. She is drawn to the idea, derived from the New Critics and T.S. Eliot, that the poem should be a complete and autonomous object, outside time, belonging to an ideal order of perfect artefacts. But she is equally drawn, from her earliest work, to a sense that poetry that controls and denies personal, emotional chaos is a kind of lie, an act of bad faith – that to write truthfully is to be true to chaos. Plath's ideal form therefore takes on the shape of the sea: defined but formless, substantive but always in motion. In her late poems, the kind of personal, emotive sensationalism that Eliot rigorously excluded from high modernism creates not only her subject but her style.

When she writes about the sea, and the edge of the land, the author of *Ariel* also writes about the edge of the poem. Throughout her work, water ambivalently signifies uncontainable, subjective feeling – resistant to formalism yet demanding to be expressed. The place from which poetry can be written is poised untenably alongside, and sometimes in, the endlessly renewing chaos of the sea. The young Plath figures herself standing on the shore, looking out across the water that stands for everything her poems cannot contain: emotion whose truth cannot be expressed in continent form, whose truth is violence and rupture, and above all, whose truth is *sensational*: personal, specific, felt.

She is by no means the first or the last poet to confront this problem. But her change of attitude towards the sea setting in which so much of her poetry operates tells us a good deal about how she came to write her later poetry. To illustrate this shift clearly, this essay focuses on three of Plath's poems, representing three phases of her style, each identifiable with a different sense of the sea, and of the boundaries and potentialities of the lyric form. What happens in Plath's work, in this analysis, is that she stops commenting on and complaining about this problem and enters it, finding a position from which to speak. This ambivalent position is expressed in its most powerful and fully articulated form in her great poem 'Ariel', where the transition observed by Shakespeare's sprite (above) is intimately experienced by the speaker herself.

The Sea as Mirror

This essay is about what the sea stands for in the work of Sylvia Plath. But this is, of course, paradoxical. The sea cannot stand, cannot be fixed. The sea represents a threat to one's capacity to end anything, whether it is a journey, a process of mourning or a poem. To take one well-known example, Tennyson writes of the sea:

> Break, break, break on thy cold grey stones, O sea!
> I would that my tongue could utter
> The thoughts that arise in me.[2]

Here, the sea 'stands for' a kind of grieving sensibility – 'break, break, break, on thy cold grey stones' evokes the painful repetitions of grieving on the level of sense and sound – yet at the same time speaks of the natural world's utter indifference to that sensibility. The sea goes on breaking on the stones, regardless of the dialogue the speaker may wish to enter into with it. The water is a mirror that enables the speaker to see himself and his own inward predicament, but through its constant shifts and repetitions exposes his desire to identify with his image as tragic or even absurd. *Break break break* is, after all, what Tennyson also does to the Lady of Shalott's mirror. As Sylvia Plath asks in one of her earliest poems, 'What ceremony of words can patch the havoc?'[3] In a way, Tennyson asks the same question. Like the mourner who has to remake his life in the full knowledge of his loss, he speaks of the impossibility of speaking, making a kind of poetry – connection, unity, aesthetic completeness – out of the knowledge of disunity and separation. The very existence of his poem is therefore a paradox.

The Tennyson example derives, of course, from the nineteenth century, but it is not hard to see the sea in modernist writing as doing some of the same work, simultaneously making and breaking the correspondences that enable the expression of personal emotion. One such moment is the conclusion of Virginia Woolf's *The Waves*: the two different, and yet similar, endings she gives the novel. Bernard's impassioned 'against you I will fling myself, unvanquished and unyielding, O Death!' is set against the quite impersonal *The waves broke on the shore* that immediately follows it. The contrast is striking on the page.

> 'Against you I will fling myself, unvanquished and unyielding, O Death!'
> *The waves broke on the shore.*[4]

We are invited to see both a resemblance and a distance between the waves' final gesture and Bernard's. He has imagined crying defiantly at the moment of death that in himself he is not vanquished, not obliterated, not, if you like, broken. The breaking of the waves can be identified with Bernard's projected death, while it paradoxically consists in the breaking of that identification. If Tennyson's lines find in the sea the paradox of speaking without authority – speaking of one's own silence – Woolf's waves hold together the same ambivalence, both enabling and radically cutting off metaphoric resemblance.

Again, the sea is literally a place without linearity – a concrete gap that consists of tide and cycle, something that breaks, breaks and breaks – which means that it troubles metaphoric connections, unmaking them as soon as they are made.

Here is the twenty-two-year-old Sylvia Plath on *The Waves*:

> Last night: finished 'The Waves', which disturbed, almost angered by the endless sun, waves, birds, and the strange unevenness of description: a heavy, ungainly ugly sentence next to a fluent, pure, running one. But then the hair-raising fineness of the last 50 pages: Bernard's summary, an essay on life, on the problem: the deadness of a being to whom nothing can happen, who no longer creates, creates, against the casting down. That moment of illumination, fusion, creation: We made this: against the whole falling apart, away and coming again to make and make in the face of the flux: making of the moment something of permanence. That is the life work. [...] I shall go better than she.[5]

The problem with Woolf's prose, for Plath, is its own failure as an artwork to live up to the aesthetic philosophy she finds in the last fifty pages: its failure to be as well wrought as she would like, as perfectly complete. (There is too much contrast, too little of the 'pure, running style'; the imagery here implies a controlled flow of water.) In fact, for Plath, the prose lacks unity. She concludes by quantifying her competition with Woolf in these terms, at least by implication. *She* somehow will make of the moment something permanent, resisting the 'flux' that has risen from the content of Woolf's book and infected her form. She will create unity where Woolf has been the victim of dispersal. 'Too ephemeral,' she writes in the same passage. 'Needing the earth.' The sea's flux and formlessness comes to stand for the flux that artistic form must respond to and – for Plath at least – must resist and contain.

On one level, this is a rather simplified, though urgently felt, condensation of ideas Plath would have derived from her reading of the so-called 'New Critics' while at school. She received Cleanth Brooks's *Understanding Poetry* (a kind of propaganda text of this modernist movement) for her school literature prize in 1948 – at her personal request. Together with Brooks's *The Well Wrought Urn* and Wimsatt's *The Verbal Icon*, *Understanding Poetry* entered her well-stocked library and was scrawled over extensively.[6]

Keats's Grecian urn, from which Brooks borrowed his title, exemplifies this view of art: the urn's artist has made of a passing moment something that can never change. It is both moving and still, present and past, cold and hot, like Kubla Khan's fire-and-ice pleasure-dome, in which Brooks detects another image of the poem as a self-contained, absolute paradox. The high priest of this post-romantic view of the poem as an autonomous object absolved of authorial investment and historical context is the *fons et origo* of poetic modernism, Ezra Pound, whose poem 'faces in the station crowd / petals on a wet black bough' is perhaps the most compressed poem ever written outside of haiku.[7] Pound's view also found an enthusiastic vocalist in T.S. Eliot, whose 1919 essay 'Tradition and the Individual Talent' famously argued that the poem exists in an ideal order outside history, speaking to and of other poems, cleansed of the personality which produced it.

The fingerprints of this post-romantic belief system are all over Sylvia Plath's early writing. But what makes her interesting is the odd undertone of Tennysonian morbidity and irrationality that accompanies her formalist language, as though – like Tennyson – even in speaking it, she cannot help but undermine it. In 'Notes to a Neophyte' (1953) she imparts a lesson to a younger writer:

> [m]etamorphose the mollusc
> of vague vocabulary
> with structural discipline:
> stiffen the ordinary
> malleable mask
> to the granite grin of bone. (p. 306)

So much about New Criticism – its idea of the poem as a self-reliant paradoxical structure, able to contain opposites, its sense that a poem is an organic form, complete as a rock or a flower – is here in this poem.

> For such a tempering task
> heat furnace of paradox
> in an artifice of ice;
> make love and logic mix. (p. 306)

We can clearly see Plath's devotion to the idea of the poem as solid and instrumental, the sort of imagery a critic like T.E. Hulme was using when he spoke of poetry as a 'knife order'. But we also sense an odd current of discontent and even violence, as the images insist on frozenness, hardness and death ('the granite grin of bone'). In the moment of advocating hard, linear, continent form, she seems to suggest there is something life-denying about it, as though she is being drawn back, by implication, to a different aesthetic, more fluid, more capable of tolerating formlessness.

Similarly, in the passage on *The Waves* where she responds to her most obvious modernist precursor, even as the young Plath seems to subscribe to a formalist aesthetic, she cannot suppress a parallel and complicating interest in the flux and smash of the sea, or of language and experience. Indeed, the very language of that passage seems to mimic the sea's tendency to collapse individuality into a generalised movement: the words themselves pick up on and repeat each other in a crashing rhythm that sounds like nothing so much as a tide: 'That moment of illumination, fusion, creation: We made this: against the whole falling apart, away and coming again to make and make in the face of the flux.' Plath is clearly in love with the destructive force she is trying to resist, or at least recognises it, like Shelley's west wind, as the power she has to harness. Moreover, and perhaps more profoundly, if the sea is iterative, breaking and breaking and breaking, so is Plath's ideal writer: she 'create[s] and creates', 'makes and makes'. Repetition, which is a mechanism of grief, is made into the figure of creativity, which literally can never stop. In this regard, it is unstable and overflowing, not unlike the sea that it resists. Like Woolf and Eliot, Plath's writing here confesses the overwhelming *presence* of chaos and fragmentation. If she is ambivalent here, she is drawing partly on an ambivalence that already exists in modernist writing itself.

The fear that the imagination will be usurped by the reality it cannot hold in check dominates Plath's oeuvre. Some of her earliest writing about her seaside childhood (she was born and raised in Cape Cod and Winthrop, Massachusetts) emphasises the need to impose on reality the power of the shaping imagination in ways that echo both Brooks and the New Critics and (perhaps via Eliot) the famous passage from Ariel's song that will later inform her major work. This is evident throughout her poetry, perhaps most tellingly in an early work, 'Full Fathom Five' (1959), and one of her final and most famous poems, 'Ariel' (1962). The clues are in the titles: the first poem focuses on the dead father, the second on the process of transformation, with Eliot always lurking in the background.

The Sea as Terminus

'Full Fathom Five', the next poem I will consider here, describes a speaker standing on a shoreline beyond which a near-mythical figure, whom s/he addresses as 'father', seems occasionally, and unpredictably, to appear. He has evidently died (the speaker remembers 'the muddy rumours / Of your burial', p. 92), and when he resurfaces from the sea it is as a kind of sinister *objet d'art*, somehow existing beyond time – yet beaten, one notes, to 'the granite grin of bone': 'the archaic trenched lines / Of your grained face shed time in runnels' (p. 92). In fact, he shares with New Criticism and its Coleridgean and Shakespearean totems – Kubla Khan's pleasure-dome, the albatross and its sea setting, Alonso's bones – the quality of representing death-in-life, even, perhaps, reality's transformation into artistic form. He appears to have undergone the sea-change Ariel observes, and enacts, over Alonso, who too will 'reappear' from the fatal ocean: huger than life, yet dead and alive, he is as cold as 'keeled ice-mountains / Of the north' (p. 92).

And yet the effect on the speaker of this curiously artificial figure of mourning is to disorient his or her sense of the very thing he represents, their shared origin. Scrutinising his or her patriarch, and trying to identify in him the source of his or her vision, speech and being, the speaker gives up:

> Miles long
>
> Extend the radial sheaves
> Of your spread hair, in which wrinkling skeins,
> Knotted, caught, survives
>
> The old myth of origins
> Unimaginable. (p. 92)

This is not just a psychological disorientation; it is an instability within the language of the poem. It is, in fact, impossible to say exactly what the speaker is looking at here. The lines invite a sexual reading – the 'spread hair' as pubic, the 'myth of origins' a phallus – while at the same time the vastness of the image ('Miles long'), and the oddly ironic hocus-pocus of the language, its artificiality ('in which wrinkling skeins'), weighty diction and gesture towards myth, make this reading feel reductive. What the speaker sees, in fact, is obscurity itself: an unimaginable origin, a limit to her vision and her language which nevertheless lies at the root of that language, at the root – literal and figurative – of the person who speaks. This father, a figure replete with mythology and significance of an obscure kind, is unreadable, unfathomable: 'to be steered clear / Of, not fathomed' (p. 92).

Naturally, to get *down* to the root, to speak from her origins, is the apogee of the speaker's desire. But it also marks his or her own death, and the death of the poem, which ends:

> Your shelled bed I remember.
> Father, this thick air is murderous.
> I would breathe water. (p. 92)

In the context of the conscious and ironic artificiality of the poem's scene, this extravagant claim represents the thanatic force given a sly, metaliterary slant. If 'Notes to a Neophyte' held in tension the opposite poles of unity and death, these last stanzas speak dramatically of the speaker's need to enter a place that combines opposites: 'Father [...] I would breathe water.' Breathing water, like walking on water, is a suspension of the laws of time and space; it is the holding in tension of that which feels constantly on the verge of splitting apart. The end of this poem puts the maximum possible pressure on the New Critical image of poetry as autonomous, self-contained and paradoxical, as cold fire, motionless time or burning ice. The essential gesture of the New Critical poem, towards paradoxical, self-sustaining unity, is figured at the end as a death wish.

If the poem talks about the borderline between psychology and literary tradition, it reflects in its diction the same crisis: both emotional and intellectual, a crisis of personality *and* form. As we read, we realise that the poem itself is self-destructive, since its language consists in constantly being just about to slip out of control, something Plath renders brilliantly visible on the page. The whole poem looks as though it has been off-set, presented at an odd and perilous angle, making its speech laboured and awkward. There is almost a gasp between the 'foam-' that ends the first stanza and the 'Capped' that opens the second, as though the poem might not quite make the leap over the stanza break:

> Where seas wash cold, foam-
>
> Capped [...]

Another awkward moment arises in stanza six:

> Your dangers are many. I
> Cannot look much but your form suffers
> Some strange injury.

The rebellious movement of the lines – sense strained, as it is throughout the poem, by the interruptions of an awkward, even brutal enjambment – makes us feel the desire of the 'I' not to participate in the narrative, to look away, only to be dragged back into the drama just in time. The obscurity the father represents makes itself felt, visibly and audibly, in all those odd and inhibiting line breaks: every blank space in the poem bears witness to his presence.

The question of who it is that suffers, and seems to die, is an open one. Ostensibly, it is the body of the father; but when that father is a literary artefact, derived from the seabed of *The Tempest*, where his bones stand for imaginative transformation, we can dimly make out poetic form itself suffering and being injured. Like Hamlet's father, whose injunction to 'remember me' this poem analogously obeys, this god who denies all other gods grows more and more fragmented the more absolutely he installs himself in control of the poem's rhetoric.

Waist down, you may wind

One labyrinthine tangle
To root-deep among knuckles,
Shinbones, shells. (p. 92)

This God, we remember, makes his own origins 'unimaginable'. Here, his threat is the threat of obscurity, he winds down into concrete fragments: knuckles, shinbones and shells. What is 'winding down' here is also the ability to make firm statements. The more the poem commits to worshipping the sea-god, the more it commits to its own fragmentation. This is the irony of the poem's conclusion: the curious crab-like progression suddenly resolves itself into the perfect, fluent, final two stanzas, with their smooth series of end-stopped lines, simply when, and because, they express despair. The poem is never more visibly confident than when it speaks of its own failure and death, when its speaker denies herself and asks to drown.

You defy other godhood.
I walk dry on your kingdom's border
Exiled to no good.

Your shelled bed I remember.
Father, this thick air is murderous.
I would breathe water.

But the poem stops there, at the edge. Plath's speaker cannot speak from underwater: she looks out across the element she longs to enter, recognising that to enter it is fatal. If it is fatal to her, it is fatal also to her poem, which experiences the father and his store of unrepresentable grief as a threat to its very form. Far more complex, 'Full Fathom Five' nevertheless remains at the decorous distance of 'Notes to a Neophyte'. The question these early works leave us with is how the concrete mess of reality can be transformed into form without following the deadly advice of the earlier poem, which would rob chaos of its quiddity: in Plath's image, how to breathe water.

It is a problem of experience and identity, which, in Plath's hands, becomes a subtly delineated crisis within the poet's relationship to poetic tradition. The poem's form suffers under the pressure of everything the sea represents for Sylvia Plath: obscene personal emotion, outside the boundaries of modernism at its most austere.

The Sea as Form

I will end by looking briefly at the poem which in some ways represents the climax of this seam of Plath's thinking. It is called 'Ariel', and rather than simply talking sadly about the impossibility of holding water, it becomes water: becomes the flux of personal experience. Rather than presenting the granite grin of the art object in 'Notes to a Neophyte', this poem focuses on movement. It is not about object but about process, making its form the sign of raw becoming and not of formal perfection. Its referent is initially, and tellingly, unclear, but it in fact describes the *process* of being carried away by a runaway horse.

> Stasis in darkness.
> Then the substanceless blue pour
> Of tor and distances. (p. 239)

As the speaker, a kind of solitary Valkyrie, gives herself over to her wild flight, she seems to enter a space where every ornament of selfhood is burned away:

> White
> Godiva, I unpeel –
> Dead hands, dead stringencies.

Initially, the shift might appear to be a shift into an embodied unity with the natural scene around her:

And now I
Foam to wheat, a glitter of seas ...

And I
Am the arrow,
The dew that flies

Suicidal. (p. 240)

But a closer look at the language here makes any vocabulary of transformation problematic, since this is a transformation which appears to have no end point but its own dissolution, its own eternal becoming and unbecoming: 'foaming' to wheat, this speaker enters a glitter of seas, which in turn transforms into an arrow, then a drop of dew, each themselves moving into a self-obliterating unity with the sun. That state figured throughout her work by the sea – a state of becoming without end – *is* the end-point, the *telos* of this poem.

It is also its narrative logic. The first thing that happens to this poem's landscape is that it turns to water: 'The [...] blue pour / Of tor and distances'. In a way, 'distances' have been the subject of this essay – the chaotic and subjective space represented by the sea. Here, Plath's speaker enters that distance itself, no longer mourning it or observing it, but becoming one with it. Objects are obliterated. Berries become shadows; the horse's neck is joined with the field's furrow:

The furrow

Splits and passes, sister to
The brown arc
Of the neck I cannot catch,

Nigger-eye
Berries cast dark
Hooks –

Indeed, the horse is never really described, only its secondary effect – motion – which it comes to represent. The phenomenon of movement – movement through space – becomes a source of speech. Where Tennyson treated the uncrossable space between him and the natural world, figured by the sea, as a kind of grief, Plath understands it as a kind of ecstasy. Indeed, as we have seen, her speaker enters that space and becomes it. 'And now I / Foam to wheat, a glitter of seas': the movement of the language becomes an ontological transition, a movement from being into becoming, into the constant break, break, break of the sea. The poem concludes with the speaker entering the liminal state of a drop of dew, being sucked up into the morning sun. She is finally breathing water, or breathing *as* water: she both has form, and has no form. Her form is space, the space between dew and sun. The poem now represents the movement between lived experience and deathly apotheosis which appeared as an irreconcilable irony in that early poem, 'Notes to a Neophyte'.

The vehicle through which Plath manages, experiences and expresses this change in her writing is, quite simply, poetic style. Here, impersonality, the holy grail of so much modernist thinking about poetry, is arrived at through the vividly, sensationally personal; sensational in the sense that the material is provocative but also that we *feel* the transition very intensely, as a result of the texture and purposefulness of the verse. Comparing her lexicon here with the language Plath uses for the sea in her critique of Virginia Woolf, it is evident how far she has come. There, her rush of smooth, flowing adjectives seemed to challenge the objectivist aesthetic she was setting out: 'Against the whole falling apart, away and coming again to make and make in the face of the flux'. Here, Plath is entirely at ease with the dissolutions and ruptured boundaries of sound: it is part of the texture of her speaker's transition. It is impossible not to luxuriate in the poem's clashing, sibilant noise.

But it would be wrong to say this poem broke free of modernism into confessional directness. The title is both direct and somewhat arch; the language is showily controlled; the poem, with its jagged edges, is a controlled plummet down the page. Plath's purpose is always ambivalent; she attempts to join together dissolution and formal completeness, to make a space for the sea's nothingness within the fixed boundaries of form. Here, Plath wears her New Critical credentials with particular obtrusiveness: the title reminds us of another text, the first line is drawn from Aeschylus' description of Klytemnestra as a lioness of God, and the final line is a lovely, ironic pun. This bouncing between texts hijacks the New Critical aesthetic in the name of the aesthetic of the gap, the rupture. It is almost giddy, reminding us that it is in the nature of nothing – no-one-thing – to rebound between positions, settling on none.

> And I
> Am the arrow,
>
> The dew that flies
> Suicidal, at one with the drive
> Into the red
>
> Eye, the cauldron of morning.

Here, Plath is speaking not only from beyond her everyday, conscious identity, not only from within 'the glitter of seas' from which she was 'exiled to no good' in 'Full Fathom Five', but also from within the blank space between the lines of that earlier poem: here, the savage enjambements speak of an endless transformation which even separates 'I' from 'Am'. To be formal, teleological even, about dissolution and circularity, is the paradox on which this poem rests, the paradox figured as the space between 'I' and 'Am'. She makes a form replete with absences the vehicle for the most vivid expression of *presence*, personal and authorial, in all her work: the gap separating 'I' and 'Am', after all, oddly lends each word an added authority and presence on the page. In this close attention to language and diction, she is the consummate New Critical poet. Plath accomplishes her plunge into formlessness through a careful, self-conscious treatment of poetic form and its histories: the paradox, repeatedly, of her late work.

'Ariel', then, represents one of Sylvia Plath's versions of a solution to the problem of breathing water, engulfing yourself in flux and speaking of it without fixing it down. The overt statement of Plath's poem can be compared both to Bernard's defiant last cry in Woolf's *The Waves*, and to the last words of that novel: it is both a declaration of absolute individuality, unchangeable form, and an acceptance of change and cyclical movement. We can almost imagine that in this poem Sylvia Plath speaks from within the gap between those two lines, those two views of being, from the unfixable space in between them which she so often figures as the sea.

Part IV

NAUTICAL STYLE

Frances Spalding

Frances Spalding is an art historian, critic and biographer. She is Professor of Art History at Newcastle University and also a specialist in modern British art. Her books include *British Art since 1900*, a centenary history of the Tate, biographies of the artists Roger Fry, Vanessa Bell, John Minton, Duncan Grant, Gwen Raverat and the poet Stevie Smith, and an introduction to the Bloomsbury Group in the National Portrait Gallery's 'Insight' series. Her study of the life and work of John and Myfanwy Piper will be published by Oxford University Press in 2009.

In the Nautical Tradition: John Piper

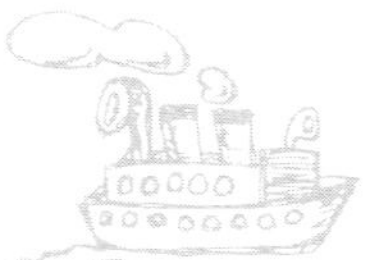

'BLESS ALL PORTS' Wyndham Lewis announced in 1914, devoting an entire page to this subject in the first issue of *Blast*.[1] From then on a maritime theme became gradually woven into the developing history of modernist theory and practice. Edward Wadsworth, Lewis's fellow vorticist, made dockyards and ports a central aspect of his oeuvre, also obtaining an intense feeling for the sea from a few pieces of bleached cork and some seashells. Readers of Le Corbusier's famous manifesto, *Vers une architecture*, an English translation of which appeared in 1927, not only learnt that a house is a machine for living in, but were encouraged to see in a steamship ('a machine for transport') an 'important manifestation of temerity, of discipline, of harmony, of a beauty that is calm, vital and strong'.[2] His famous desire that form should follow function led him to argue that a modern dwelling, in its use of space, should be conceived as economically as a ship's cabin. By the 1930s this association of good design with a ship's architecture had become so accepted that when King George V's yacht, R.Y.S. *Britannia*, was broken up, the art dealer Rex Nan Kivell bought some of its parts and incorporated them into the new premises of his Redfern Gallery in Cork Street.

In this context it is not difficult to see why John Piper's interest in the trimness, purposefulness and swagger of seaside architecture and maritime design chimed nicely with the modern movement. Both had a strong functional basis. 'On the coast waves break and salt foam scatters and denudes, gales blow stronger and the rain is more searching,' Piper writes. 'Buildings must be sturdy and close to the earth.'[3] '"Modern" architecture', he insists, 'has a pull by the seaside, because its straightforwardness, its clarity and functionalism are in the nautical tradition.'[4]

These remarks can be found in his razor-sharp essay 'The Nautical Style', first published in the *Architectural Review* in January 1938. Here he revealed his full responsiveness to the seaside manner in all its cultural manifestations. Though this article has been acknowledged as seminal, it has played surprisingly little part in recent debates about English modernism in the 1930s. Today, its significance also lies in the fact that it was ahead of its time in dealing with issues of style under the generous embrace of visual culture. Whereas Paul Nash, whom Piper regarded as his 'artistic father', saw in the modern movement a recovery of the architectural values of classicism, Piper was to evolve a rougher, more demotic and inclusive aesthetic, operative over a wide visual spectrum. Certainly, anyone offering a critique of modernism in Britain in the 1930s can find in 'The Nautical Style' a text that has both resonance and accuracy. My intention in this essay is to position this article within the wider context of Piper's involvement with the coastal subjects and to point up its connection with a slightly earlier article in the *Architectural Review*.

The seaside was a subject close to John Piper's heart. This is signalled in his early journalism, in 1933, by his remark that the sea is a 'powerful emotive force' in English art.[5] Two years earlier, he had filled a sketchbook with coastal subjects, drawing the hulls of boats, buoys stranded on the shore, shoreline buildings and a lone painter with his easel on the beach (see Figure 18). From the shape of the boats in this sketchbook, it can be inferred that he was working somewhere on the Suffolk coast. But during the early 1930s, while he had a base at Betchworth in Surrey, he had relatively easy access to the south coast. We know that he made visits to Bognor Regis, Dungeness and Newhaven, to Portland and Chesil Beach in Dorset, later going further afield, to Aberaeron in Wales, and to Cornwall. For a period he rented the black-painted Rose Cottage, on the edge of the beach at Rye Harbour. But, as he pointed out in an article in *The Listener*, there is no place in England more than seventy miles from the sea: 'The sea is the mystery that lies beyond the flat fields and the woods, the downs, the rough moors and the Black Country recesses: never far away'.[6]

What began as one of the pleasures of his childhood became in adulthood a passion. And there were many aspects of the sea that he loved: remote and empty beaches; rocky coastlines; the forthrightness of coastal buildings; the

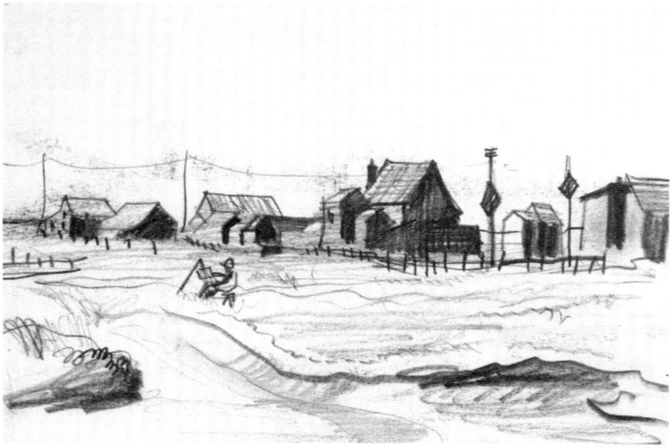

Figure 18
The artist on the beach, from John Piper's 1931 sketchbook

romance of lighthouses; the appearance of strength in nautical machinery; fishermen's huts and signal masts; and the elegant sweep of the grander seaside resorts such as Brighton and Scarborough. He was more broadly responsive to maritime subjects than any other artist at this time and returned to them time and again in his art of the early 1930s.

Often the sea appears in his pictures as a view through a window. This use of the window to frame a view was a popular trope at this time, particularly among painters associated with the 7 & 5 Society. Offering a picture within a picture, and therefore permitting a modernist play upon reality and illusion, it was a motif that Piper used repeatedly, sometimes adding a shutter or paper doilies which stood in as witty substitutes for lace curtains. Sometimes too the doilies acted as stencils for crisp, delicate patterning on curtains and still-life objects. In one picture, he paints over silver foil to suggest the glitter of light on the sea (see Plate 3). This playful inventiveness extended to collages of cliff and beach scenes incorporating newspaper, marbled paper and scrim (see Plate 4), as well as vividly detailed engravings of shells and fish, cut out of aquarium catalogues, which charge the picture with a surreal quality reminiscent of Max Ernst. Then, too, in some of these early coastal subjects the eye snags on the home-port lettering and numbering which, for Piper, had 'the same punch and prominence as "LE JOURNAL" in a Picasso still-life'.[7]

At a personal level, the early 1930s were a period of disappointment and frustration for John Piper. His marriage to Eileen Holding was failing. The couple were moving towards an agreed separation before John met Myfanwy Evans. Suitably enough, this meeting took place at the seaside, both having been invited by the painter Ivon Hitchens, in June 1934, to spend a weekend at Sizewell on the Suffolk coast. Sent to collect Evans from Leiston station, Piper was smitten the moment she stepped out of the train. As it was a warm evening, they went for a swim in the sea before joining the rest of the party and this proved a propitious start to their relationship. Shortly afterwards, Piper took Evans to Dorset, where they stayed at Abbotsbury, nine miles from Weymouth, and walked for miles along the shingle on Chesil Beach.

When Evans disappeared to Devon and Cornwall for a holiday in July 1934, Piper wrote to her: 'Send me some S. Devon lighthouses from Dartmoor and other intimations of your existence.'[8] A similar request followed her to St Ives. 'Don't miss it,' he wrote, referring to the lighthouse, 'and postcards of all angles please.'[9] Another postcard, which Piper sent Ben Nicholson in May 1934, reads: 'Paris must be interesting now. We are going in June.'[10] But turn the card over and there is Beachy Head lighthouse, beckoning in another direction.

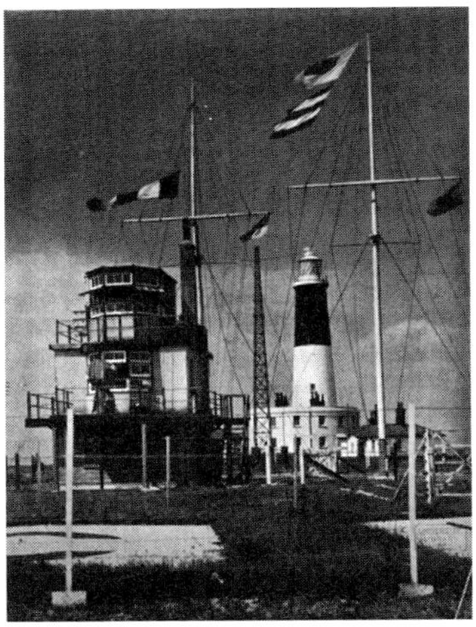

Figure 19 Gaiety and contrast: the lighthouse at Dungeness, photographed by John Piper

Lighthouses figure significantly in 'The Nautical Style'. Piper points out that though they are 'the most obvious of many functional buildings' at the seaside, they do not entirely banish the shaping ingredient of taste.[11] One quality he associated with them was gaiety. Certainly his photograph of the black-and-white striped lighthouse at Dungeness (see Figure 19), with the nearby signal masts hung with blown flags, conveys this mood, a gaiety that he also encountered in sea shanties and early naval prints. Two other qualities which he found in lighthouses and coastal architecture, in general, are strength and strong contrasts. Lighthouses, in

Piper's words, 'cut water and air with sharp edges', but if they have an absence of nuance, they do not lack romance.

His 'Nautical Style' essay owes its existence in part to J.M. Richards, who had taken over from John Betjeman in 1935 as assistant editor at the *Architectural Review*, under Hubert de Cronin Hastings. It was Richards who, on learning of Piper's interest in Romanesque and Saxon carving, had commissioned him to write the essay 'Early English Sculpture' (1936), which became a landmark in the growing appreciation of early English art. Richards was also the person who, in 1937, recommended Piper to Betjeman as a potential Shell Guide author. The commission that resulted – to write a 'Shell Guide' to Oxfordshire – proved to be a task that helped detach Piper from abstraction and returned him, in his own work, to an art that acknowledged place, history, memory, native traditions and the significance of English heritage. As the political situation in Europe worsened, and the threat of war became an increasing reality, the need to stand back from the imperatives of high modernism, in order to let other things come into view, became more urgent. Piper's realignment, however, appalled Ben Nicholson, Herbert Read and others who regarded him as a turncoat and a traitor to the modernist cause.

Certainly it must have baffled the modernists, with their interest in pure form, when in 1939 Piper published an illustrated book on a famously seedy and aesthetically very impure seaside town. *Brighton Aquatints*, an album of architectural images, found him using a medium more usually associated with the eighteenth century. But those who had read his essay on 'Nautical Style' the year before might have been prepared. For it was here that he first extolled the pleasures for the eye offered by Brighton and also the need, at the seaside, for contrasts and differences:

> Brighton has these more than any other place. The great yellow and white façade of Brighton is ranged along the Parade, to face the incoming breakers. The piers, the fishing boats pulled up on the shingle, the bandstands and shelters, the Georgian and Victorian and Edwardian hotels and lodging houses all act up. The bow windows and porticoes, the wide pediments and bargeboarded bays of Regency Square, the great Black Rock and Brunswick Square curves and sweeps, the late Victorian yellow brick at the far end of Hove – all these keep up the seaside spirit. They make thousands of people remember Brighton, and long to

> return to it. The Regency architecture is worth fighting for not only because it is good Regency but still more because it is good 'seaside'.[12]

No mere antiquarian, Piper was a man not just in love with the past, but profoundly sensitive to the ways in which that past challenged, thickened and enriched the present. In 'The Nautical Style' the modern shakes hands with the traditional, as J.M. Richards was one of the first to recognise.

Cyril Connolly once famously warned of the dangers to creativity presented by the pram in the hall. But the arrival of children helped to bond Piper and Richards as both, by the late 1930s, had wives and small infants. 'There's such a lot I wanted to talk to you about', Peggy Richards once wrote to Myfanwy Piper, ' – but I couldn't get a word in edgeways for Jim and John's non-stop archi-talk.'[13] This talk continued on the tours the two men made together in connection with articles for the *Architectural Review* (nicknamed 'The Archie'). Both, Myfanwy Piper observed, had 'an insatiable interest in people, places, buildings, and ways of life'.[14] Richards himself recalls:

> Piper and I made a number of expeditions together in his car, taking photographs and working out ideas for articles notably on the vernacular types of building that histories and historians for the most part ignored. We covered much of England, and out of our expeditions came articles (some written by me but most by Piper, and illustrated by his photographs and sometimes his own drawings) on such subjects as pubs, lighthouses, country railway-stations and Nonconformist chapels.[15]

One of these articles formed a prequel to Piper's 'The Nautical Style'. Written by Richards and illustrated with his and Piper's photographs, it is entitled 'Black and White: An Introductory Study of a National Design Idiom' and was published in the *Architectural Review* in November 1937. Its subject is workaday black-and-white surface decoration, an idiom seemingly timeless in style and peculiar to this country. They found it, for example, in Belisha beacons, chequered kerbs, road signs and bollards, but its origin, Richards states, almost certainly echoing Piper's point of view, is nautical. He was referring to the tradition of painting boats black and white, with white lettering on black gunwales; and to the use of black and white in the paraphernalia found on quaysides: posts, capstans, signalmasts and railings, not to mention lighthouses and beach huts.

Many of the qualities that Piper held up admiringly in 'The Nautical Style' – such as 'rightness' and 'gaiety' – are also significant here. Both men liked the 'rightness' this black-and-white idiom of broad surface design had for the English climate. Despite its severity, the result is paradoxically (I quote Richards) 'a gaiety that seems able to survive even the gloomy English skies and grey winter light' and which maintains in mild English sunlight 'a robuster richness than any bright colour could manufacture'. One of the photographs that illustrates his article shows Rose Cottage, the black-painted house which Piper rented on the beach at Rye Harbour. Whitewash and tar are two principal decorative means in seaside architecture. 'Limewashed walls', writes Richards, 'are characteristic nearly all round the coast, combined with tarred plinths and black-painted window-frames'. Furthermore, as Richards points out, the restraint inherent in the use of black and white 'allows the satisfactory geometrical forms from which the buildings are composed their maximum effect'.[16]

This analysis of black-and-white surface decoration would have sharpened Piper's appreciation of nautical design, for it is a decorative style that permits maximum visibility and is therefore often used on lighthouses, such as the old one at Dungeness, today painted entirely black but which, when photographed and painted by Piper, was both black and white. When striped black and white, lighthouses are clearly seen through the fisherman's binoculars, regardless of the background against which the lighthouse is seen.

While developing an interest in vernacular architecture and design, Piper was simultaneously looking for a way to reintroduce the subject in art, after an intensive period working with pure abstraction. Around 1936, he began making return visits to the coast, taking with him a folder filled with coloured papers which he began cutting and tearing into shapes that could be used to create beach and seascapes, also at times employing scratchy pen-work to convey a blustery mood. This re-engagement with coastal subjects and with collage forms the background to his writing of 'Nautical Style', which was first published in the *Architectural Review* in January 1938 and then ten years later republished in revised form in his book of essays *Buildings and Prospects*. The later version is more insistently framed by his awareness that along much of the south coast, from Kent to Cornwall, villas now stretched inland as far as the eye could see and seaside character was fading fast.

In seeking to explain this development in his revised version of 'Nautical Style', he writes: 'People wanted a change when they went to the sea, but a change with home comforts; and that meant buildings (or so the builders thought) that looked as much as possible like the houses that visitors lived in all year round.' And the result is inland-towns beside the sea, or, as Piper neatly observes, 'seaside snuggeries'.[17] But between the rows of bungalows and along the expanses of open coast, he still thought it possible to find examples of maritime pride and efficiency. He urges his reader to look at useful coast objects, praising for instance the spare geometrical quality found in marine furniture, and the way in which seaside bandstands and other ornamental structures can assimilate foreign influence without losing their character. Another passage in this essay brings out his fondness for that seemingly desolate and forgotten place, Dungeness, an area dotted with coastguard huts, cottages, stores, railways and flagpoles, all of which offered a wide range of maritime structures and appliances. 'The whole area looks like an oversized nursery floor,' he writes, 'very untidy at first sight, but having an underlying pattern.'[18] Visitors who, today, go in search of Derek Jarman's cottage at Dungeness, can affirm the accuracy of Piper's description, and can find here an area rich in maritime architecture, even though it is nowadays, like Sizewell, haunted by the overpowering presence of a nearby nuclear power station.

Later, in 1957, when Piper was working through ideas for his enormous stained-glass window for the Baptistery in the new Coventry Cathedral, he toured France looking at modern churches and modern stained glass. Among the places he visited was Le Corbusier's Ronchamp which he noted was 'self-conscious'. Indeed it is, and this epithet is not necessarily derogatory. But what Piper liked most about seaside style was its unselfconsciousness. The trimness of coast building, he argues, reflects the trimness of boat building. And because many of the man-made objects at the seaside have been determined by seafarers and engineers, they are unselfconscious and ingenious. As has been noted, there is a strong vein of functionalism in the maritime design. But alongside this functionalism is a certain swagger and gaiety, the jauntiness of a sailor's jig. Piper writes: 'It is not simply the sea air that is such fun and such a change, it is the whole gamut of heightened contrasts that the seaside provides, and is strong enough to make life there seem fuller and gayer.'[19] Timothy Mowl rightly remarks of Piper's essay: 'No-one had written from quite such an anarchic, wonderfully persuasive viewpoint before'.[20]

Whereas most people go to the coast in search of refreshment and escape, Piper went because the experience returned him to the present, with a sharper awareness of its needs. 'Our epoch is fixing its own style day by day,' wrote Le Corbusier. 'It is there under our eyes.'[21] Piper not only discerned it, but brought to his perception of it a broad and generous vision. By giving attention to anonymous vernacular buildings and objects, he encouraged readers to look more intently at their surroundings. The underlying purpose of his writing and photography for the *Architectural Review* and the Shell Guides, together with the extensive work that he did for the latter in an editorial capacity over many years, was to empower readers. He encouraged them to take nothing for granted, and instead to decide for themselves what matters, what should be kept or torn down, thereby strengthening the demotic in our environments. Behind his seemingly casual and entertaining promotion of coastal gaiety lay a deep-rooted commitment to a common heritage, to English identity and English style.

Bruce Peter and Philip Dawson

Bruce Peter and Philip Dawson's book *Ship Style: Modernism and Modernity at Sea in the Twentieth Century* will be published by Conway Maritime Press in 2010.

Bruce Peter lectures in design history and theory at the Glasgow School of Art. His recent publications include (with Peter Quartermaine) *Cruise: Identity, Design and Culture* (Laurence King and Rizzoli, 2006) and (with Philip Dawson and Ian Johnston) *QE2: Britain's Greatest Liner* (Ferry Publications, 2008).

Philip Dawson is the author of many books on nautical history. The most recent is *The Liner: Retrospective and Renaissance* (Conway Maritime Press, 2005).

Modernism at Sea

Ocean Liners and the Avant-garde

A MAJESTIC PASSENGER LINER AT SEA – viewed from a low angle and surging towards the picture plane – remains one of the most compelling images of twentieth-century design and engineering achievement, symbolising the epitome of luxury and hospitality. Le Corbusier, in particular, was fascinated by ocean liners as exemplars of floating technology. In his iconoclastic *Vers une architecture*, published in 1923, he used a Cunard Line publicity montage showing its flagship, the *Aquitania*, to be longer and taller than the most famous triumphal buildings in Paris. The young architect was clearly intrigued by the ability of the ocean liner to be at once technically fit for purpose, yet somehow awe-inspiring. He wrote of 'new architectural forms; elements both vast and intimate, but on man's scale; freedom from the "styles" that stifle us; good contrast between solids and voids, powerful masses and slender masts'.[1] For the modernist architect, liners also demonstrated the potential of highly-serviced mega structures to provide ideal living conditions – a potential that was realised by Le Corbusier when he designed the Unité d'Habitation at Marseilles.

Le Corbusier was a frequent liner passenger. In 1929, he voyaged to South America, returning to France aboard the *Lutétia* in the company of the Parisian cabaret star Josephine Baker. As a homage to Baker, on the night of the costume ball, Le Corbusier 'blacked up' and dressed in a costume of bananas and feathers. Later, in 1933, the Congrès International d'Architecture Moderne (CIAM), of which Le Corbusier was a founding member, chartered the steamer *Patris II* to sail from Marseilles to Piraeus en route to their Athens conference. But unlike the glamorous *Lutétia*, the *Patris II* was a rather perfunctory passenger-cargo ship of moderate size and speed, built in 1926 on the Tyne by the Greek-owned Byron Steamship Company, based in London. Powered by reciprocating engines rather than turbines it was, in terms of naval architectural design, even a little old-fashioned. Modernist architects who expressed enthusiasm for ships as models for the future of architecture on terra firma, however, seemed to be largely uncomprehending of naval architecture as a distinct discipline with its own heritage, established traditions and modern concerns. To the members of CIAM, a ship was just a ship; it did not matter who designed it and it did not matter how it was propelled, so long as it had a white superstructure with those uninterrupted lines of promenade deck windows and sunny expanses of teak decking with black caulking between the planks.

Two years after chugging along to Piraeus on the *Patris II*, Le Corbusier crossed the Atlantic once again, this time to New York during the maiden season of the magnificent *Normandie* (see Figure 20). He travelled first class and evidently found the liner to be very exhilarating. No wonder: the *Normandie* was unquestionably the most sumptuous passenger ship ever built – a floating modern-day Versailles, containing grand vistas of highly wrought art deco to showcase all that was best in the French decorative arts, but finally commissioned ten years after the Paris *Exposition des Arts Décoratifs et Industriels Modernes*.

Costume balls in the grand salons of France's most famous liner seem strangely at odds with our perceived image of mainstream modernism in general, and of Le Corbusier in particular: the liner's ornate interiors were the antithesis of his concept of a *machine à habiter*. But liner design was already changing so radically that by the early 1950s, when Le Corbusier was working on the Unité d'Habitation, he would be looking to ships for inspiration. The modern spirit was in the air on board the *Normandie*. Le Corbusier's attempts to learn English aboard, with the help of the American surrealist painter Abraham Rattner, capture something of the mood. The list of words and expressions he learned included 'swimming pool', 'sunbathing', 'people who bore me', as well as 'shoulders', 'breast', 'figure', 'drunk', 'cockeye' and 'here's looking at you'.[2]

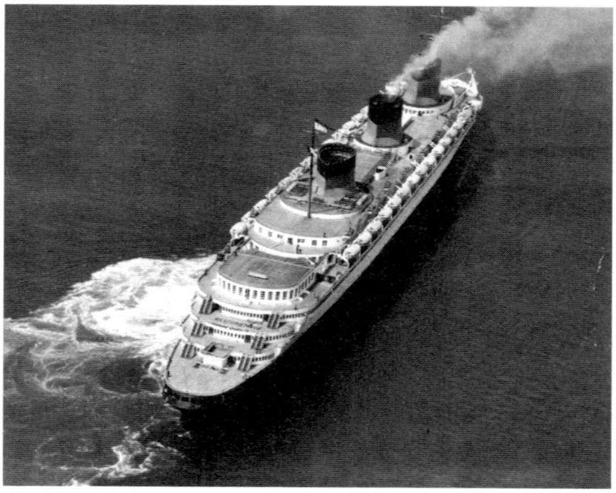

Figure 20
Sweeping lines and uncluttered expanses of teak decking are evident in this aerial view of the *Normandie*, photographed at sea in the late 1930s

Pioneers: The *Ile de France*

The great turning point for shipboard design throughout Europe was the 1925 Paris *Exposition*, where the established beaux-arts style was fundamentally challenged. Highly ornamented decor was no longer the only way to impress passengers. Grandeur, hospitality and commercial pride might be better expressed through progressive aesthetics more in keeping with contemporary taste. As the French Line's president John Dal Piaz asked rhetorically, 'Why Mesdames, would you, with your short skirts and bobbed hair, want to sit down on Louis XVI bergères?'[3]

Of all the new liners designed in the wake of the Paris *Exposition*, the *Ile de France* caused the greatest sensation on account of its fashionable interior design (see Figure 21). Introduced in 1927, the liner brought the spirit of European modernity to the New World on its maiden arrival in New York. The decoration and furnishing of the first-class spaces were carried out by a cadre of prominent French designers and artisans, largely in the style and character of Jacques-Emile Ruhlmann (1879–1933), whose work featured prominently at the *Exposition*. Influenced, in part, by the Arts and Crafts movement and by the *Weiner Werkstätte*, Ruhlmann followed an elitist view of his art, believing that high-quality furnishings had to be individually hand-

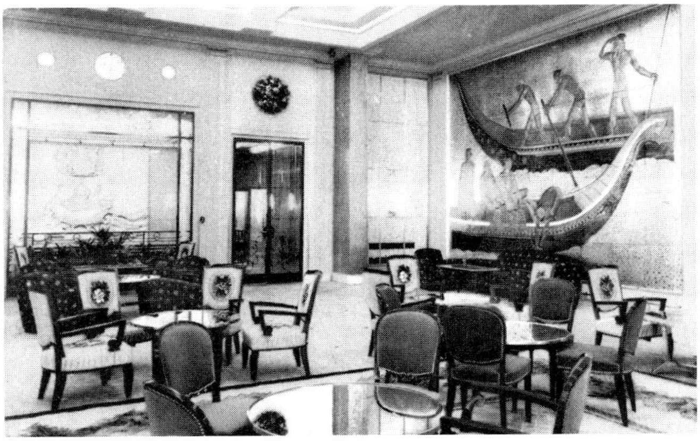

Figure 21 The *Ile de France* brought the glamour of the 1925 Paris Exhibition to New York

crafted by skilled artisans as unique one-of-a-kind pieces, made to order for each client. Many of his contemporaries, however, held the opposite view: that modern furnishings could – and, indeed, should – be manufactured so as to be affordable to greater numbers of people. Ruhlmann was consulted on the choice of architects and designers for the *Ile de France*'s first-class interiors – Richard Bouwens de Boijen, André Mare, Henri Pacon, Pierre Patout and Louis Süe – and even developed concepts for a number of the spaces himself.

While the internal spaces aboard the *Ile de France* were, for the most part, already defined by the naval architects, the vibrancy of the ship's first-class public interiors, and of many of the higher-grade cabins and suites, was noteworthy. This was achieved through the use of vivid saturated colours and in the textures and patterns of the carpets, furnishings and artworks, rather than through historicist decoration. Gone were the cornices, beadings, dados, elaborate leaded glass domes and art nouveau flourishes of previous French liners in favour of a far less embellished approach which seemed brilliantly to capture the spirit of the era. The *Ile de France* was among the first ships to make significant use of indirect architectural lighting at sea. Then, before the advent of cold-cathode fluorescent lighting and the widespread use of air conditioning, reducing the number of tungsten lamps also helped to keep these spaces cooler through the summer months and on tropical cruises. In short, the *Ile de France* was the most modern and stylish ship yet seen and immediately rendered its predecessors hopelessly unfashionable.

From the time of its maiden voyage to New York in 1927, the *Ile de France* proved so popular that, for the first few years of its career, it was said to have carried more first-class passengers than any other ship on the North Atlantic.[4] Yet the majority of those who sailed aboard the liner did so in its 'cabin' and tourist-third accommodation. Here was another major feature of the modern ship: the new generation of liners was far more egalitarian than Edwardian predecessors like the *Titanic*. Responding to the huge rise in the number of tourists wanting to travel from America to Europe, and wanting to get there on the most glamorous ship they could afford, the new transatlantic liners offered comfortable tourist (or 'cabin') class accommodation, instead of 'the steerage' with its open-plan dormitories that had previously carried migrants in the opposite direction – from Europe to new homes in America.

With its newly democratic ethos, the liner even found its way into popular song: 'You're just as hard to land as the *Ile de France* / I haven't got a chance / This is a fine romance!'[5] As the United States emerged into an era of prosperity, at least until the 1929 Wall Street stock market crash, greater numbers of people found themselves with the money and available free time to travel overseas. The *Ile de France* quickly became the ship of choice for those Americans who had read about France in books such as Hemingway's *The Sun Also Rises* and Fitzgerald's *Tender is the Night*. The ocean liner historian John Maxtone-Graham later wrote of the *Ile de France* as 'the original whoopee ship symbolising an abandonment that was unthinkable [...] The absence of traditional frills and the relentless modernity, coupled with the seductive Parisian dream, guaranteed her success.'[6]

The Spread of 'Ocean Liner Style'

The kind of glossy, streamlined design found aboard the *Ile de France* quickly became known as the 'ocean liner style' and, as the 1930s progressed, elements of shipboard design began to appear in modern buildings on terra firma. One of the first in Britain to sport this fashionable new look was the 1935 De La Warr Pavilion at Bexhill-on-Sea, designed by the émigré architects Erich Mendelsohn and Serge Chermayeff.

A great deal of Mendelsohn's architectural output in Germany incorporated ship-inspired details, such as portholes, ribbon-windows, sweeping curves, tiered external balconies and deck railings. This aesthetic may have been inspired by his experience of sailing to New York in 1924 aboard the *Deutschland*. Mendelsohn had toyed with the idea of visiting America since 1920, but the unstable German currency of the early 1920s presented financial obstacles. In July 1924, however, a wealthy client, the Mosse publishing firm, sponsored his trip, presumably in the expectation that Mendelsohn would write a book about his experience which they could publish.

One of the most interesting fellow passengers on board, and the one with whom Mendelsohn spent the most time, was the filmmaker Fritz Lang. Mendelsohn wrote humorously about Lang to his wife, gently mocking his elegant monocle and hoping that it would 'fall overboard at the next opportunity'. 'Apart from the monocle and similar Viennese affectations,' wrote Mendelsohn, 'Fritz Lang [...] is a thoughtful, active and bold person.'[7] On the approach to America, Mendelsohn turned his attentions to the shoreline, and recorded his powerful first impressions of New York from the *Deutschland*:

> Around noon land in sight [...] Suddenly appearing for a moment in the evening fog – the Woolworth Building. Like a phantom towering up in the sky. No one ever thought that high [...] Lights just above the bay, ascending, stretching up to the sky – red light – the top of Woolworth. The ship turns – Babylon. Ghostly in the moonlit darkness. Towering up with verticals of light. Rapid entry, turns, curves – a battle of space in the darkness, in the light of the embedded streets. A thrust to the heart, lost in such dimensions – the tragedy of madness, insane power, the power of space, the unending intoxication of victory.[8]

With such intense responses to the city from the first, it is not surprising that on his return to Germany Mendelsohn did indeed publish a book of his expressionist photographs, *Amerika: Bildbuch Eines Arkitekten*, while Lang made his celluloid masterpiece, *Metropolis*.

Chermayeff actually had hands-on experience of shipboard interior design by the time he tackled the De La Warr Pavilion project. As a result of the sudden fashion for art deco amongst the fashionable set after the Paris *Exposition*, the London-based society decorators, Waring & Gillow, had established 'Modern Art Studios' in London and Paris to carry out private commissions and contract work in the art deco manner, effectively selling art deco back to the French. As a well-connected, youthful and forward-looking designer, Chermayeff was employed to oversee their success. Waring & Gillow had an established reputation for shipboard interior design and, as this was an increasingly regulated specialist discipline, involving fitting out spaces with sheer and camber, the firm was employed by numerous European shipyards and owners. By this means, Chermayeff came to design the first-class grill restaurant aboard the grand French South Atlantic liner, *L'Atlantique*, delivered in 1931.

With its sycamore panelling and luxuriant patterned carpeting, the room was both plush and intimate – but *L'Atlantique* was more fundamentally radical in its design than mere surfaces and furnishings. This was the first transatlantic liner to achieve a fully open-plan interior layout, the funnel casings and service shafts being separated in order to free up space along the centre line.

Quite apart from the axial plan of the public rooms, *L'Atlantique* was perhaps most notable for its remarkable ocean-going *rues*, whole streets which ran through a triple-height atrium space, facilitating a very workable single centreline corridor cabin plan for so large a ship. With the greater emphasis on modern hotel-grade accommodation with en-suite bathrooms in post-First World War ship design, *L'Atlantique*'s designers had better opportunities for creatively using space inboard of the bedrooms. Apart from merely providing a simplified cabin plan, *L'Atlantique*'s central *rues* also offered something of a pedestrian street life of their own, with the E-Deck *rue* widening into the embarkation hall's various shops and other communal services and its D-Deck counterpart emerging into a gallery around the atrium's mid-level.

Unfortunately, *L'Atlantique* suffered the grave injustice of being a little-known masterpiece. The liner never attained the public attention of North Atlantic service, and the opportunity to show off in the United States, where the modern design and supreme luxury would undoubtedly have attracted great interest. *L'Atlantique* also suffered the misfortune of a tragically short service life when, only fifteen months after the September 1931 maiden voyage to Rio de Janeiro, Santos, Montevideo and Buenos Aires, fire broke out onboard in January 1933 while sailing from Bordeaux for a routine drydocking at Le Havre with only a skeleton crew onboard. The ship lay adrift for days in the English Channel while the flames completely consumed its innards, leaving but a charred hulk to be written off. As the *L'Atlantique* fire – and, later, a devastating blaze on the similarly open-plan *Normandie* – both proved, an open-plan liner did not offer the best fire protection and was, in fact, extremely vulnerable to total destruction. This meant that *plan libre*, one of the central tenets of

Corbusian modernism, was best not applied to ships. Later on, however, retractable fire doors were developed to enable a certain amount of open planning to occur without compromising safety.

As with architecture on terra firma, it tended not to be the most prestigious or glamorous ships on which the most radical ideas were tried out but, rather, smaller vessels for secondary routes where national prestige was not at stake in the same way as on the highly competitive North Atlantic run. This situation also reflected that of avant-garde design at the Paris *Exposition*, where Le Corbusier's *Pavillion de L'Esprit Nouveau* was a relatively small structure, crammed onto an awkward, peripheral site, some distance from the imposing art deco edifices of the most prestigious pavilions. While the *Ile de France*, *L'Atlantique* and the *Normandie* are similarly remembered as prestigious icons of art deco, the thinking behind smaller, less well-known ships – such as the *Panama*, *Ancon* and *Cristobal* of America's Ancon Line – perhaps better reflects *L'Esprit Nouveau* in naval architecture. These three liners, designed by George G. Sharp and Raymond Loewy and delivered in 1939, neither flew the flag of some famous line nor plied the North Atlantic. They were not even privately owned or operated, but rather creations of government necessity to serve the Panama Canal Zone. Seldom have three ships introduced more new and novel features, inside and out (see Figure 22).

Their design emphasised simplicity and harmony of line, co-ordination and rationalisation of elements, and concealment of clutter. A long, low superstructure and a streamlined funnel capped the beamy hulls. Following the example of *L'Atlantique*, these were the first American liners without sheer; having level decks throughout did away with expensive shipboard joinery. The funnel was internally guyed, another first for an American liner, which avoided the need for tensioned cables cluttering the upper decks, as on the *Queen Mary*.

For vessels rigidly subdivided by watertight and fireproof bulkheads, their 'wide open' feeling was a remarkable accomplishment. To facilitate the fire zone concept, as well as spaciousness, these were the first American liners with divided funnel uptakes. As the funnel was far forward, the amidships engine hatch was sited on the port side and the staircase on the starboard side so as not to break the vista aft. Raymond Loewy's interior design comprised pastel or neutral grey tones, clean, uncluttered surfaces, an emphasis on structural

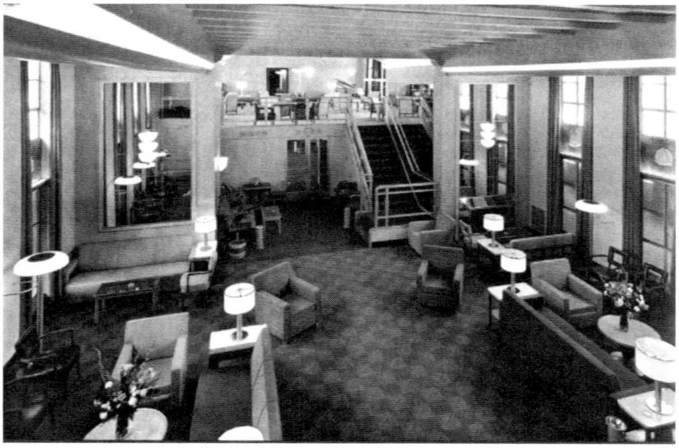

Figure 22
The Great Hall of the *Panama*

elements, rather than on decoration, and superbly designed and comfortable furniture. According to Loewy, 'Planning the interior of a ship is not a matter of "interior decoration", but of design.' The *New York Times* praised his 'avoidance of period encumbrances and decorative claptrap'.[9]

From being so lacking in confidence about its ability to make any kind of contribution of its own to modern architecture and design at the 1925 Paris *Exposition*, America had by 1939 become a style leader in its own right. American liner design never looked back and, from being regarded as conservative – even puritanical, due to prohibition laws – ships flying the Stars and Stripes came to be viewed as being amongst the most glamorous of the postwar decades.

British Modernism at Sea

During the 1930s, Britain neither built ships as glamorous as the French nor as technologically progressive as the Americans. The *Orion* of 1936, with interiors by Brian O'Rourke, was probably Britain's best effort and was the result of Orient Line's chairman, Colin Anderson, being a leading member of the Design and Industries Association. During the 1950s, Orient Line continued to build ships more forward-looking in design than its rival, P&O, and the postwar *Orcades* was chosen to represent Britain's resurgent passenger fleet in Basil Spence's 'Sea and Ships' pavilion at the 1951 Festival of Britain.

The Festival brought to prominence a group of moderate, herbivorous British modernist architects and designers – Hugh Casson, Misha Black and James Gardner – each one of whom was to co-ordinate the design of one of Britain's three great 1960s flagship liners: the *Canberra*, *Oriana* and *Queen Elizabeth 2*. Shipping line directors, who invariably represented old money, the British establishment and commercial culture, could never have brought themselves to employ a Lubetkin, a Lasdun, a Smithson or a Goldfinger, but the Festival of Britain, in contrast, represented the acceptable face of British modernism and could, therefore, be applied on board British ships.

In the later 1950s, the two principal British lines in the Australia trade, Orient Line and P&O, joined forces, each ordering a new flagship for the Southampton to Sydney route, via Suez. First to enter service was Orient Line's *Oriana*, delivered in 1960 (see Figure 23). This remarkable vessel caused a mild sensation by breaking the record for the fastest passage to Australia, taking just under four weeks to reach Sydney on its maiden voyage. Built by Vickers-Armstrongs at Barrow-in-Furness, the liner had a powerful-looking hull with soaring lines and a slender entry at the waterline. However, this was surmounted by a most unusual, almost constructivist, superstructure treatment, in which the various volumes – containing public rooms, promenades, officers' quarters, the navigation bridge and air-conditioning plant – were expressed individually and piled up amidships with a small funnel at the summit. From any angle, the *Oriana* was utterly unique and certainly memorable, but hardly beautiful in the conventional sense. Instead, the liner's grace lay within, as it had a very effective and distinctive layout and some exquisite public spaces. Misha Black's Design Research Unit drew up most of the first-class accommodation, as well as creating a uniform graphic identity for the entire ship. Many cabins, on the lower decks, were arranged around internal 'courtyards', so that even those deep within the hull had a window, looking onto a communal space, illuminated by natural daylight. The public rooms were also bright and airy, with high ceilings, uncluttered surfaces and numerous contemporary art installations.

P&O's *Canberra*, designed by the naval architect John West, working in conjunction with Casson-Conder, was equally spacious – but with a very sleek and

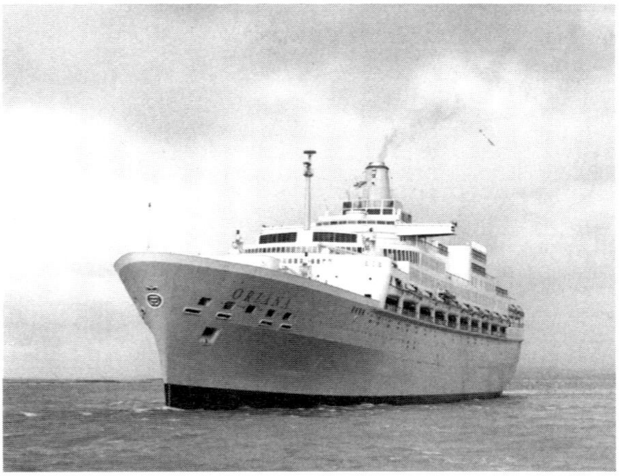

Figure 23
Bulky but business-like, the *Oriana* eschewed streamlining altogether in favour of a more constructivist approach to the arrangement of the superstructure

streamlined silhouette, featuring smoke stacks located towards the stern and a superstructure formed of a series of receding layers, piling up towards the bridge structure, just forward of amidships. As with the *Oriana*, much of the *Canberra*'s upper works were fabricated from aluminium alloy to save weight. Inside, the *Canberra* had many striking public rooms – indeed Casson-Conder's interiors were a *tour de force* of British modernism at its very best. For example, the Club Bonito and Bonito Pool formed a single indoor / outdoor space, which acted as a lido by day, but became a ballroom after dark. Moving forward, the main public rooms in each class were open-plan, and those in first class were connected by a dramatic spiral staircase, with under-lit treads. Amongst the *Canberra*'s many memorable interior spaces, a teenager's room called the 'Pop-Inn' stood out on account of its graffiti-style wall murals by a youthful David Hockney. Alas, these delightfully witty decorations were quickly panelled over, perhaps because the ship's rather conservative owners feared that their design might inspire youthful passengers to draw their own versions elsewhere onboard. Both the *Oriana* and *Canberra* set a very high standard for British shipboard design and the two vessels proved extremely popular, first in liner service and, later on, as cruise ships. Indeed, both survived well into the 1990s, the *Oriana* latterly in a static role in the Far East.

By the mid-1960s, the shipping industry was in a state of flux due, in part, to major social and economic changes on terra firma and to the advent of jet aircraft and mass car ownership. New ship types – car ferries, cruise ships, container ships and bulk carriers – rendered traditional passenger and general cargo liners obsolete. In this process, even famous established shipping lines came under intense financial duress. Britain's Cunard, not surprisingly, was amongst the worst hit. The transatlantic flagships *Queen Mary* and *Queen Elizabeth* had been a winning formula for the company, but the Boeing 707 rendered both hopelessly *démodé* almost overnight. As with many successful businesses which experience a sudden change in trading conditions, at first Cunard seemed unable to decide what best to do. Some of its existing liners were converted to cruise ships, but with limited success. Clearly, the only solution would be to build anew.

During the first half of the 1960s, Cunard worked to develop its new liner, known under the code name 'Q3' – but events overtook the project and it quickly became clear that the design thinking was not sufficiently radical to reflect the rate of change in lifestyles and visual culture taking place ashore. Meanwhile, Britain's increasingly confident design community heaped pressure upon Cunard to build a ship fit not only to compete in the jet age, but also the supersonic age and, even, the space age. The company's existing chairman, Sir John Brocklebank, retired in 1965, to be replaced by Sir Basil Smallpeice, who was drafted in from British Overseas Airways Corporation (BOAC) – meaning that Cunard gained a new sense of direction from an airline man with fresh ideas about how the old steamship line ought to be run.

The Q3 project was quietly abandoned, and a new vessel code-named 'Q4' was developed instead. This was to be a dual-purpose transatlantic liner and cruise ship of a very daring design, both technologically and aesthetically. As with the recent *Oriana* and *Canberra*, it was to have a superstructure largely made of aluminium, meaning that it could have more decks than its predecessors, due to the weight saved and, consequently, a lot more onboard space per passenger. Where the old *Queens* had had limited outdoor deck spaces, the new Q4 would have vast lidos because, in the jet age, it was de rigueur to return from holiday with a suntan. In terms of overall layout, the Q4's cabin decks were to have central service casings running the length of the ship between the hallways. On either side of these, there were parallel corridors and, thus, around 75 per cent of the cabins had portholes, an unprecedented proportion for so large a vessel. Unlike before, all of the public rooms, including the restaurants, were in the superstructure and featured large windows and open planning.[10]

The new liner was built by the famous shipyard of John Brown & Co at Clydebank, near Glasgow, and, as construction progressed, it became clear that it would present a radical break with the past. Launched in September 1967 and named *Queen Elizabeth 2*, the vessel not only represented the hopes of Clydeside, but also the entire British shipping industry. Although undeniably well constructed, upon entering service, the *Queen Elizabeth 2* immediately caused controversy on account of its novel appearance. Unlike its Cunard predecessors, the new liner did not have lofty red and black funnels but, instead, a single, slender smoke stack, with an air scoop at its base. The mast, which leaned slightly forward, resembled a space probe and the upper decks had a unique, chiselled appearance, all resulting from James Gardner's careful design work and attention to detail. Traditionalists were horrified, however, and the fact that the new liner suffered a mechanical failure on the shake-down cruise only seemed to add to a growing backlash against the modern movement in Britain. To the reactionary, it was not surprising that a ship without even a single 'proper funnel', let alone two or three, would be a failure.

On the contrary, after the initial teething troubles were ironed out, the *Queen Elizabeth 2* went on to be an outstanding success and to enjoy a peerless forty-year career as both an express ocean liner and a luxurious cruise ship. Over the years the original late-1960s 'Swinging London' interiors were gradually removed and replaced by pastiches of Edwardiana and art deco. But such superficial changes did not significantly alter the general arrangement, or the very sophisticated hidden servicing which, back in 1969, had made the ship by far the most advanced of its kind in the world. The *Queen Elizabeth 2* represented the apotheosis of modernism at sea. Nearly all subsequent cruise ships have been retro-styled from the outset. Indeed, the postmodern aesthetics of Las Vegas nowadays more or less define the design identity of today's mass-market cruise industry.

Fred Gray

Fred Gray is author of *Designing the Seaside: Architecture, Nature and Society*, published by Reaktion Books in 2006. He has a long-term interest in all things seaside and seaside architecture in particular – for example he curated an Arts Council national touring exhibition on the subject in the 1990s and he is the honorary historian for the Brighton West Pier Trust. In his spare time he is Professor of Continuing Education and Dean of the Sussex Institute at the University of Sussex.

1930s Architecture and the Cult of the Sun

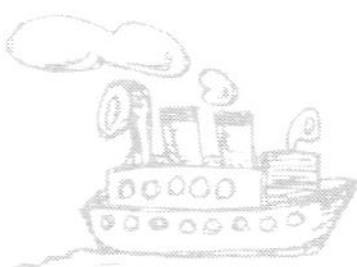

THE 1930S SAW A GROWING OBSESSION with sunshine and sunbathing, which led to radical changes at the seaside. The sun was at the centre of a broadly based social movement which involved holidaymakers, the medical profession, social reformers, designers, architects and even governments. Modernist design and architecture – often distrusted by the dominant architectural orthodoxies – found a warm welcome in the modernizing and transforming coastal resorts. Seafronts and coastal townscapes were redeveloped with the sun in mind, while a host of innovative resort buildings deployed a newly sun-oriented architecture.[1]

The new seaside architecture included sun terraces, communal beach bathing stations, solariums, glass-clad entertainment pavilions, holiday camps and beach chalets. Seafronts might be remade with wide new promenades and with parks designed for sunbathing, sport and pleasure. Most iconic of all, the interwar open-air swimming pools and lidos reflected the new belief in sunshine, exercise and the open air. By the end of the period the relationship between the architecture and clothing of the seaside moved into close alignment: the stripped-down, clean-lined, modernist lidos of the 1930s went hand-in-hand with the development of minimal, figure-hugging costumes for swimming and sunbathing.[2]

Contemporary architectural histories have little to say about the flowering of modernist architecture at the seaside, with the exception of a few iconic, architect-designed buildings such as Bexhill's De La Warr Pavilion.[3] Perhaps lidos and beach chalets are too far removed from orthodox architectural forms to put historians at their ease. They tended to be designed not by professional architects but by developers and borough engineers, and although the structures might be modern, they can be dismissed as an inferior seaside vernacular rather than properly and authentically modernist. And yet many 1930s seaside buildings respected the basic tenets of modernism, their form following their function and their structures freed of unnecessary embellishment. Seaside modernism, in all its diversity, was also able to make a special contribution to the modernist genre, often incorporating into designs both nautical themes and the coastal setting. This approach to the modernist aesthetic had been endorsed by Le Corbusier, who linked resort architecture with ocean liners in 1923: 'A seaside villa, conceived as are these liners, would be more appropriate than those we see with their heavy tiled roofs'.[4]

This essay explores the neglected history of modernist architecture at the British – and particularly the English – seaside. It relates the growing appreciation and use of the sunshine to the production of radically different seaside buildings designed to accommodate new forms of seaside leisure and seaside living.

The Cult of the Sun

Until the early twentieth century English seaside holidaymakers had little interest in the sun, preferring the natural qualities of sea air, sea views and the pleasure of bathing in the sea itself. The pier, the winter garden and the bathing machine were the architectural manifestations of the Victorian seaside; timber and cast and wrought iron were its classic construction materials.

The coming of the sun to the English seaside was a gradual process. Segregated by gender on their beaches, the English could look across the Channel, often in admiration, at the mixed bathing common on French beaches. Holidaymakers increasingly rejected the bathing machine, a structure that regulated and individualised the medicinal use of the sea. The discovery and growing enjoyment of communal swimming was architecturally expressed with new buildings on the beach and pier, as well as pools (indoor and out) designed for swimming rather than bathing.

Most significantly, however, in the late nineteenth century the sun emerged as a attractive accompaniment to sea air, and it became, by the 1930s, the dominant force shaping what people did and built at the seaside. Early in the twentieth century the medical profession promoted the therapeutic use of the sun, particularly in combating tuberculosis (or consumption), then still a scourge of many parts of the Western world (despite earlier beliefs that it was preventable or curable through the use of seawater or sea air). Heliotherapy, the direct exposure to sunlight combined with fresh air and relaxation out of doors, became an accepted medical treatment. Within three decades the medical benefits of the sun were widely acknowledged; in 1939, one British commentator described the 'profundity and prodigality' of the sun's ultra-violet radiation.[5]

The sun seized more than the medical imagination, however. It had strong class and gender dimensions as well. Elite groups had previously privileged white skins for reasons of status, health and gender, regarding the suntan as distasteful because of its connotations with degrading physical labour. But the coming of the sun reversed these existing values. The suntan became a 'distinguishing trait' for the elite, 'a new symbol of modern times, an external manifestation of prosperity'.[6] For social reformers, architects and town planners, a 'dream of health, sunlight and the body reformed' was bound up with a quest for a new social order.[7] In the intense 1930s debate among architectural and planning commentators the established resorts were repeatedly criticised for what one 1935 review called 'shoddy buildings steeped in Victorian mediocrity'.[8] A modern architecture of leisure was needed, something that would respond to the increasing number of people making the 'great movement seawards' in search of health, fitness and sunshine.[9]

The government gave enthusiastic support to the sunny seaside and all that went with it in terms of a healthier nation. From 1928, for example, it provided financial backing for local authority spending on health-promoting building projects such as pools and lidos. Another functional designed structure, the deckchair, a seemingly insignificant piece of beach furniture introduced in Margate in the late nineteenth century, came to represent the idling away of time in the sunshine. In the process, the seaside resort was increasingly focused on the summer season: a critical if all-too-brief annual period making for the success or failure of individual resorts.

Professional, political and official support apart, there was strong popular appreciation of health, physical activity and pleasure in the open air. People came to enjoy the sun, this pleasure extending, at its extreme, to the nudist or naturist movement and, more moderately, to a growing realisation of the joys of sunshine and warm air on the bodies of beach-goers and those paddling in the sea. A complicated web of cultural networks propagated the cult of the sun and the new forms of seaside leisure. Some of the strongest proponents of modernism were also regular contributors to the new 1930s naturist magazines with, for example, Eric Gill (centrally involved in the decoration of Morecambe's Midland Hotel) and G.B. Shaw (a stout defender of Bexhill's De La Warr Pavilion) both enthusiastically writing for the *Sun Bathing Review*.

By the mid-1930s, however, architectural and planning critics were ambivalent about the massive coastal changes taking place. On the one hand the 'democratisation of the coast' could be praised, but on the other hand the concreting over of vast stretches of scenic coastline was causing understandable anxiety. In 1936, the *Architectural Review* set out 'the programme the architect has to follow in planning for leisure spent at the seaside', arguing that the 'newly appreciated' virtues of light and air provided architects with the maximum opportunity of 'achieving a characteristic modern expression'.[10] A particularly powerful influence for seaside designers was the symbolism of Nautical Moderne, with its references to ocean liners, brave new modern engineering and construction and to other distant places. Architects and planners imported from across the Channel ideas about what to build at the seaside.

Both local authorities and the private sector were involved in reconstructing the coast. While municipal bodies concentrated on designed public buildings such as pavilions and lidos and open spaces, remodelling promenades and building new seaside parks, the private sector focused on speculative residential developments, amusement parks and holiday camps. The local authorities were also increasingly active in selling the seaside to holidaymakers.[11] Visual publicity on railway posters and in resort guides emphasised a number of elements including the sun, health and physical fitness. Increasingly, though, an important theme in the representation of the seaside was the image of the young woman – 'the seaside girl' – displayed against a background of the new seaside architecture. Apart from guidebooks and publicity posters, she sometimes appeared etched in glass or in bas-relief as part of the decoration of the buildings themselves. The coming of the sun and the new resort architecture was, then, also bound up with the explicit exposure of supposed gender and sexual relationships at the seaside.

Bathing Pavilions and Sun Terraces

With bathing machines increasingly redundant (some were reused as beach huts, with wheels removed and located at the landward edge of the beach), British resorts developed a new architecture of bathing stations and pavilions. Copied from resorts in other Western countries, the bathing station had the utilitarian purpose of providing holidaymakers with a place to change and store their belongings before venturing onto the beach and into the sea. Many also included refreshment rooms and sun terraces. The architects tended to be municipal engineers and the architecture mediated between land and sea, society and nature.

Margate claimed its Marine Bathing Pavilion of 1926 to be the first of its kind in Britain, taking 'the place of the old-fashioned "machines"'.[12] The long rectangular structure was built on a steel frame to take it well above sea level. It included a surrounding promenade with a pitch pine deck and flights of stairs to the sands, hot-water showers and a café providing beach trays for 'afternoon tea on the sand'. At Margate, and at some other resorts where the sea receded at each low tide, the pavilions and their users were inconveniently separated from the sea itself. The response in Margate in 1937 was to construct unadorned pools on the foreshore, the simple structures replenished by the sea with every incoming tide.[13]

The resorts most able to respond to the demands for this sunny architecture were the newest and fastest-expanding seaside towns. In the 1920s and 1930s, Poole on the south coast developed an array of new beach structures for sea and sunbathing and for summer and winter use. The corporation was particularly proud of the Branksome Chine Solarium, designed by the borough engineer following a visit to similar facilities in Germany, boasting that it was the first of its kind built in Britain: 'In summer the Solarium [...] is used as a bathing pavilion; in winter one may enjoy within its walls artificial sunshine

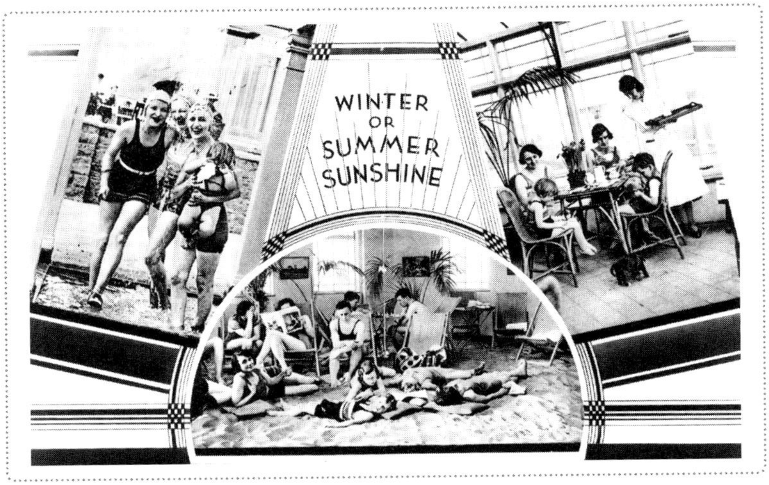

Figure 24
An advertisement for the Branksome Chine Solarium in the council's *Official Guide to Poole*, 1934

and summer heat.'[14] The sheltered flat roofs of the building gave 'undisturbed facilities for basking in the sun' and so allowed 'concentrated sunbathing' (see Figure 24). The café 'was designed in order to introduce something of the continental "touch" to the country'. Branksome Chine and the other bathing pavilions became the centrepieces of a radically new seafront architecture, 'designed for the crowds who come here for bathing, picnicking and other seaside delights', and including a new sea wall doubling as a broad promenade, chalets and day bungalows for hire, boating pools for children, parks and gardens and a 'Motor Park' for the increasing number of visitors driving to the seaside.[15] The private sector also got to work, producing in Poole a series of modernist houses featuring flat roofs that doubled as sun terraces. This was architecture that helped reinvent and transform the English seaside into a location for modern and increasingly affluent and child-centred families to appreciate and consume the sun.

Lidos and Open-air Pools

As society fell in love with the sun and with physical exercise and relaxation out of doors, the open-air pool and lido emerged as the pre-eminent architectural symbol of the British seaside in the first half of the twentieth century.[16]

New popular ways of utilising nature – sunbathing, swimming and diving and watching other holidaymakers – demanded new architectural structures (see Figure 25).

The government avidly supported the open-air pool building movement, asserting that swimming and sunbathing were in the national interest, contributing to improved public health and promoting physical and mental fitness. Opening Weston-super-Mare's new swimming pool in 1937, the MP Sir Edward Campbell announced the government's determination 'to do their utmost to encourage physical exercise for all classes and ages', with exercise taking 'no better form than swimming in clean sea-water open to the sun and air'. Sir Edward hoped the spectators would be so stimulated by the prowess of those using the pool that they would emulate their example, helping to build a 'Fitter Britain'.[17]

The larger and more impressive the open-air pool, the better it reflected the forward-looking stance of its designers and planners. Resorts tirelessly promoted the attractions of their own pools and lidos through their official handbooks and guides. The dimensions of their pools, the number of gallons of water held, the depth of the water and the height of the diving boards were all-important. Hastings Corporation argued of its new pool in the 1935 visitors' handbook that 'there is certainly no finer or better equipped pool in England'; four years later it had become 'the finest open-air swimming pool in Europe'.[18]

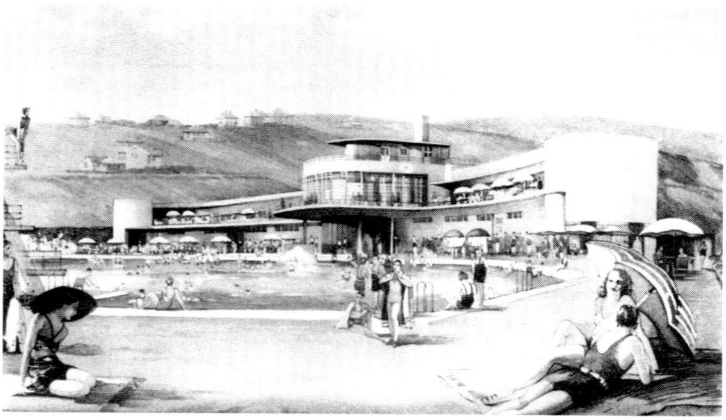

Figure 25
At Saltdean Lido 1930s seasiders could bathe in resolutely modern, open-air surroundings

Visual representations of swimming pools and lidos laid great stress on the new pools as sites of spectacle and display. These were places of modernity, social and sexual equality and liberation. Shorn of their everyday clothing, the pool users appeared classless. Typically in these images, women were numerically and visually dominant and often seemingly unattached, suggesting that at the new pools men would meet fun-loving young women with the promise, perhaps, of much more. One popularist and salacious social historian, George Ryley Scott, seemingly disapproved of the role adopted by women, 'merely displaying, for the edification of the other sex, their physical charms with the aid of daring and attractive bathing costumes'.[19] Respectable Southport Corporation on the north-west coast of England proclaimed its Sea Bathing Lake was 'the only place in the country where the question of Sun Bathing has been successfully dealt with'. It seems unlikely that the Corporation's provision of separate sunbathing areas for men and women, each in 'complete privacy', was fully in accord with the wishes of many of the sunbathers.[20]

Commenting in the late 1930s, S.D. Adshead, one of Britain's most influential architects and town planners, believed the sea was losing its attraction and that swimming pools were a necessity for a modern resort: 'In a modern swimming pool, diving, the attractions of fashion in bathing costumes, refreshment accommodation, sunbathing and shelters set in garden surroundings are the accompaniments of a great show.'[21] The 'great show pools' became a central element of the new forms of seaside leisure and in turn demanded a radically different theatrical architecture.

Pools, lidos, sunbathing terraces and promenades became amphitheatres. The diving boards, water chutes and fountains were props, while the water-cleansing plants, changing rooms and car parks were essential backstage facilities. As to the bathers and spectators, they were transformed into performers and audience although sometimes the prone sunbathers were as much a part of the performance as the swimmers and divers. Amongst the most popular performances (continuing well into the postwar period) were bathing beauty contests. The new structures were built as close to the sea as possible, and ideally on the foreshore. The pools touched and used nature, taming and remaking it as a modern synthetic creation suitable for social use.[22]

Architecturally, the earliest open-air pools drew on classical and neo-Georgian design themes including domed pavilions, columns, colonnades and pediments.[23] By the 1930s, however, classical designs fell from favour and the cult of the sun was literally reflected in modernist pool designs: flat roofs were designed for sunbathing; the extensive use of glass allowed light into buildings; tiled surfaces, often in white, refracted the heat and light of the sun. The Nautical Moderne style was especially redolent of the international avant-garde. It was at this point that 'lido', suggesting the style and glamour of the Venetian beach resort and representing the modern, the adventurous and even the exotic, was often used instead of the more mundane and traditional 'pool'.

Hastings' open-air bathing pool of 1933 was one of the first more modernist structures, with a range of innovative features that included underwater floodlights, three promenades, space for five thousand spectators, a sunbathing beach that faced and allowed access to the sea and provision for deck games, copied from the sports and pastimes on ocean liners.[24] Reporting on nearly twenty-five thousand Whitsun visitors rushing to 'the new luxury bathing pool', the local newspaper described how

> Under a clear sky and dazzling sunshine the great pool and its surrounding terraces made a brilliant picture with its ever-moving crowds of gaily clad bathers and spectators in cool summer garb. Though there was no limit to the variety of bathing costumes worn, they were uniform in one feature – they revealed the utmost of the wearer's form to the beaming rays of the sun. The gayest of colours splashed and darted in the bright blue water and 'dressed' the gleaming white terrace in a pageant of bold tints. Many of the bathers had already achieved a magnificent tan. Others were doing their utmost to follow suit.[25]

The Hastings pool and others around the coast revealed society, architecture and nature in powerful new relationships.

Pavilions and Amusement Parks

The most complete architectural expression of modernism and the cult of the sun was the 1935 De La Warr Pavilion at Bexhill-on-Sea, Sussex.[26] Earl De La Warr, the aristocratic but socialist mayor of the town, was the driving force behind Bexhill Corporation's architectural competition for a new pavilion in the relatively young but increasingly unfashionable resort. The Earl believed that the architecture of recreation should be a significant force in local and national regeneration, with the building at Bexhill intended to perform a local role as a centre for entertainment and the community and to act as a futuristic exemplar for other resorts.

The winners of the competition, the German–Russian architectural partnership of Mendelsohn and Chermayeff, made a radical break from the resort entertainment pavilions constructed in the 1920s. With the southern side presenting large expanses of sheet glass to the sea and sun, the building made use of nautical symbolism. It was the first public building in Britain designed and built on International Style principles. Running parallel to the coast, the Pavilion included a large flexible theatre, restaurant, library, conference room and lounge. Outside there were terraces for sunbathing and listening to music and a rooftop sundeck for sports and games reminiscent of those on ocean liners. Behind this startling appearance lay some innovative construction techniques: this was the first large building in Britain with a welded steel frame.

As he laid the foundation stone of the building, Lord De La Warr claimed that the Pavilion was the means of achieving a new form of cultural and social provision:

> How better could we dedicate ourselves today than by gathering round this new venture of ours, a venture which is going to lead to the growth, the prosperity and the greater culture of this our town; a venture also which is part of a great national movement, virtually to found a new industry – the industry of giving that relaxation, that pleasure, that culture, which hitherto the gloom and dreariness of British resorts have driven our fellow countrymen to seek in foreign lands. We are rightly proud of ourselves today.[27]

For the most part the Pavilion was praised by architectural critics and the national press, although there was also vociferous local and national opposition to the building and its architects from, respectively, conservative ratepayers and fascists.[28]

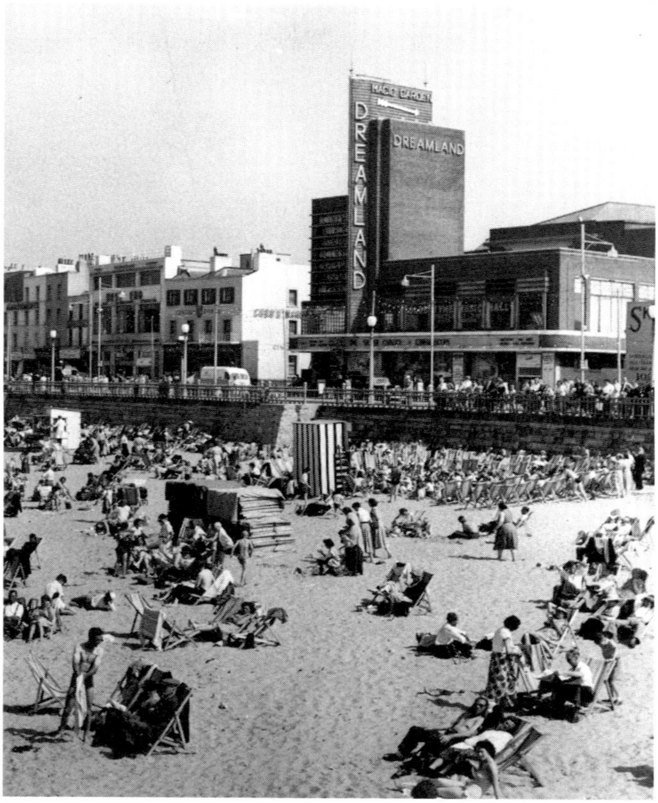

Figure 26
'Margate at its merriest': the entrance to Margate's Dreamland in the 1930s

Modernism also made its mark on the private enterprise amusement parks. The two best examples, both remodelled in the 1930s, are Margate's Dreamland (see Figure 26) and the Pleasure Beach in Blackpool. In Margate, an essentially Victorian pleasure garden was transformed into a modernist artificial entertainment and amusement park modelled on the example of America's Coney Island. The Scenic Railway of 1920 was followed by new, innovative rides and, as the park became more successful and permanent, original wooden buildings were remade in brick and concrete. In the early 1930s, Dreamland, with 'all the fun of the fair', was 'where Margate is at its merriest'.[29] The success of the park and need to respond to new entertainments

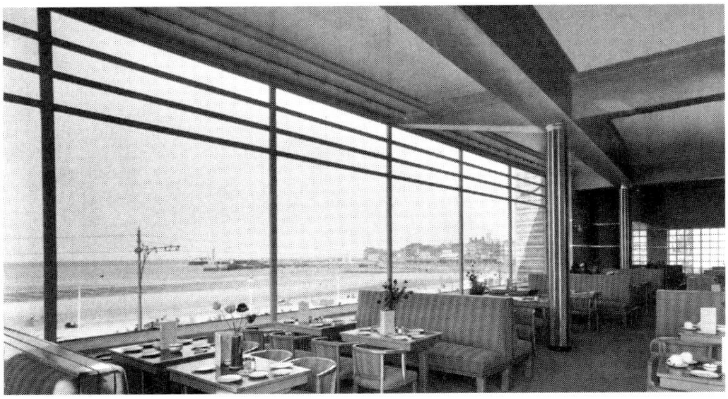

Figure 27 The Sunshine Café, Margate

led to a radical remaking of Dreamland's seafront between 1933 and 1935 and the construction in modernist style of new entertainment buildings. The aim at Margate was 'the erection of one of the finest and most comprehensive entertainment buildings in the country'.[30] The transformation included a new wider entrance from the promenade, a deluxe cinema with 2,200 seats, and The Sunshine Café, 'with big windows overlooking the sea, and seating for 500 people' (see Figure 27).[31]

Unlike Margate's Dreamland, Blackpool's Pleasure Beach, with its early-twentieth-century origins, was on the edge of holidaymaking Blackpool, distant from the Tower, the 'Golden Mile' and the resort's other attractions. Increasingly, from the 1930s, commentators emphasized the modernity and distinctiveness of the Pleasure Beach in contrast to the traditional nature of the larger resort.[32] There was a sense, too, that the Pleasure Beach had a particular role to play:

> It is the final solution of the periodical need for an orgy, a safety-valve for the high-spirits of mankind, set in a scene of extra-ordinary beauty, made doubly beautiful when night falls and the flares are lighted, and little rows of fairy lights hang on strings from booth to booth, and all along the perilous convolutions of the aerial railway.[33]

Between 1933 and 1939 the amusement park was radically restyled to a modernist design by Joseph Emberton. The purpose was 'to present all these machines and devices in such a way that they look interesting to the English public and at the same time to tie all these devices together by a certain continuity of architectural form so that the place looks like an Amusement Park and not like a factory'.[34] The work extended throughout the Pleasure Beach but one of the most significant changes involved the demolition of the 1913 Casino entrance building and its replacement by a new reinforced concrete structure bearing the same name and completed in 1939. Even the animals on the Noah's Ark attraction were restyled in cubist design.

Staying by the Sea

The coming of the sun had consequences for how and where people stayed by the sea. Modernist hotels, bungalows and villas sprang up to meet the needs of the new holidaymakers and seaside residents. Perhaps the most iconic of the new buildings was the 1933 Midland Hotel, constructed to the designs of architect Oliver Hill, on Morecambe's decidedly Victorian seafront, although three years later it was to be joined there by the modernist Super Swimming Stadium.[35] The structure reappeared cloned and relocated to the south coast just a few years later with the opening of the Ocean Hotel at Saltdean, the fast-expanding coastal suburb of Brighton.

Uncompromising modernist apartment blocks were sometimes located in the middle of Regency or Victorian terraces. The architecturally innovative Embassy Court apartment building of 1935 was ill-placed next to the glories of Hove's earlier neo-classical Regency Brunswick Town. Constructed in reinforced concrete, Embassy Court proposed a futuristic 'new design for living' in mansion flats, including the first penthouse flats in England, making much of the sun and sea views. Thirty-five miles to the east, the nautically themed Marine Court of 1938 (see Figure 28) was in one authoritative view 'the first modernistic affront to the English seaside', looming over the early-nineteenth-century resort of St Leonards.[36]

Another result of the coming of the seaside sun was the development of holiday camps as permanent, complete and planned resorts offering a radically different holiday experience from the traditional resorts.[37] The private enterprise and competitive holiday camp business boomed and both the

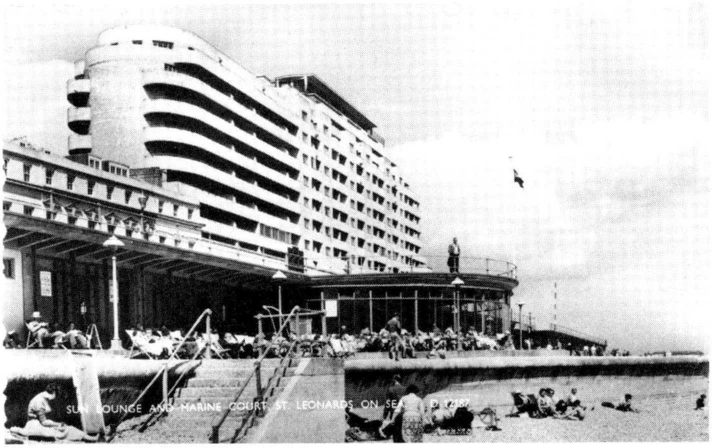

Figure 28
The Sun Lounge and Marine Court at St Leonards

small-scale independent camps and large-scale enterprises added a significant new dimension to the landscape and architecture of the seaside.

At Skegness, on the east coast of England, Billy Butlin, the most famous of the camp entrepreneurs, opened his first holiday camp in 1936.[38] Designed by Butlin himself, the camp was initially able to accommodate two thousand people and eventually five times that number. The Butlin's enterprise, replicated around the coast, proved immensely attractive.[39] The architecture, from the decorated façades of the modernist communal buildings, to the manicured lawns and gardens and iconic pools with playful fountains, provided a unique environment for a participatory holiday compared with what was offered in the old seaside resorts. The most widely applauded holiday camp design was that of the Prestatyn camp, opened in North Wales in 1938. The venture was portrayed as progressive and modern. Designed by the railway architect William Hamlyn, Prestatyn was 'based on sound architectural precepts': 'There was to be no piecemeal building, no sprinkling of chalets to destroy the symmetry of the camp plan.'[40]

Making much of the fashionable nautical style, the spectacular centre of the camp was the Sun Court, a large landscaped square with swimming pool and sixty-feet high observation tower, both for judging beauty and other competitions and for viewing the sea. Close by, the Prestatyn Clipper 'gives the impression of a ship on land, which indeed it is! [...] You can sit in one of the quaint barrel seats and imagine yourself on the high seas in the bar of a luxury liner.'[41] The Clipper experience is one example of how theming, particularly of interiors, was used to evoke other exotic and luxurious places and times.

Although enlivened by grand architectural gestures and façades, the communal halls were monolithic (constructed using modern industrial building techniques), and the chalets for sleeping were usually set in serried rows. From the air the overall layout was more reminiscent of the light industrial factory estate or military barracks and parade ground than the traditional seaside. Nonetheless, the holiday camps were an ideal solution to the holiday problem of contemporary society, with the much-loved commentator Godfrey Winn, for example, believing these 'playgrounds of the man-in-the-street' would solve the 'holiday problems of literally thousands of human beings [...] in the healthiest and happiest kind of manner'.[42] However, other middle-class voices (including that of George Orwell) criticised the synthetic holiday camps for commercialisation and for cultural, moral and spiritual decline.[43]

The War and After

The project radically reshaping the English seaside came to an abrupt standstill with the start of the Second World War in 1939. Many resorts, especially on the south and east coasts of England became part of the front line. Although the seaside reopened quite quickly from 1945, an age of austerity had set in and postwar reconstruction necessarily focused on the devastated inland cities and on damaged ports such as Portsmouth and Plymouth. Coastal resorts had to rely on the existing architecture and infrastructure. With hindsight it was clear that the interwar building for the sun represented an important watershed in the English seaside holiday and its architecture: the transformation of the seaside in the 1930s had a lasting impact on the townscape of many English resorts. The new buildings and designed open spaces – especially those most proudly modernist – often remained defining features of the seaside well into the postwar period. And in the early years of the present century, they re-emerged as an important aspect of the debate about the future of seaside resorts.

In the 1950s and 1960s the English seaside continued to prosper on the whole, even if the prosperity depended on investments in an environment that had been created during the interwar years. But the cult of the sun, so eagerly exploited in English resorts in the 1920s and 1930s, also contained the seeds of the English seaside's own postwar downfall. From the 1970s English holidaymakers were increasingly lured away to sunnier, warmer and often cheaper holidays on the shores of the Mediterranean and more distant coasts. Although the fortunes of individual resorts and the life histories of specific structures varied, the consequences for the interwar architecture of the sun were, in many cases, devastating. As fashions changed and visitor numbers fell, many of the structures became outdated and unattractive, and expensive to maintain. Decline and stagnation sometimes led to demolition, and in other cases to a feeble half-life, a poor shadow of what had been originally intended.

From the 1990s a string of official reports charted the decline of the English seaside resort while arguing that regeneration might be achieved through investment in the built environment and architecture. The titles of these reports – *Shifting Sands*, *Sea Changes* and *Turning the Tide* – suggested a natural process of uncontrollable movement, and they reflected an uncertain optimism that architecture, including the restoration of heritage buildings and designed spaces, could form the basis of the renewal of the seaside, contributing to the physical, social and economic regeneration of a resort.[44] As the twentieth century ended and the new century began, some of the interwar seaside buildings were identified as 'iconic' and therefore worth restoring, either as exceptional examples of a building style or because of their assumed potential to assist in the regeneration of a resort. Ironically, the products of what began in the interwar period as a radical challenge to the English seaside and the architectural manifestation of new ways of holidaymaking by the sea have, in such cases, now become 'heritage'. They are part of the contemporary debate about how we might use the past to regenerate the English seaside for the future.

Increasingly obsolete and out of tune with the late twentieth century, bathing stations declined in the postwar decades, although some structures were reused as seafront restaurants. While open-air pools and lidos continued to attract visitors into the 1950s and 1960s, they became less attractive to holidaymakers more interested in the relaxing warmth of overseas holidays or the comfort of the enclosed 'sub-tropical water paradise'. Just three survived into the new century, lauded as outstanding seaside structures. As to the amusement parks, seven decades after Emberton's modernization the Pleasure Beach successfully continued to isolate itself from Blackpool's declining fortunes. While there was serial investment in new rides, the Pleasure Beach also celebrated the heritage of the remaining modernist structures. After the war Margate's Dreamland prospered, entertaining more than forty thousand visitors on a busy day in 1948.[45] From the 1970s, however, despite investment in refurbishing and changing the use of the entertainment buildings and the installation of modern rides, Dreamland slowly if erratically declined as Margate's iconic amusement centre. By 2008 the park had closed. Only the modernist entrance buildings and the Scenic Railway survived to form part of the proposal for a new heritage seaside amusement park.

After decades of stagnation Morecambe's Midland Hotel was reopened in 2008 following a radical restoration scheme, while Saltdean's Ocean Hotel became the centrepiece of a large-scale residential development. By the new century the grand architect-designed holiday camps had been removed, although three Butlins holiday camps survived as reimagined 'beach resorts'. These remade holidaymaking sites included significant architectural innovations (such as white-tented 'Skyline Pavilions' visually dominating the local landscape) designed to combat the rival attractions of sunny overseas holidays.

As for the most iconic of modernist seaside buildings, the innovative De La Warr Pavilion seemed to soak up the character of postwar Bexhill. The resort was transformed into a residential town by the sea, with one of the highest proportions of retired people in Britain. Rather than functioning as a vehicle for regeneration, the Pavilion slowly decayed. By the early twentieth century, however, the De La Warr Pavilion was increasingly eulogised as a 'modernist masterpiece looking out over the sea [with] a sinuous elegance that has rarely been surpassed', 'arguably the most beautiful 20th century building in Britain' and 'the most beautiful work of art in Britain'.[46] In the minds of cultural commentators and architectural critics, it had become an iconic building. In 2002, the Arts Council and Heritage Lottery Fund awarded a new charitable trust £6 million to restore the structure. The contemporary restoration plans were curiously reminiscent of the original thinking behind the building. Stripped of the accretions of the previous seven decades, the restored Pavilion was intended to have an internationally significant new role as a centre for contemporary art, architecture and live performance. On the reopening in 2005 the success of the new regeneration project remained to be tested.

In the first years of the new century, the surviving modernist buildings that resulted from the interwar cult of the sun at the British seaside have, as the De La Warr Pavilion example illustrates, increasingly been labelled as iconic, preserved as heritage and given a role in the regeneration of individual resorts. There are intriguing indications, however, that a new twenty-first-century version of seaside modernism may be developing. The most significant Butlins investment at its resort at Bognor in Sussex is in a seafront hotel in a present-day version of the Nautical Moderne so prevalent in 1930s seaside buildings. Elsewhere round the British coast other designers, especially those building houses and apartments, also draw on the modernist imagination, albeit in new ways and with new materials. Modernism on Sea remains an unfinished story.

Part V

SOCIAL CHANGE ON THE PROMENADE

Edwina Keown

Edwina Keown lives in Dublin. She holds a BA in literature from Cardiff University and an MPhil and PhD from Trinity College Dublin. She is a teaching fellow at St Patrick's College, DCU, Dublin. She co-organised the first conference on Irish modernism and is currently working on a collected edition of essays, *Irish Modernism: Origins, Contexts, Publics*, to be published by Peter Lang, and a monograph on Elizabeth Bowen.

The Seaside *Flâneuse* in Elizabeth Bowen's *The Death of the Heart*

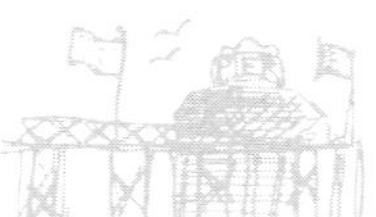

ENGLISH NOVELISTS HAVE LONG CELEBRATED the seaside as a cornerstone of Englishness, but it is only recently that cultural critics, such as the novelist and art critic Michael Bracewell, have recognised the special role of English seaside resorts in representing cultural transformations in English society. Bracewell describes a heady scene of art deco architecture, surreal arts, music and popular entertainment: a setting that mixes style and vulgarity, grandeur and seediness, permissiveness and morality. He lists 'the seers of British modernism': T.S. Eliot; Paul Nash; W.H. Auden and Graham Greene 'who set out a particular – and enduring – relationship with the ritual landscape of the English coastal holiday'.[1]

Elizabeth Bowen is a troubling and enlightening addition to Bracewell's seaside seers of British modernism. An Anglo-Irish writer with homes in both England and Ireland, Bowen was always alert to the significance of crossing-points and boundary spaces. She responded to the English seaside as a place of shifting identities, and made it the site of her most probing investigations of class mobility and consumerism between the wars.

Although Elizabeth Bowen was born in Dublin in 1899 she grew up on the Kent coast between 1906 and 1918 and was an eyewitness to the transitions between the Edwardian and postwar worlds. She was a member of the Anglo-Irish gentry with an ancestral house in Cork. But as a young girl in England she lived a rootless and vulnerable life with her mother, renting villas in Folkestone and Hythe. When her mother died in 1912 Bowen lived with her aunt in Hythe before attending boarding school. She witnessed 'Fashionable Folkestone' becoming popular Folkestone as the English aristocracy started holidaying abroad following the invasion of middle- and working-class punters.[2] For Bowen, the Kent coast was imbricated with 'the pageant' of British history, and Folkestone was a miniature theatre for modernity and change.

Bowen's sixth novel *The Death of the Heart* (published in 1938, the same year as Graham Greene's *Brighton Rock*) is set in London and at the fictional seaside resorts of Seale-on-Sea and Southstone, modelled on Hythe and Folkestone respectively. This novel is her masterpiece, and at its centre is a south coast resort. More than all her novels, it explores the fears of the upper classes and the intellectuals that English standards are slipping and that people are becoming more common – that the middle classes are invading and making the cultural spaces of their betters mediocre. However, Bowen does not give a black-and-white 'us and them' depiction of the class war. Instead she mocks the modernists' fears of commercialism and mass culture, using wicked irony and exaggerated stereotypes.

By focusing on *The Death of the Heart* this essay will investigate some of the central tenets of British modernism. First it will explore the importance of the seaside in relation to the chattering class's fear of mass culture, by looking at Bowen's background and the historical and cultural context of Folkestone between 1843 and 1938. Second, it will consider the sixteen-year-old heroine Portia Quayne as a *flâneuse*, suggesting that her 'roving eye' enables Bowen to critique English society between the wars, aided by her own Anglo-Irish identity – at once insider and outsider in England. The product of an unfortunate liaison between a lower-middle-class divorcee and an upper-class philanderer, Portia is outside the English class system. Through her, Bowen satirises the mass culture of the working classes, the aspirations of the middle classes and the closed mindset of the upper classes, while also exploring intellectual paranoia about social change and the rise of popular culture. Ironically, *The Death of the Heart* nearly made Bowen a popular writer. Fellow modernist Ivy Compton Burnett quipped that 'people keep writing to her about the death of their hearts'.[3]

All Change in Folkestone

Bowen's Folkestone first came to life in 1843 when the Southern Eastern Railway opened a line from London to Dover and inaugurated a steamer service from Folkestone to Boulogne – directly connecting the seaside with European cultural influences. Folkestone and Boulogne provide the setting for important scenes of sexual permissiveness between classes in Bowen's preceding novel *The House in Paris* (1935). In this novel, the upper-class Englishwoman Karen Michaelis escapes the stultifying values of her own milieu by embarking on an affair with her friend's fiancé, the Anglo-French Jew Max Ebhart. For Karen, the sea and France offer a passage into 1930s modernity and life: 'The long line of quay-side hotels and cafes smiled, expectant of the incoming ship. France met her approach coquettish, conscious and gay'.[4] And she chooses a hotel in the English resort of Hythe, down the road from Folkestone, to consummate the affair.

In 1844, Folkestone's first hotel, the Pavilion, was built for upper-class and continental travellers; it was soon renamed the Royal Pavilion signifying the town's rising status under Queen Victoria. A number of upper-class amenities were built under the auspices of the local aristocracy: Folkestone Estate; the Leas and Promenade; a bathing establishment; ornate concert pavilions featuring European orchestras, French and Viennese in particular; the Pleasure Gardens Theatre; and the Victoria Pier. H.G. Wells moved to Folkestone in 1900 bringing with him the 'buzz' of the Edwardian literary scene: Joseph Conrad, Ford Madox Ford, Henry James and George Bernard Shaw. By 1903 Folkestone had reached its peak as 'Fashionable Folkestone' with concert fees and the Earl of Radnor's policemen keeping the Promenade and Pier exclusive.

After 1903, Folkestone underwent a sea change, however, as middle-class visitors poured into the resort on a tide of commercialism. The years just before and after Bowen's arrival in Folkestone were crucial markers of this cultural intrusion and the modernists' counter-guard response. High and low culture flirted with each other on Victoria Pier as the new century dawned. In 1898, the famous music hall star Miss Marie Lloyd delivered a song at the Royal Pavilion about the snobbery of 'Fashionable Folkestone':

Twenty girls, and I was one of them,
All intent on having a spree,
Went to Folkestone for a holiday,
Bathed our tootsies in the sea.
It's a place where Costers seldom go,
They look upon us as low,
They're a stuck up lot you know.[5]

T.S. Eliot was a fan of Marie Lloyd, distinguishing her artistic and moral superiority from her fellow 'popular' artists because of her 'understanding of the people and sympathy with them'.[6] Eliot wrote his influential essay 'Marie Lloyd' as the last of his 'London Letters' for the *Dial* and then reprinted it in his new journal for modernist writing, the *Criterion*, in 1923. For Eliot, the middle classes are 'morally corrupt' and are infecting the upper classes with their apathy and corruption: 'The middle classes, in England as elsewhere, under democracy, are morally dependent upon the aristocracy, and the aristocracy are subordinate to the middle class, which is gradually absorbing and destroying them.'[7] The working classes are currently saved by Marie Lloyd, who embodies and therefore inculcates their virtues. But if Marie Lloyd is replaced with mass entertainment like the cinema and the revue there is a danger that 'the lower classes will tend to drop into the same protoplasm as the bourgeoisie'.[8] Eliot's rhetoric of eugenics and degeneracy echoes Friedrich Nietzsche's critique of the rising middle classes in his influential 'Third Essay on Aesthetics' in *On the Genealogy of Morals* (1887). Nietzsche writes about middle-class culture and capitalism at the *fin-de-siècle*: 'Anyone whose sense of smell extends beyond his nose to his eyes and ears detects almost everywhere he goes something like the air of the asylum, the hospital.'[9] For Nietzsche 'Man is *the* sick animal', but the working-class 'herd', the 'masses', can be saved by a new type of artist: a strong man who, acting as an 'aesthetic priest' and 'herdsman', will 'heal' and channel the working-class virtues and life-force. Eliot views the highbrow literary-cultural spaces of the *Dial* and the *Criterion* – and Marie Lloyd's music-hall art – in a Nietzschean sense as moral imperatives against the rabid commercialism of the middle classes.

Virginia Woolf echoes Eliot's sentiments in a letter she planned to send to the *New Statesman* in 1932 as part of a media debate between high and popular culture.[10] Woolf protests against the middle classes and their presumption to be the moral arbiters of taste, as opposed to Woolf and Bloomsbury – the 'highbrows'. Woolf classifies the aristocracy and working classes as 'lowbrows' and admires their 'thoroughbred vitality'. The enemy of both is the middlebrows – the middle classes – who are lost in no-man's-land between the upper and lower classes. 'They are neither one thing nor the other.'[11]

Between 1903 and 1938, Folkestone reflected the battle of the brows. Victoria Pier and the Royal Pavilion became increasingly commercialised for a certain middle-class clientele. 'Popular prices', Arts and Crafts programme designs and new booking stalls on the pier itself pushed out 'Fashionable Folkestone' but also kept out the working classes. In 1906, the year that the seven-year-old Bowen moved from Dublin to Folkestone, Edward VII's mistress Lillie Langtry performed at the Pavilion but was booed by the increasingly middle-class crowd, supposedly for being the King's mistress.[12] Importantly, when Bowen arrived in Folkestone in 1906 the resort was at its fashionable zenith and she witnessed at close quarters the encroachment of popular culture. This cultural transition left a fundamental impression on her sense of Englishness.

> Then, what about Folkestone? True, not a city but really a quite large town, my first English one. Folkestone, self-christened 'Queen of the South', had hardly yet overdrawn on what had been a highly fashionable reputation. Henry James characters, for instance, had stayed there (though that I was not to know).[13]

From 1907 to 1934, Folkestone's crown slipped under the management of the Forsyth Brothers who made no bones about turning the resort into a commercial enterprise by wooing the middle classes with 'Dainty Afternoon Teas', 'Bouncing Dillon's Comedy Gymnasts', 'Strong men wrestling', 'Ladies' Orchestras', 'Covent Garden Opera'. In 1907, the brothers launched the first-ever seaside beauty contest which became the highlight of the summer season and a staple of other English resorts.[14] Significantly, they made the Royal Pavilion one of the first venues in town to show films, renaming it the Pier Hippodrome to mark its cultural change and the new type of acts and customers it would attract.

Bowen revelled in the new entertainment and thrills, 'the sensation' of Folkestone and the encroachment on high society of popular, middle-class culture – speed, consumerism, moving-picture shows. Bowen remembers in 1906 delighting in the 'sea-viewing promenade, up and down which sailed scarlet or pink silk parasols [...] The shops were showy, and hummed with custom'.[15] Folkestone made Bowen a writer. It was her first impression of England, but more importantly 'Kent, and, above all, Kent's dramatisable coastline' was the opposite of Dublin's grey Georgian houses or her classical Bowen's Court and the wet, green Cork landscape. 'Everything, including the geological formation, struck me as having been recently put together [...] And this *newness* of England, manifest in the brightness, occasionally the crudity, of its colouring, had about it something of the precarious. *Would* it last?'[16] Folkestone's newness contrasted with her sense of the Anglo-Irish decline, claustrophobia and political tensions associated with Ireland. Significantly, Bowen valued the seaside over London as the scene of fast-paced modernity and social change.

The *Flâneuse*

Bowen's fascination with the particularly English sense of class consciousness, and her fellow modernists' obsession with the dumbing-down of culture in the hands of the middle classes with their penchant for popular culture and light entertainment, comes to a head in *The Death of the Heart* where the seaside is set in contest with London – and the seaside wins.

Bowen draws upon her own experience to create the literary figure of the *flâneuse* in the sixteen-year-old orphan, Portia Quayne. Portia acts like a 'roving eye', moving between the two social spheres of upper-class London and lower-middle-class Seale-on-Sea. Portia and her stepbrother's employee Eddie remain outsiders in the two societies (Eddie lacks a surname, indicating his classlessness). *The Death of the Heart* opens on an icy January morning in Regent's Park, and the iciness outside penetrates 2 Windsor Terrace, the home of Anna and Thomas Quayne. Inside, where Anna lives her mannered, stylish and morally vacuous life, all is quiet, repressed and 'edited'. The ice acts as a metaphor for the state of the upper middle classes in the 1930s: the dying heart belongs (in one sense) to the British establishment, and its demise is caused by the imperial decline and loss of self-belief following the First World War. Neil Corcoran describes Thomas Quayne as the stereotypical 1930s upper-middle-class Englishman who is profoundly conscious of discontinuity, realising that the imperial 'game' is over and yet still attempting to keep the 'game up'.[17]

In Anna's version of events, Thomas is the broken product of the union of his upper-class rock-solid paterfamilias and Portia's lower-middle-class mother, Irene. Divorced and then rendered impecunious by his wife, Mr Quayne senior was condemned to live a classless, rootless life on the French Riviera. Significantly, it is only at Folkestone that Mr Quayne could meet Thomas and Anna. The resort signifies not only Mr Quayne's outcast status – 'he did not behave at all like Thomas's father, but like an off-the-map, seedy old family friend' – but also the shift in Folkestone's reputation in the 1920s and 1930s into a dangerously permissive cultural space where the upper and middle classes can mingle (p. 15).

Irene and her lower-middle-class spontaneity invade Windsor Terrace through her daughter Portia, who fits into neither the Quaynes' upper-class world, nor later, the Heccombs' lower-middle-class world. English, yet born outside England, with an insider's and an outsider's perspective, Portia writes about Englishness and unfavourably compares Thomas and Anna's straitjacketed, mannered marriage with her former free-roaming life with her mother in France and Switzerland. 'Precarious high-upness had been an element in their life up there [...] They would lie down covered with coats leaving the window open [...] at four o'clock Portia would make tea. They ate in alternate mouthfuls, block chocolate and *brioche*' (p. 34). Portia's recollections mock Anna's attempts to make Windsor Terrace artfully casual.

Although Portia is Thomas Quayne's stepsister, society will always suspect her of vagrancy, of dangerously mixing class boundaries. She feels (and is) watched all the time for signs of being common, read as 'hotel habits' (p. 56). Unlike her fellow pupils who are driven to and from school, Portia walks, again a sign that she is not 'quite-quite'. As Janet Wolf argues, polite girls could not be *flâneuses* in 1930s England.[18] Portia's real education is watching the masses on the streets of London. But she remains an observer. It is when she visits the Heccombs at Seale-on-Sea that she partakes in the Englishness she has hitherto merely observed. Now she can put Windsor Terrace in perspective and gain a clearer picture of the Quaynes and the Heccombs and the stratification of English society as a whole. As Anna says at the start of the novel, 'Experience isn't interesting until it begins to repeat itself – in fact, till it does that it *is* hardly experience' (p. 11). Portia only begins fully processing life into experience in her diary when she arrives at Waikiki, Seale-on-Sea, and repeats the process of trying to adapt to English life that she began in Windsor Terrace.

It is this process of simultaneous adaptation and critical observation which, in Declan Kiberd's eyes, makes Portia (and Bowen's many other transient characters throughout her fiction) a *flâneuse*: a female literary embodiment of Charles Baudelaire's and Walter Benjamin's figure of the artist-*flâneur* and doomed heroic dandy. In his essay 'The Painter of Modern Life' (1863) Baudelaire declared that the writer of modernity should be a *flâneur*: a man of the crowd who both observes and mingles with the crowd. For Baudelaire the figure of the dandy best characterises the crisis of modernity – the transition between an old order and the new. Witnessing the rise of the bourgeoisie and increasing consumer culture in the 1860s, Baudelaire saw in the dandy the 'characteristic quality of opposition and revolt' who 'appears above all in periods of transition when democracy is not yet all-powerful, and aristocracy is only just beginning to totter and fall [...] Dandyism is the last spark of heroism amid decadence'.[19] In his modernist compendium of consumer and popular culture in nineteenth-century Paris, *The Arcades Project*, Walter Benjamin explores the figure of the *flâneur* as a defiant dandy at home on the streets and in shopping malls – 'a spy for the capitalists, on assignment in the realm of consumers'.[20] Declan Kiberd sees Bowen's penchant for rebellious outsiders, in particular orphaned young females, as a late modernist development of Baudelaire's and Benjamin's dandified *flâneur*. In his essay 'Elizabeth Bowen: The Dandy in Revolt', Kiberd argues that Bowen's dandy figures highlight the 'breakdown' in a performance that relies on style and the tenets of an older pre-First-World-War social order: 'The Dandy who begins with a taste for the heroic soon finds that there is no theatre in which to enact heroism, and so he or she is driven back into the studio and drawing-room, there to bemoan such frustration'.[21] In *The Death of the Heart*, Portia leaves the enclosing spaces of Windsor Terrace behind, turning to the colourful blare and recreational pleasures of the British seaside resort. At Seale-on-Sea she becomes a 1930s version of Walter Benjamin's *flâneur* who wandered through the shopping malls of nineteenth-century Paris.

'Life at its Highest Voltage': Seaside Vitality

Maud Ellmann notes that the first section of *The Death of the Heart*, set in Windsor Terrace and appropriately named 'The World', draws on a mixture of classical and gothic styles to signify the clash between Anna and Portia.[22] The second section, 'The Flesh', is set at the seaside and is a confusing pastiche of 1930s modernity. Seale-on-Sea and Southstone are a riot of colour, commercialism and sexuality where the life of the sensations is unedited and raw energy is on display. Anna and Thomas Quayne holiday in Capri but pack Portia off to the coast to stay with Anna's former governess, Mrs Heccomb, suggesting that this is where Portia belongs.

From the start, Portia is enraptured by Seale-on-Sea's boldness and energy. On arriving she finds that 'the view of sea, town, and plain' seem to be 'tilted up to meet her eyes like a mirror' and she finds that the shops are 'lively, expectant, tempting, crowded, gay'. She is immediately entranced by the Heccombs' exotically named villa Waikiki, which faces the sea 'boldly, as though daring the elements to dash it to bits' (pp. 131, 133). The sea itself 'seemed an annexe of the living-room' with its 'energetic and briny smell' heralding their arrival at the house (pp. 134, 133). Portia is liberated by her new watery home, feeling that 'a new life' has begun, and the next morning she 'boldly' lets herself out of the glass door to gaze at the sea, taking on the boldness of the house. She brings this new confidence to bear on her relations with Londoners, fearlessly inviting Eddie to come and stay.

In this energetic seaside setting the vulgarity of the middle classes becomes enticing. From Anna's snobbish perspective 'Miss Yarde' has married down by marrying Doctor Heccomb and moving to villa life at the seaside. But Bowen plays with the English obsession with the niceties of class difference and behaviour, taking revenge on the upper-class snobbery of Anna and Thomas. For all her foibles, Mrs Heccomb is a happy widow, holding onto gentility by giving piano lessons and renting out Waikiki during the summer. She talks merrily, knows everyone and loves to shop at the 'crowded, gay' Seale stores (Bowen even lists the fanciful purchases that go into her hive-shaped basket). She too is a snob though, and is mocked in her turn, with Bowen also poking fun at Mrs Heccomb's aspirational middle-class anxieties. She worries that her stepchildren, Dickie and Daphne, are rough and 'common'. Their mother 'had not been quite-quite' and now they are found 'in rinks, in cafés, cinemas and dance halls' (p. 128).

In her presentation of Dickie and Daphne Bowen portrays seaside life at its most vulgar and its most enticing. At every turn we see evidence of the working-class proclivities that Mrs Heccomb dreads, but we also see evidence of their vitality. Dickie works in a bank in Southstone, a solid commercial occupation; Daphne works in the local library, is wilfully dismissive of all the books around her and terrifies the genteel clientele who come to borrow nice novels, taking revenge on middlebrow culture and economic necessity: 'Portia realised later that the tomb-like hush of Smoot's library, where she had to sit all day, dealing out hated books, was not only antipathetic but even dangerous to Daphne' (p. 137). Bowen places Daphne as a member of the 'decent and contented' working classes who wave flags at red-carpet affairs and society weddings. She is 'the bad old order's principal stay'; but still there worryingly lurks in Daphne 'a touch of the *tricoteuse*' (pp. 143–4).

Bowen's celebratory parody of class prejudice and stereotyping reaches its comical climax when Portia witnesses the breakfast ritual at Waikiki. Daphne and Dickie let off steam noisily and colourfully in their leisure time. At Windsor Terrace Thomas's intimate life is muffled and edited out, his presence is only felt when he uses the internal phone; seaside Dickie, however, is 'uncompromisingly vigorous' in his morning routine, making his masculinity felt throughout the house. He makes such a noise in the bathroom as to make Portia think he must be enormous; he 'polishes off' his breakfast with a bit of egg on his chin, and then plunges out, with a 'satisfied, civic' air, to keep the wheels of English commerce rolling (p. 142). Daphne (who even manages to *sleep* voraciously) is even more of an over-the-top parody of the modern working girl. She bangs objects; she makes up her mouth – tangerine lipstick – like someone cutting her throat; she snaps at her toast, dribbling marmalade (of a brilliantly orange variety) on her lips; eats in the lounge; has the eyes of a shark. 'Daphne's person is sexy, her conversation irreproachably chaste' (p. 144). Daphne's sexuality is associated with fast cars; she perches in the passenger seat of the racing car owned by her current boyfriend, Bursley. Bursley nearly strays from Daphne to Portia at the Saturday jive the Heccombs hold in the Waikiki lounge, and Daphne gets her own back on Portia when she steals Eddie from her. The two erotically rub each other's hands in the local cinema (conforming to Eliot's belief in the cinema as an immoral force) while witnessed by the mesmerised Portia.

Bowen portrays Seale-on-Sea with a more comic and parodic style than the sections set in London. But her comedy is liberating. It is as if Bowen, like Mrs Heccomb, 'may even have got a sort of holiday pleasure from letting Daphne rip': 'The degree of blare and glare she permitted Daphne may even have been Mrs Heccomb's own tribute to the life force it had for so long been her business to check' (p. 138). Like the child Bowen, breaking loose from memories of her claustrophobic life in Anglo-Irish Dublin to embrace the vitality of Folkestone, the novelist Bowen takes a break from the modernist literary scene in London and presents the seaside as an energizing cultural space for modernism. She parodies the highbrow's fixation with class, even as they aimed to be classless in their vision, and the English obsession with status, which the intimate spaces of the seaside made more apparent. Portia's vision of Southstone is overlaid by a worldly omniscient narrator's perspective as she looks over towards the Hotel Splendide with its gilt dome where 'the flying flags receive at about sunset their full glory, and distantly glitter, a plutocratic heaven, for humbler trippers on the Seale esplanade' (p. 147). Waikiki makes Portia re-evaluate Windsor Terrace. However, while upper-class London is found wanting in favour of Portia's sense of the seaside as the 'fount of spontaneous living' and life 'at its highest voltage', Bowen is still a conservative who, like Eliot, wants to keep the classes in their place (p. 133). The Heccombs do not want to exchange Seale for London or even the plutocratic heaven of Southstone. They have marked out their territory, but will not overstep the mark.

Svetlin Stratiev

Svetlin Stratiev is the author of a study of modern British comic novels entitled *Philistines Beware: The Class Humour of Saki, Max Beerbohm, Martin Amis and David Lodge* (Sofia University Press, 2006). He has a DPhil in English from the University of Oxford and has taught English language and literature and Canadian studies as a full-time lecturer at Sofia University. Currently he works as a translator and lives in Luxembourg.

The Margin of the Printable

Seaside Postcards and Censorship

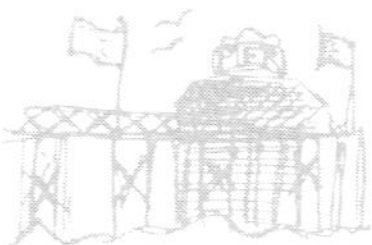

IN 1941, GEORGE ORWELL expressed surprise at the vulgarity of the comic postcard. Analysing the work of postcard artist Donald McGill, he found that 'at least half McGill's postcards are sex jokes, and a proportion, perhaps ten percent, are far more obscene than anything that is now printed in England.' Somehow the comic postcard artists were escaping the rigid censorship that had resulted in a total dearth of 'popular literature specialising in the "vulgar", farcical aspects of sex'; only on the postcard was 'really "low" humour [...] considered to be printable'.[1]

Orwell does not stop to ponder the explanation for the postcard's evasion of the censors and leaves several questions unanswered. What made these postcards printable? How did artists and publishers avoid the pitfalls associated with printing such jokes in Britain at that time? The obscene postcards survived with relative impunity in a society that expected its customs officials to seize Henry Miller's *Tropic of Cancer* in the 1950s and, as late as 1960, prosecuted Penguin for publishing *Lady Chatterley's Lover*.

This essay will suggest some answers to these questions, examining the British comic seaside postcard as a fascinating case of the printed word and image perched precariously on the very margin of the printable. It will examine some of the moral, aesthetic and legal pitfalls facing postcard artists and publishers and then explore their survival strategies. It will consider the comic postcard over the course of its long and sturdy life, from its Edwardian infancy until its vital old age, after it had outlived the demise of most censorship committees in the 1960s and 1970s. This was a life untroubled by the need for change; there is a surprising continuity in the subject matter of the postcards. The infamous Little Willie joke appears on cards from 1907 to the 1960s and many jokes were redrawn a number of times, decades apart, with a few adjustments for changes in clothes or superficial detail, so that the flirtatious chambermaids who still populated the postcards of the early 1950s were eventually replaced by secretaries.[2]

The Enemies: Snobs and Censors

Authors and publishers attempting to disseminate vulgarity in print came up against three major categories of obstacle in this period: social, aesthetic and legal. Socially, vulgarity was countered by simple prudery; certain topics and forms of expression were seen as taboo. In the eighteenth century Dr Thomas Bowdler had published editions of Shakespeare and Gibbon with all the bawdy jokes cut out; his legacy ran on into the twentieth century when 'the Polite Conspiracy' prevailed and censors attempted to protect the tender sex from the crude or the vulgar.[3] Aesthetically, the nineteenth century saw the privileging of 'high' culture over the 'low' humour of the sixteenth century, when Shakespeare could afford to spice up his works with obscene jokes that would have been unthinkable for Dickens.[4] This favouring of elitist culture continued into the twentieth century when the high modernists tended to favour the arcane over the bawdy.

When society ostracises certain content, the next step is to enshrine the prohibition in law. There was, indeed, legislation that caused concern to comic postcard artists and publishers well into the 1980s. First and foremost, the 1857 Obscene Publications Act gave magistrates the power to issue warrants allowing police to enter premises and seize and destroy obscene materials. This was modified in 1959, resulting in an act that is still in force today. The 1959 Act defines any article as obscene if its effect is such 'as to tend to deprave and corrupt' the persons likely to see it.[5] In addition, the retailers and indeed the senders of comic postcards could be prosecuted under the Post Office Acts of 1908 and 1953, which prohibit the transmission of indecent materials by post. And a host of other acts sprang up to join in the witch-hunt. Publishing and selling comic postcards could qualify as committing the common law offences of Blasphemy, Conspiracy to Corrupt Public Decency, Conspiracy to Corrupt Public Morals, Conspiracy to Outrage Public Decency, Exhibiting Indecent Activities, Pictures or Things, Obscenity, Outraging Public Decency and the Scottish common law offence of Shameless Indecency.[6]

In addition to this liberally repetitive list of statutes, various local authorities produced their own by-laws designed to catch the humble postcard unawares. In 1887, the Blackpool authorities announced that no person could sell or produce material 'of an obscene, indecent, or offensive nature or referring to any disease of a loathsome or secret kind'.[7] Inevitably, these laws became a minefield for publishers and retailers, largely because they failed to define their key terms. One person's obscenity will be another's indecency and a third person's vulgarity. A Lord Chief Justice is reported to have attempted a definition, placing indecency 'at the lower end of the scale' of impropriety, and obscenity at 'the top end'.[8] Vulgarity was perhaps deemed to be just lamentably bad taste, which sadly could not be prosecuted.

The Triumph of the Comic Postcard

The success of the comic postcard, attested by the fact that D. Constance Ltd (McGill's publisher) sold four million cards in 1954 alone, can only be understood in conjunction with the role of the seaside holiday and its adjacent myth of sexual liberation and unbridled hedonism.[9] Since the turn of the twentieth century Britain's working class had benefited from comparatively high wages, guaranteed holidays and cheaper travel. Consequently, British seaside resorts welcomed ever-increasing numbers of working-class holidaymakers. The annual week or two in the relative anonymity of the seaside resorts – and the relative state of undress on the beach – produced a liberation from the daily grind and from the social norms prevailing at home.

The idea of sexual licentiousness by the seaside was largely mythical but extremely potent among holidaymakers. It was even tacitly welcomed by local authorities, as researchers from the 1930s sociological project Mass-Observation reveal:

> the amount of extramarital intercourse is negligible, less than on a Saturday night in Worktown. When we told reporters that 'Blackpool was the most moral town in England', this seemed positively to annoy the municipal authorities. The sexual myth must be preserved. Although the imputations of the brassiered belle on postcard and brochure bear little relation to the real thing, they are nevertheless true in the minds of innumerable Worktowners.[10]

Comic postcards capitalised on that mythical atmosphere of liberation and loosening morals. It is commonly assumed that they served as a vent for the socially unacceptable impulses – what Orwell calls the 'Sancho Panza' in every human being:

> the voice of the belly protesting against the soul. His tastes lie towards safety, soft beds, no work, pots of beer and women with 'voluptuous' figures [...] There is a constant world-wide conspiracy to pretend that he is not there ... a dirty joke is [...] a sort of mental rebellion, a momentary wish that things were otherwise.[11]

This passage restates in figurative language the Freudian idea of 'tendentious' jokes functioning as vents for repressed desires, as encoding such impulses through a dreamlike process of condensation and displacement. In Freud's *Jokes and Their Relation to the Unconscious* the joke form is seen as rendering smut more socially acceptable.[12] To be able to serve as a vent and thus continue to sell, the comic postcards had to transgress some taboos. Thus artists and publishers were forced to manoeuvre on the margins of the socially acceptable, caught between the need to transgress norms and the threat of censorship, paying lip-service to taboos while flouting them, thumbing their noses at society yet taking care to avoid prosecution.

Several attributes of the comic postcard assisted its survival in this precarious position. First of all, the postcard itself was a marginal printed object: small, cheap and seemingly insignificant. Postcards had rarely been the object of commentators' attention or scrutiny, with Orwell's essay remaining the exception until the 1970s. In libraries, postcards are still sometimes classified as 'ephemera'. In addition, the comic cards were marginal geographically, socially and temporally: they were *seaside* postcards aimed at working- and lower-middle-class holidaymakers. This meant they were sold on the margins of polite society, members of which probably never set eyes on them. Orwell thought it 'a curious fact that many people seem to be unaware of the existence of these things or else have a vague notion that they are something to be found only at the seaside, like nigger minstrels or peppermint rock'.[13] This dismissive attitude was one of the postcard's survival tools.

Second, the postcards' obscenity, where present, tended to be obscured by their 'overpowering vulgarity', to use Orwell's expression. Vulgarity may transgress good taste and 'high' art but it is not a legally punishable offence. It was therefore valuable to the postcard artists, enabling the working-class tourists to say 'ya boo' to the Polite Conspiracy. The impression of vulgarity was conveyed both by the content of the jokes and the quality of the drawings. The anatomical and physiological references focused on disproportionately large body parts (huge breasts, fat bottoms, pot bellies), physical ugliness in older men and women bordering on the grotesque, unromantic ailments (lumbago, piles, ill-fitting false teeth), bad eating habits, bad food, excretion and vomiting. Beyond these, there were references to marital drudgery, henpecking, drunkenness, bad smells, practical jokes, embarrassing situations and laziness at work. The other dimension of seaside comic postcards' vulgarity was purely visual – created by the exaggeration and stylization of the outlines, by the simple, crude drawing and by the garish, cheeky primary colours, chiefly red and yellow (witness the characters' bright-red bulbous noses). The card's naturalistic relish may often have served as a smokescreen, confusing the censor's glance through the frontal assault of vulgarity and deflecting attention away from elements that could really be construed as obscene.

Comic postcards were also aided by their use of smutty innuendo, or *double entendre*. The archetypal instance is the Little Willie joke, in which the caption says something like 'I do wish I could see MY LITTLE WILLIE' and the picture is that of a worried pot-bellied gentleman in a bathing suit, under whose belly a little boy stands, completely blocked from sight. In most cases the ambiguity could be deduced from the text and the drawing provided grounds for both the innocent and the obscene meaning, as in this example. Sometimes the drawing was necessary for the correct interpretation of the *double entendre*: the caption 'Aye, she's top heavy and she wears her funnels too high – but she's OK for pleasure' is explained by the image of two sea captains discussing a steamship visible in the distance, while the smutty subtext is suggested by a woman with huge breasts and a scandalised expression, passing by. A variation on this is the malapropism ('My old man suffered from conscription ever since he was demoralized from the Army')or misunderstanding ('There's the Vicar at the window sponging his Aspidistra.' 'Horrid old man! He ought to do it in the Bathroom!').

The value of the *double entendre* lay in the fact that it was perfectly transparent but difficult to prosecute. Before the judge, the defence could claim that the innocent meaning was the correct one and accusers could even be charged with being dirty-minded themselves in looking for a second interpretation. Thus Lord Goddard C.J., quoted in the case of *Thomson v. Chain Libraries Ltd*, said that

> with regard to [allegedly obscene] postcards [...] it is only confusing the justices to have anything said to them about innuendoes. 'Innuendo' means a secondary meaning; a meaning because of something that is known to particular people ... If a thing has a secondary meaning I should say, prima facie, that it would not be obscene.[14]

Yet the *double entendre* did not always work so well, especially with pre-censorship. Local censorship committees rejected captions whose references were deemed too blunt. 'I'm tired of the same old diet – I fancy a few tit-bits', says a fish to its companion below a girl swimming in the nude. This caption was rejected as late as July 1966 and substituted with the almost meaningless: 'Fancy anything for afters?' A similar card including the word 'tit-bits' was published ten years later.[15] The pre-censorship committees often made arbitrary and wildly inconsistent decisions about what to reject in the case of, say, innuendoes referring to male sex organs. While the Little Willie joke was ubiquitous from 1907 until the 1970s, other references to penises and their sizes were routinely disallowed. One design, rejected in 1968, showed a disappointed bride in a transparent nightie saying, 'Blackpool Tower isn't as big as I thought it would be either.' Elfreda Buckland notes that in order to be made passable, these references were often transposed to children or nude statues. A drawing of a little boy in a full bathtub, one hand holding a Union Jack, the other submerged in front, with the caption 'What we have, we hold!' was quite popular. But a similar picture of a boy up to his waist in water saying, 'I've lost it!', was rejected in Hastings. References to statues were rarely problematic in the 1960s, but the drawing of a charlady looking at a fig-leaved male statue, saying 'Until I took this job I thought these 'ere feelings had died within me', was rejected in September 1953.[16]

The final tool in the postcard's survival kit was its typography. In a typical 'Bamforth comic' a fat white margin surrounds the picture and within it is a ruled border enclosing the drawing in a box. Sometimes there are rectangular 'flaps' drawn on both sides of the box, which do not have any apparent communicative, aesthetic or symbolic value. Perhaps this elaborate system of borders was meant to stress the fictional character of the design, creating a safety margin or *cordon sanitaire* around the problematic picture as if to insist that it was an inoffensively artificial object, safely isolated from reality. The printed words themselves often formed part of the border: 'A "BAMFORTH" COMIC'. This statement in itself is another defence tactic, reinforcing the message of the margin and border, reassuring the world that this is only a joke. Versions of this message appear also on the backs of many cards by Bamforth and other publishers: '"Comic" Series', 'Comicard', 'Inter-Art Comique Series', a picture of a smiling cat, a grinning mask. All of these have the same effect of arguing the innocence of what is purportedly only a joke.

Buckland's description of the way McGill submitted his originals to the censorship committees highlights the full significance of typography. He apparently sent the drawings in pencil, with the caption on the reverse side, accompanied by various technical instructions for the printers; this was perhaps the case with the majority of postcard artists and publishers. In this way the separation of caption from picture, and the typographic uniformity of the caption, went some way to neutralising the innuendo. Once printed, the captions probably looked much cheekier, because of the colours, layout and typeface. The average caption was printed in large capitals with blunt outlines, often in bright colours, immediately catching the attention. Typography was used to suggest intonation or to draw attention to the innuendo: key words were singled out through bold type or a different colour. 'QUICK, MUM, LOOK AT BASIL – HE'S GOT ONE **A FOOT LONG!**' is the caption to a drawing of a picnic trio. The girl refers to the fish her friend has just caught; the girl's mother, facing the other way, starts with a scandalised expression and drops a knife. Undoubtedly the phallic shape of the knife is also significant.

A similar effect was achieved by a larger font size (Reporter: 'WHAT DO YOU THINK ABOUT UNO, MISS?' Shapely beauty: 'I NEVER THINK OF ANYTHING ELSE MISTER!'), by the alternation of upper- and lower-case words and by underscoring.

In conjunction with the typeface, the postcard artists exploited the potential of line breaks. Here is an example of a temperance activist's speech losing its forcefulness:

> Gentlemen! Reconstruction means
> no **BITTER** feeling, **STOUT** hearts,
> plenty of **SPIRIT**, and your sup-
> **PORT** in every way!

Typically the key pun came on a new line ('My wife's about to become a / mummy!' a man thinks, watching his wife commit adultery beside a pyramid). The caption to a joke about seasickness on a boat, which was often considered screamingly funny, is arranged in an inverted pyramid to mimic the rocking of the boat and the vomiting:

> 'AREN'T YOU COMING
> DOWN TO UNPACK
> MA?'
> 'U-U-N-P-A-A-K,
> YRRUP? I'VE
> DONE NOTHING
> ELSE FOR
> HOURS!'

One of the most suggestive layouts of a caption is to be found on the picture of a buxom beauty, by whose side the words are arranged in a thinning column with the font becoming smaller and smaller, which may be taken as mimicking the act of stripping or penetration: 'Got / this / one / Lined / Up for you! / Come / here / and / Live it / Up!'.

The ultimate instance of defensive mimicry by the postcard artists and publishers was that they themselves took the initiative in setting up voluntary examining bodies in the various seaside resorts. McGill himself is reported to have demanded censorship before the printing stage to avoid subsequent legal complications.[17] This voluntary submission to pre-censorship, together with the low profile of the postcard, the smokescreen of vulgarity, the slippery innuendo and the suggestive typography helped the postcard survive and thrive in British seaside resorts. It coexisted in uneasy symbiosis with social and legal restrictions and in dialectic with censorship – each useless without the other. If holidaymakers by the seaside found the seaside comic postcards funny and liberating, it was because there were restrictive social norms to fight against; norms that the seaside postcard ultimately upheld by happily taking up a marginal position. Many authors hail the comic postcard as the slayer of the Polite Conspiracy but they make the mistake of forgetting that the margin is often also a fence, a boundary enclosing the space within. Unlike *Lady Chatterley*, the seaside postcard with its posture of marginality failed to challenge the status quo; in a sense it even assisted censorship and perhaps helped define the margin of the printable.

Paul Rennie

Paul Rennie is Head of Context in Graphic Design at Central Saint Martins, London. He is a specialist in British print culture and has written widely on aspects of British modernism: the Festival of Britain, postwar reconstruction and the idea of the seaside. These interests form the basis for *Rennies Seaside Modern*, a gallery and shop in Folkestone (by the sea), directed by Karen Rennie. Paul is currently working on a project about design and the Post Office.

Postwar Promenade

Pleasure, Reconstruction and the Festival of Britain

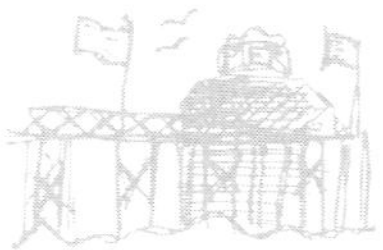

THE FESTIVAL OF BRITAIN, which took place between May and September 1951, conceptualised a uniquely British form of postwar modernism. Conceived as a celebration of the British people, and timed to mark the centenary of the Great Exhibition, this promised to be a first sighting of the sunlit uplands of reconstruction. The main Festival site was on London's South Bank, laid out between Westminster and Waterloo bridges and to each side of Hungerford Bridge. The layout was planned so as to offer a riverside promenade with views across to Big Ben and round to St Paul's. This Thames-side walk took its inspiration from the English seafront (see Plate 6 and Figure 29). The Festival gardens, too, referred to the gardens of spa towns and resorts. With their fun fairs and water gardens, the pleasure grounds at Battersea gestured towards the hedonistic pleasures of the seaside. Here was a carnivalesque version of modernity.

It is perhaps not surprising, given its waterside location, that the brand of cultural modernity exemplified by the Festival should take its cue from the seaside promenade. What needs more explanation is how the seaside came to be viewed as an ideal modern space – so much so that its benefits were transplanted to the centre of London. The English seaside resort appears to us, not withstanding its various excitements, as perhaps the least likely of modernist or utopian environments. For most of the last fifty years, English resorts have been deemed unfashionable. Yet many of the émigré modernist architects who arrived in Britain in the 1930s immediately recognised the major seaside leisure resorts as exemplary and uniquely British

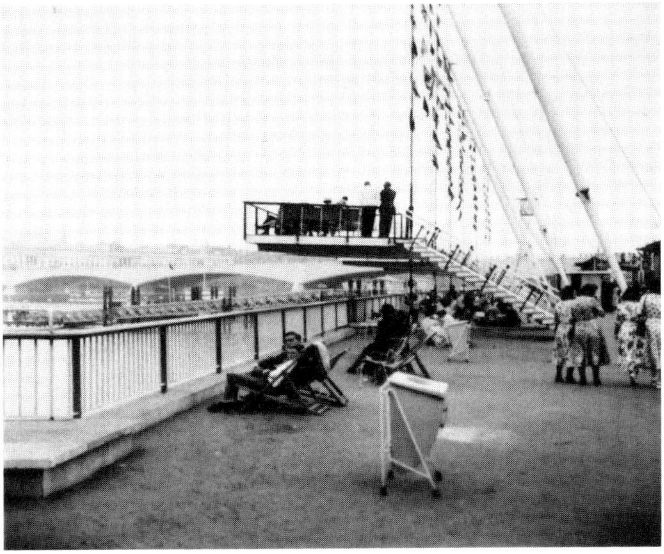

Figure 29
The Festival of Britain turned London's South Bank into a seaside resort, complete with deckchairs and bunting

manifestations of modernism. Among them were Serge Chermayeff and László Moholy-Nagy, both from landlocked Central Europe and keenly interested in the potential of the coast. In order to understand what it was that so appealed to them, we need to look briefly at the historical development of the seaside resort.

Early Promenading

In the eighteenth century the seaside was promoted for its medicinal benefits. The therapeutic qualities of fresh air and salt-water bathing were much in demand. The promenade was developed as a space where the elderly and infirm could benefit from sunshine, sea air and breezes. But not all seaside activities were so gentle. The promenade also served as a place for recuperation after the shock of the period's violent and sensational salt-water cures. For women these involved being plunged under the water just as a wave broke, thereby inducing the sensation of suffocation. Men, on the other hand, were made to battle against the relentless power of the sea until literally exhausted.

So the seaside promenade began as a space for post-shock recovery and for the horrified observation of other people's aquatic therapies. In his history of resort development, Alain Corbin observes that here, by the sea, 'sheltered by the therapeutic alibi, a new world of sensations was growing out of the mixed help and pleasure of sudden immersion'.[1]

It is understandable, given these circumstances, that the promenade became an observation point for 'bathing beauties'. And from there it was a short step for it to become a parading ground for wealth, privilege and glamour. In nineteenth-century resorts aimed at an aristocratic clientele, like Folkestone for example, the promenade was removed from the immediate seafront so as to preserve gentility. Indeed the parkland seafront at Folkestone, 'The Leas', was policed as a semi-private environment with a dress code enforced by local stewards. These precautions indicate that unseemly things were happening on the 'pleasure beach' which, in Folkestone, was removed to the foreshores and developed as a place of mass-market leisure facilities, sun lounges and entertainments.

From its very beginnings the seaside resort conceptualised itself as an alternative to the prevailing constraints and disciplines of civil society. Accordingly, and notwithstanding its origins as a place of medical therapy, the seaside resort was quickly identified as a place of exoticism. Given the association of aquatic cures with sexual pleasure, the resort could promote itself by appeal to a more relaxed and sexually liberated environment.

By the beginning of the twentieth century there were four big seaside resorts (Blackpool, Southend, Brighton and Bournemouth), each one connected by an extensive railway network to a large urban hinterland. These mass-market leisure resorts encouraged a powerful sense of liberation. A continuous sense of carnival distinguished the holiday crowd, which conformed to Mikhail Bakhtin's theory of the carnival as a series of sanctioned transgressions. The particular carnivals of the modern seaside have been examined more recently by Darren Webb, who argues that it was in the Tower Ballroom at Blackpool that 'class distinctions came closest to being suspended, that communication came closest to being free and frank, that the crowd came closest to fusing into the immortal mass body of people'.[2]

For European modernists the appeal of the seaside lay in the interaction of function, leisure and mass-market egalitarianism. Aristocratic isolation was of little appeal when set against the vital excesses of a bank holiday by the sea. The potential of seaside modernism was explored in the pages of the *Architectural Review*, under the editorship of J.M. Richards. The *Review* played a key role in introducing bold continental experiments to Britain, while also promoting a specifically British form of architectural modernism. Richards assembled a group of writers whose sympathetic intelligence, ranging in opinion from Nikolaus Pevsner to John Betjeman, appreciated the possibilities of modern transformations in the native tradition.

A special issue in 1936 was devoted to the seaside, outlining the history of the British resort and asking how its future could best be shaped. This issue was designed by Moholy-Nagy, whose dynamic observation of buildings and people was reflected in his use of coloured card pages with cut-out windows. Moholy-Nagy also provided a series of striking seaside photographs, paying particular attention to the De La Warr Pavilion at Bexhill.[3]

The Pavilion was a prime example of the way in which the evolution of steel, concrete and glass materials allowed for the separation of load-bearing elements from the traditional forms of structure. The new seaside architecture was characterised by dramatic scale, open spans and the relative transparency afforded by very large apertures. The transparent potential of the new building materials and new calculus of structural engineering became powerfully symbolic of social progress and personal emancipation. For Moholy-Nagy writing in 1936, the transparent, interconnected social spaces of the promenade and pavilion at Bexhill were an exciting manifestation of utopian modernity.

Gordon Cullen and Reconstruction

Discussion of these ideal spaces did not stop with the coming of war. In fact they became ever more prominent as the articulation of war aims began to extend beyond military concerns and to engage seriously with plans for reconstruction. And with the end of the war these theoretical considerations became urgent practical problems. The *Architectural Review* led the way, publishing influential writing on the future of town planning. Among the most significant of these articles were those by the *Review*'s own art director, Gordon Cullen.

During the 1930s Cullen had been a well-established member of the modernist community, working with Berthold Lebetkin for Tecton and playing an active role in the Modern Architecture Research Group (MARS). Now, as thoughts turned to reconstruction, he developed a sophisticated new project called 'Townscape'. He began by revisiting the pioneering work of Steen Eiler Rasmussen, who had examined the social construction of metropolitan London through the analysis of its various architectural styles. Cullen used the degradations of war to revisit the Georgian square, as theorised by Rasmussen, and to reclaim it as a pedestrianised public space. So, for example, the removal of railings as part of the war effort could become an opportunity to open the square and to remove the implicit reference to privilege contained in the visible enclosure of space.

At the heart of Cullen's 'Townscape' project was the idea that the movement of people through public spaces should express a meritocratic and egalitarian politics. In a cultural context defined by the social and military exclusions of previous years, the radical impact of this idea is clear.

In November 1947 Cullen presented a detailed proposal for the creation of a civic space around Westminster. It was to be modelled on the collegiate examples of Oxford and the Inns of Court and distinguished by its bias in favour of the pedestrian. Cullen called the proposal 'Westminster Regained'. Then, in 1949, Cullen responded to the announcement that the South Bank was to be the site of the Festival of Britain. In a second proposal, this time called 'Bankside Regained', he suggested a bold and permanent extension of the Festival spirit right along the embankment from County Hall to Bankside.[4]

The South Bank at this time was still a densely packed area of wharves, warehouses, tenements and slums. It existed in sharp cultural and architectural contrast to the London of the North Bank. Cullen's conceptualisation of South London accepted the existing architectural jumble and stylistic eclecticism. He proposed a promenade as an extension, in length, along the river frontage. The modernist pontoons would be embellished with architectural details of flags, rigging, and sails. The South Bank would, in effect, become a seaside pier and promenade combined.

In the event, neither of Cullen's proposals was accepted in full although, as I will show, significant parts of 'Bankside Regained' were incorporated into the Festival. It was to be another fifty years before Cullen's Thames-side walkway became a reality. In the twenty-first century it is now possible to walk along the river from Westminster Bridge to Tower Bridge.[5]

Seaside Design at the Festival of Britain

The site of the Festival on the southern riverside, opposite Whitehall and the Adelphi, was dominated by the expansive sweep of the Thames. The absence of the smoke and soot usually associated with railways (Waterloo was, in the main, served by electric trains) greatly enhanced the open spaces of the Festival, and meant that the riverside promenade could become a defining feature of the South Bank site. But the decision to turn the South Bank into a promenade was far more daring and risky than it might seem. In 1951 it was not obvious that promenading by the river was the attractive proposition that it would become.

The river was still an industrial highway with levels of traffic far beyond those that we see today. The smog of 1952, which killed over four thousand people, showed the air quality in London to be so poor as to make any outdoor activity practically impossible. In 1951 the air quality was just good enough, during the summer months, to make an outdoor promenade a possibility. It took courage on Hugh Casson's part, however, to adopt Cullen's theoretical proposals and to conceive of the Festival as a trip to a modernist seaside resort on the banks of the Thames.

The designers of the Festival recognised that the most dramatic approach to the South Bank was from across the river. The Westminster and Waterloo bridges were at either end of the site and gave only a partial view of the whole, but a temporary bridge was installed in the lee of Hungerford Bridge to bring visitors directly to the heart of the Festival site. This new bridge was accessed from Northumberland Avenue, where the approach was illuminated with large Festival Star lights above the street. The bridge itself was decked with bunting, so that the experience of arriving at the Festival was similar to the excitements of the seaside pier. By the time visitors reached the South Bank, they were in high spirits.

This limited access to the site would tend to create congestion points, but the problem was solved by splitting visitors into two groups, embarking on their festive promenades in opposite directions. Accordingly the exhibition was designed to be seen from two separate routes: 'People' and 'Land'.[6] In addition to this urban promenading, there were many other explicit celebrations of Britain's coastal heritage. Chief among these was Basil Spence's 'Sea and Ships' pavilion, designed with large-span open spaces and elevated walkways so that it could accommodate large maritime exhibits.[7] Appropriately, there was also a 'Seaside Section', which displayed lettered rock and saucy postcards. But perhaps the Festival's most valuable borrowing from the seaside came in the form of typography.

The Festival's typographic identity was constructed through the rediscovery of eighteenth- and early-nineteenth-century display types, and the resulting signage, underpinned by its historical references to English vernacular style, helped orchestrate the crowd to the happy rhythms of democratic diversity associated with seaside holidays.[8] The Typographic Panel included Gordon Cullen and Nicolete Gray, both closely involved with the modernist avant-garde while also promoting nineteenth-century display types. The panel commissioned from Philip Boydell a three-dimensional shaded letterform called 'Festival Titling'. The resulting letter was a perfect complement to the fluttering dazzle effect of the Festival bunting: it alluded to the cut-letter sharpness of classical tradition while simultaneously embracing sans-serif modern style.

Legacies

Notwithstanding its popular success, the Festival was immediately dismantled. The template proposed by Cullen and the Festival designers thereafter existed within the context of continuing postwar austerity as a theoretical construct rather than a reality. The Coronation of 1953 recast the 'New Elizabethans' as subjects of a monarch rather than citizens of the promenade.[9]

The immediate demolition of the Festival, with the exception of the Royal Festival Hall, has obscured the conceptual sophistication of this ephemeral architecture. In fact, as the pages of the *Architectural Review* make clear, and as Gordon Cullen's drawings show, the Festival was an attempt to integrate modernism into the emotional reality of the British architectural scene. Nowhere was this more successful than in the appropriation of seaside vernacular in all its detail. The seaside promenade was recast, in its Festival form, as an emancipatory experience of fun and social mobility. The conjunction of pleasure and modernity as a template for reconstruction deserves closer inspection, and Gordon Cullen deserves lasting recognition as the guiding intelligence behind the Festival's pioneering seaside style.

Part VI

MODERNISM AND AFTER

Alan Powers

Alan Powers is Professor of Architecture and Cultural History at the University of Greenwich and Chairman of the Twentieth Century Society. He has published widely on twentieth-century British art, architecture and design, including *Britain* in the series 'Modern Architectures in History' (Reaktion, 2007).

The Destructive Element

Benjamin Britten and Aldeburgh

MODERNISM CAME TO ALDEBURGH in 1948, with the first annual Festival of Music and the Arts, conceived by the resident composer, Benjamin Britten, and his creative circle. The sea had a lifelong importance for Britten, and the Festival deepened this relationship, drawing a new type of visitor to the small Suffolk town.

Aldeburgh is representative of a genre of seaside town favoured by artists. It has in common with St Ives and the smaller ports of the East Neuk of Fife the presence of a small local fishing industry, which provides economically and socially independent 'characters' as well as a picturesque paraphernalia of nets and boats. For Britten, this was significant. During his boyhood at Lowestoft, the Britten children found the docks the most interesting part of town, and they listened to the songs sung by the itinerant Scottish herring girls as they worked on the quay gutting the fish. As a resident of the town, he befriended Billy Burrell, one of the fishermen who was photographed by Kurt Hutton for *Picture Post* in 1950 with Britten and E.M. Forster on board his fishing boat at the time they were working on the opera *Billy Budd*.

Aldeburgh enjoyed an influx of titled visitors in the first period of English sea bathing during the Napoleonic wars, and a few large houses remain as evidence, together with George Crabbe's descriptions of them in 'The Borough', 1810, the poem that drew Britten back from America to Suffolk in 1942 and provided the basis for his most famous opera, *Peter Grimes*. The town had the potential to become a popular resort with a pier, amusements and streets of boarding houses as the nineteenth century proceeded, but such moves were resisted. Newsom Garrett, a local businessman and property owner, controlled the development of the town after 1850, and, despite the arrival of the railway in 1860, he and his family retained their grip. Aldeburgh had no reputation as a centre for the arts. Its population of summer visitors and retired professionals were attracted by golf and sailing, and there was some opposition to the Festival within the town among a group that the Festival organisers named 'the antibodies'.

The local topography helped, for the town offers a relatively narrow strip of land for construction between the shoreline of the sea, the bend of the River Alde at Slaughden and the marshes to the north. For similar reasons of topography, Southwold, the only other town on the sea between Felixstowe and Lowestoft, has also retained a pre-Victorian scale and hence an anti-populist exclusivity. Like Aldeburgh, it now has a problem of too much money trying to come into the town rather than, as happens with larger resorts, especially Lowestoft, too little. Unlike Southwold and Walberswick (where Wilson Steer, Charles Rennie Mackintosh, Margaret Mellis and many others worked as painters), Aldeburgh had little history of the visual arts. Eric Ravilious passed through in the summer of 1938 and painted three watercolours of the bathing machines on the beach and the lifeboat. Connie Winn, who was born at Uplands, opposite the church, ran her family house from the 1930s into the 1960s as a bohemian private hotel which would not have been out of place in Ronald Firbank's imaginary seaside resort of Valmouth. She was a good amateur landscape painter in an expressionist style, and during the 1950s ran a summer school for painters which included the young Peter Blake among its teachers.

'The Borough' provides one reason why the Aldeburgh Festival was not the Southwold Festival, but Britten's purchase of Snape Mill in 1937 at the age of twenty-four, is the other. 'The country is grand', he wrote, 'none like it in England'(see Figure 30).[1] Looking south downhill, one surveys the upper part of the Alde estuary, a wide tidal expanse of reed, saltings and islands made from surviving fragments of medieval river wall, almost devoid of visible buildings below the Snape Maltings, built after 1850 by Newsom Garrett at the head of navigation by Snape Bridge. This estuary is the strangest of the four great tidal rivers of Suffolk, owing to the configuration of the river, which almost reaches the sea at Aldeburgh, but takes a right-angle bend and continues southwards between the mainland and an uninhabited shingle

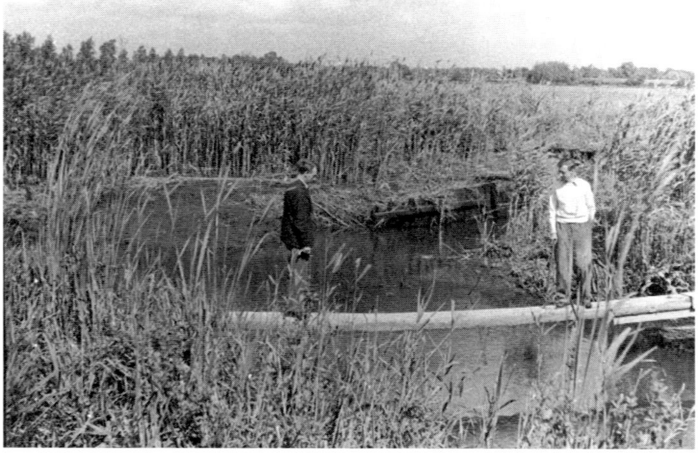

Figure 30
Benjamin Britten and Montagu Slater on the marshes near Snape, c. 1944

spit for a further twelve miles. Not many aesthetes seem to have savoured its quality before the 1930s, but Julian Tennyson, a local writer killed in the Second World War, wrote: 'there are things beyond the reach of man, and to me the Alde will always be the river of my boyhood and the loveliest river in England.'[2] Tennyson's book involves much activity in small boats, which became a form of escape for many men between the wars, often representing childhood companionship, as in Arthur Ransome's novels, or male solitude and endurance. Britten knew a different part of the estuary in his childhood, when his family regularly rented a farmhouse for holidays close to Butley Creek. The experience was evoked by Britten's colleague Imogen Holst in her book on the composer:

> As they went on their way, the tall reeds and rushes moved with them, leaning over with a swishing sound, while high overhead the curlews and redshanks called to each other. Beyond the marshes, the farthest walks led to Shingle Street, a small row of cottages on a pebbly beach, where there was nothing in sight except a vast expanse of sea and sky [...] on a still day the light can have the delicate outlines of a Japanese picture. On a stormy day, even in summer, the grey sea batters itself against the shelf [of pebbles], dragging the shingle down with a

> scrunching, grating, slithering sound. To anyone born on the Suffolk coast, this sound means home.[3]

This passage shows the dualism of the actual seaside shore, and the half-way condition of the tidal rivers, where the ebb and flood of the tide is a daily spectacle.

There were two years between Britten's arrival at the Mill and his departure for America, in company with the singer Peter Pears, in April 1939. He was living in Escondido, California, when he read the issue of the *Listener* magazine of 29 May 1941, with the article 'George Crabbe: The Poet and the Man' by E.M. Forster. Britten and Pears found a second-hand copy of Crabbe's poems and read 'The Borough', with its series of character studies, two of which would provide much of the substance for *Peter Grimes*. Crabbe wrote as an anti-romantic, almost defying the reader to enjoy the squalor of the town and its surroundings that he knew as a boy and escaped, and thereby appealing more strongly to the anti-romantic temperament of the modern age. Forster used words similar to those used later by Holst:

> It is a bleak little place: not beautiful. It huddles round a flint-towered church and sprawls down to the North Sea – and what a wallop the sea makes as it pounds at the shingle! Near-by is a quay, at the side of an estuary, and here the scenery becomes melancholy and flat; expanses of mud, saltish commons, the marsh-birds crying. Crabbe heard that sound and saw that melancholy, and they got into his verse.[4]

The effect of this text on Britten was probably the most important single event of his life. He immediately made plans to return to England with Pears, despite the dangers of a wartime Atlantic crossing, and face the consequences of his pacifism at home. He came back to Snape Mill and began work on the opera *Peter Grimes* with the librettist Montagu Slater. Its premiere in 1945 took place only a few weeks after VE Day, and symbolically represented a new direction for postwar culture (see Figure 31). It surpassed previous English operas in refuting claims that only composers of other nationalities could successfully work in this form, and offered audiences a kind of modern music which they could understand and enjoy. It also happened, *inter alia*, to be about the sea and its symbolic and practical role in the life of an ordinary community.

Prior to *Peter Grimes*, the sea played a role in Britten's music, but its effect became stronger over time. He grew up within sound of the sea, as his mother sang him to sleep. The first significant piece of modern music he heard was Frank Bridge's orchestral suite *The Sea*, in 1924, and later he told how he was 'knocked sideways' by it.[5] In 'Marine', one of the settings of Arthur Rimbaud, made in the autumn of 1939 as part of the song cycle *Les Illuminations*, the words and music evoke the breaking waves and the intermingling of sea and land. Christopher Palmer writes that 'it is perhaps the most thrilling song in the series; fired by the idea of "tourbillons de lumière", by the clash and convulsion of light on water'.[6] In another essay, Palmer identifies the key of A major with a 'Lydian sharpened fourth' as denoting this effect of light on water in *Peter Grimes*, and even in pieces not ostensibly connected with the sea.[7]

Much has been written about the meanings contained in Britten's reaction to reading Forster's *Listener* piece, and seldom can an artistic turning point of such significance be so accurately pinpointed. While there are generic aspects of the sea involved, the specific ones of Suffolk and Aldeburgh are more salient. It is a homecoming of the archetypal kind described by T.S. Eliot in *Little Gidding*, published in 1942, that involves self-knowledge after seeking. For Britten's intellectual mentor, W.H. Auden, journeys were never circular, but it was during the three years that Britten spent in the States, often in Auden's company,

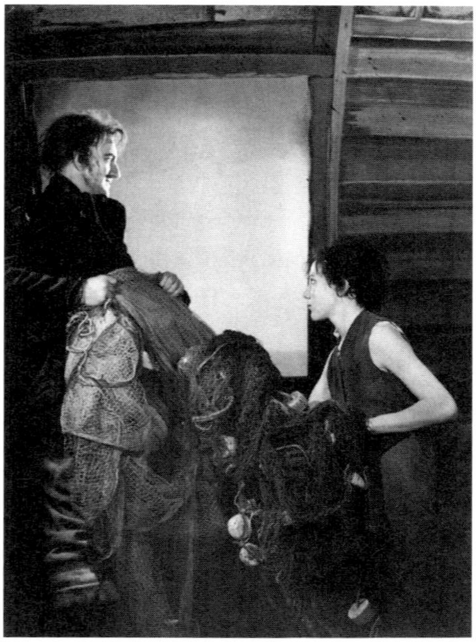

Figure 31
Peter Pears as Grimes with Leonard Thompson as the apprentice in the first performance of *Peter Grimes*, Sadler's Wells, June 1945

that he understood the significance of England for his own creativity. His essay 'England and the Folk-Art Problem', published obscurely in 1941 in the American magazine *Modern Music*, helps in understanding Britten's own sense of his position as a successor to composers who, in trying to create a national style, looked to folksong but struggled to make it speak independently of the European tradition. As Britten wrote, 'their fault lay not in the influences but in the lack of talent and inability to assimilate them'.[8] At the end of his essay, Britten quoted from Auden, adding his own gloss that 'The attempt to create a national music is only one symptom of a serious and universal malaise of our time – the refusal to accept the destruction of the "community" by the machine.'[9] His action in returning to England, and more specifically his decision to create the Aldeburgh Festival, was a direct attempt to refute this pessimistic conclusion.

The 1930s in England was a period when a portion of the avant-garde in each of the arts underwent a transformation towards localism and romanticism, tendencies that were strengthened by the isolation of the war, and incorporated in the policies of new cultural institutions of the postwar years, such as the Arts Council. The most representative creative figure in this respect was the painter John Piper, whom Britten met first in 1937 in connection with the Group Theatre, the avant-garde and left-wing troupe that produced the verse dramas of Auden and Christopher Isherwood, among others. Piper became an artistic director of the English Opera Group, together with Britten and his librettist, Eric Crozier, in 1947. He designed the sets for *The Rape of Lucretia* in that year, and for most of the subsequent Britten operas, and the ballet *The Prince of the Pagodas*. Piper's artistic progress from abstraction to predominantly topographical representation lost him some old friends, such as Ben Nicholson, but won him new ones, such as Sir Kenneth Clark, a board member of the English Opera Group and a presence at the Aldeburgh Festival as a lecturer and exhibition curator. Coincidentally, Clark also had the Suffolk coast and the Alde estuary imprinted on his early experience, and wrote evocatively about them in the volume of essays presented to Britten on his fiftieth birthday, a text that was later incorporated in his autobiography, remarking that the quality of light in Aldeburgh had always made him feel more intensely alive than in other places.

Piper's short book *British Romantic Artists*, 1942, represented his new declaration of allegiance, opening with the assertion 'Romantic art deals with the particular.' If Britten were to return to England at all, then Suffolk was the obvious place since he still owned the Mill, but this gesture was reinforced by the composition of *Peter Grimes*, and then by the commitment to the Festival in a place with no special facilities or reputation for music or other cultural activity. Piper's view was shared by a wide circle of thinkers in the war years, many of them in reaction against the presumption that modernism required a break from the coordinates of time and place, as well as an exclusion of content in favour of form.[10] Piper was in fact riding on a rising tide of interest and re-evaluation of English art, which aimed at an objective appraisal, avoiding sentimentality or jingoism on one hand and unthinking dismissal on the other.[11]

The Aldeburgh Festival has always made the most of local experiences and histories, from guided walks and visits to lectures and exhibitions. The range of subjects has included the Middle Ages (richly represented in the parish churches), and, as a recurrent feature, the literary and social circles of east Suffolk in the mid-nineteenth century, especially the poet Edward FitzGerald, famous as the 'translator' of *The Rubáiyát of Omar Khayyám*. FitzGerald lived near Woodbridge but sailed upriver to Aldeburgh on occasion to visit Edward Clodd, a populariser of Darwin and Huxley, at Stafford House on Crag Path. FitzGerald and Crabbe are minor figures of the first order, a cultural level that seems appropriate for unpretentious Aldeburgh: FitzGerald not Tennyson; Crabbe not Wordsworth. Thomas Hardy was one of Clodd's visitors, and was embraced as part of Britten's canon of stoic pessimists when his poems were set for the song cycle *Winter Words* in 1957. Clodd was one of the founders, in 1892, nine years after FitzGerald's death, of the Omar Khayyam Club, which included Henry James (whose stories provided material for two of Britten's operas). James came to east Suffolk and declared that Saxmundham, a small market town on the Ipswich to Lowestoft road, was the most beautiful place name in the language.

We might deduce from this, and from other readings of local history, that Suffolk is, as its monuments demonstrate, a country whose glory days passed with the Reformation, leaving a lingering sense of loss and regret. Indeed, the brutality of iconoclasm in the sixteenth and seventeenth centuries is emphasised by the few survivals of painted screens or stained glass. Its attraction in the 1950s was its lack of development. Such incursions of modernity as occurred (such as the Richard Garrett Engineering Works at Leiston and the nuclear power station at Sizewell), have either been limited in their effect on the wider economy and landscape, or, in the case of Sizewell, have simply completed the effect of the sublime suggested by the bleakness of shingle and sky.

Suffolk is prey to a different sense of loss through coastal erosion, and one of the first things a visitor to Aldeburgh learns is that half the town, as depicted in Tudor maps, is now under water. Indeed, as with other seaside places, erosion cannot fail to become a form of spectacle, with postcards showing, for example, 'The Last of the Three Mariners', with the waves pounding the solitary inn serving Aldeburgh's river port, Slaughden, and a few helpless onlookers. To the north, Dunwich is a more extreme case, since only a scrap of a town remains. It was here that Claude Debussy found his inspiration for his piano prelude of 1910, *La Cathédrale Engloutie*, a work linked to Britten by its evocation of Javanese gamelan.

By 1948 Britten had moved from Snape into the town of Aldeburgh itself, purchasing Crag House in the summer of 1947. The house fronts onto Crabbe Street, but backs onto Crag Path, the Aldeburgh equivalent of a promenade, with the shingle beach beginning only feet away. The sea is close to the houses, and, unlike Southwold which is raised on a modest cliff, it is almost at the same level, contributing to the intensity of reflected light, especially before noon. Britten would swim in the sea as many as five times a day (or night) during the summer.

The chorus in *Peter Grimes* sings of the townspeople's fear of the storm and part of the town was badly flooded in 1953, including Crag House, although Britten was absent at the time. One might choose to follow Hans Keller's interpretation of Britten as an aggressive pacifist, whose music contained both sadism and a 'violent repressive counter-force against his sadism'.[12] The struggle to maintain the coastline provides a metaphor for these oppositional forces of man and nature. In the post-Freudian age, the attraction of this landscape of 'the destructive element' was patent, as was the contrast of mood between the seasons and the ultimate futility of resisting fate.

While the darker side of the location was reflected in Britten's work, his presence in the area was a personal attempt to make something positive, but in doing so he built on some existing foundations. One of the Festival's founders was Margery Spring-Rice, the owner of Iken Hall on the upper Alde estuary, who had been active in Suffolk Rural Music Schools, part of a federation of county-based groups founded in 1929 for the benefit of beginners and amateurs. This was an aspect of music-making that Britten enthusiastically embraced at Aldeburgh. He played the viola, his second instrument, in the Aldeburgh Music Club, and in his own compositions he found ways to include professionals, amateurs and children. There was a strong belief among educationalists, represented in the book *Culture and Environment*, 1933, by F.R. Leavis and Denys Thompson, that the homogenisation of culture, particularly under American influence, should be actively resisted by the maintenance of a core of distinctively English values represented in selected books. This process had begun, in a far from provincial way, at Dartington Hall under Leonard and Dorothy Elmhirst, who became the primary financial supporters of the English Opera Group and the Aldeburgh Festival. There were also rare enthusiasts for contemporary arts in the Anglican Church who made common cause with neo-romantic localised modernism and used it as a national alternative to the *art sacré* movement in France. The Revd Walter Hussey commissioned a Henry Moore *Madonna and Child* and a Graham Sutherland *Crucifixion* for St Matthew's, Northampton, during the war, and then Britten's cantata *Rejoice in the Lamb*, 1943, to words by Christopher Smart (which, coincidentally, had been rediscovered in a private library in Suffolk and published only in 1939). The ability of modern art to illuminate historic institutions and places without destructive confrontation was at the core of the policies of newly created wartime bodies such as the Council for the Encouragement of Music and the Arts (CEMA, the embryo Arts Council) and the British Council.

After *Peter Grimes*, Britten's next opera, *The Rape of Lucretia*, was commissioned by John Christie of Glyndebourne, but it was not a happy relationship. The English Opera Group was created in 1946 as a way of detaching Britten's next opera commission, *Albert Herring*, from a contractual commitment to Glyndebourne, and this in turn was the springboard for launching the Aldeburgh Festival. While music and opera festivals have existed in various regions of Britain for many years, and in a few cases were built around the works of living composers, Aldeburgh was intentionally different. As Humphrey Carpenter writes in his biography of the composer, 'Aldeburgh seemed a highly eccentric location, a tiny town remotely situated in East Anglia, with poor railway and even worse road connections to London'.[13] In 1948, nobody could predict where the audiences would come from. But, to the surprise and delight of the organisers, local people attended many events, as well as Londoners and others from further afield. Aldeburgh needed to draw a wider audience owing to its sparsely inhabited catchment area (half of which, as has been remarked, was populated only by fish). But with Britten in residence and, from 1952, Imogen Holst who came there from Dartington, it had performers and creators in the community throughout the year. At an early stage, Britten declared his private ambition to make the Festival the means of establishing an educational programme for musicians, something that has come to fruition since the 1970s with the Britten-Pears School at Snape Maltings. In 2009, building work is in progress (the architects are Haworth Tompkins) to convert a derelict part of the nineteenth-century building complex into enlarged premises for the school.

The size of the Glyndebourne stage favoured 'chamber opera', especially Mozart, and *The Rape of Lucretia*, first performed there, was conceived as a chamber opera, unlike *Peter Grimes.* From this point the scale of Britten's operas indicates the level of spatial and financial resources available. *Billy Budd*, 1951, and *Gloriana*, 1953, were both written for Covent Garden and scaled accordingly, but the majority of his operas were conceived for the Jubilee Hall at Aldeburgh, a few hundred yards south of Crag House, and similarly backing onto Crag Path. This was considerably smaller than Glyndebourne, and even the modest requirements of *Albert Herring*, which was the centrepiece of the 1948 Festival, required extra precision by the cast to avoid collisions. With *A Midsummer Night's Dream*, launched at the Jubilee Hall in June 1960, the compression was even harder to achieve, as diaphanous costumes were imperilled by Piper's spiky scenery, which was intended to appear later at Covent Garden. Even with the construction of a larger stage and auditorium in the converted Snape Maltings in 1967, the sense of domestic scale, which had become part of the Festival's character, was preserved. At the Maltings, something was lost in terms of the performance happening in the middle of the town, with the audience dropping into the Cross Keys pub during the interval, although the Jubilee Hall has continued to be used for many Festival events. The sensitive conversion of the Maltings, led by Derek Sugden of Arup Associates, was, finally, the moment when the ethos of the Festival found architectural expression, and it has remained completely fresh over the course of forty years. In 1957, tired of 'the gaping faces and irritating publicity' of Crag House that came with increased social and physical mobility after the war, Britten and Pears exchanged it with their artist friend Mary Potter for the Red House, on the north edge of the town.[14] Some friends and Festival-goers regretted that this betokened a new way of life.

A small orchestra and a reduced number of singers suited the development of Britten's musical language. In 1958, *Noye's Fludde* was performed in Orford parish church, downriver from Aldeburgh, with its tall, broad interior and good sightlines. With a text from the Chester Play of the Deluge, this was the first of Britten's non-liturgical works specifically intended for church performance. The piece was devised to include children from local schools in the chorus of animals and in the percussion and recorder sections of the orchestra. The parishioners of Sudbourne and Orford were offered free tickets for the premiere, and found themselves participants, singing familiar hymns such as 'Eternal Father, strong to save' during the storm, and the Old Hundredth at the end. With *Curlew River*, 1964, he began the cycle of three 'Church Parables', all given their first performances at Orford, using sparser resources than *Noye's Fludde*, but to similar effect, in that the audience is invited to step back in time as the singers enter in monks' costume and frame the piece with their 'mediaeval' comments. *Curlew River* borrowed its stylisation from Japanese Noh drama, which Britten had experienced first hand. It confirms an affinity between watery coastal landscapes a hemisphere apart from one another, and thus becomes the most striking example in Britten's oeuvre of the familiar being re-illuminated by means of the exotic.

Since Britten's death in 1976, in parallel with changes in academia and society at large, commentators have felt free to comment on themes of homosexuality in Britten's work. It was clear that Peter Grimes was transformed in the opera from the psychopath described by Crabbe into a visionary artist-misfit in fisherman's clothing, although audiences may have found the transformation puzzling. The people of the Borough resent Grimes's disturbance of their settled existence, and propel him on his course of self-destruction. The plot of the opera parallels and even predicts tensions between Britten and parts of the arts establishment during his working life, and the passive-aggressive 'retreat' to Aldeburgh can be seen as part of his desire, tacitly at least, to make a point about his own independent position. For Philip Brett, one of the first scholars to bring these issues forward, there was a self-evident connection between Britten's left-wing affinities and his sexuality, both of which cast him as an outsider.[15] His collaboration with E.M. Forster on the libretto of *Billy Budd*, perhaps the most overtly homoerotic of the operas, linked him to an earlier generation of men whose sexuality was repressed in their work and he was able to bring such issues closer to those who understood them.

It has been suggested that Britten did not remain an outsider for long, other than in his own mind. *Gloriana*, his coronation opera about Elizabeth I, was criticised for its critical enquiry into the dilemmas of power, but royal patronage came during the 1960s, helping to win local acceptability for the Aldeburgh Festival, while losing Britten some credibility among his more radical friends. In a parody of the folksong 'The Foggy, Foggy Dew', which formed part of Britten's and Pears's performance repertory, the cabaret duo Michael Flanders and Donald Swann sang of Britten's work,

> T'was applauded by the masses,
> The middle classes too,
> And even by the Harewoods and the County Set,
> Yes, even by the Doggy, Doggy Few.[16]

Yet as Brett points out, following the defection of Guy Burgess and Donald Maclean in 1951, the pre-existing condition in which homosexuality was tolerated provided it remained largely invisible changed, and the incident set off a new round of official hostility, ending only with the conditional legalisation of gay sex in 1967.[17] Does Britten's identification with Aldeburgh have any meaning in this context? In 'Political Action and Artistic Endeavour', Brett starts from the premise that music may either be abstract and autonomous or referential, in terms of content. Abstraction was the mode linking romanticism and modernism, detached from social reality and therefore suitable for imperialist dissemination. The Festival of Britain, one may note, was inherently anti-imperialist in its presentation of national identity at a time when the mainstream expectation was the reverse, and partly for this reason most of its physical traces were quickly expunged by the incoming Conservative government of Winston Churchill in the autumn of 1951. Britten was one of several artists (his near-contemporary Michael Tippett was another) whose political and sexual instincts led them to reject this majority view, and therefore to seek subject matter liable to subvert it. Place is important in Britten's work as a composer, performer and cultural *animateur* because it leads to real issues. Hence the preference for 'alternatives', as Brett describes them in 'Britten's English Predecessors', in order to blow open the unthinking consensus about folk-music prevailing in the previous generation, that mistook its real significance and value.

The choice of Aldeburgh, Brett suggests, was satisfactory owing to his love of the place coupled with various forms of ambivalence about the people in it. The outsider Percy Grainger took the place of Vaughan Williams as his preferred master of folksong adaptation, an activity in which he was as active as his predecessors. In Brett's words:

> once having distanced himself from Vaughan Williams and Co. [...] he was nevertheless concerned to infiltrate and dominate their chosen fields of activity on his own terms. [...] The invocation of the powerful British sea myth, again on the composer's own terms, in *Peter Grimes* and *Billy Budd*, and the substitution of Aldeburgh, Suffolk and East Anglia for Hereford, Gloucestershire and the West Country, all seem to fit the pattern.[18]

One reference Brett does not make is to Auden's poem 'In praise of limestone', understandably, perhaps, since there is no limestone to be found for miles, yet Auden's linking of a mutable 'inconstant' landscape with the nature of gay love seems much more appropriately applied to the crumbling Suffolk coast, which is only waiting until the passionate sea breaks further into its frail defences.

Do these ideas resonate still in the Aldeburgh of today? After Britten's death in December 1976, there were momentary questions about the continuation of the Festival, but the succession plan has worked well and the operation has become more professional without losing its personal touch and local flavour. Even in the early 1980s the town was old-fashioned. There was hardly anywhere to eat lunch other than in one of the hotels, and this was part of the charm. The summer visitors, it appeared, mainly came because they had come there as children, and perhaps their parents before them. Outside the three weeks of the Festival in June, cultural activity was semi-dormant. Then everything began to change with the rising tide of new money, some of it in the pockets of the children of old Aldeburgh. Holiday houses, especially on Crag Path, began to go up in value and spanking new paintwork resisted the salt air. Old-fashioned food shops closed, as they do, and were replaced by smart boutiques, art galleries and restaurants in the High Street. The Aldeburgh Bookshop, a long-standing resource, began to win newly created national awards for excellence.

None of these things need be regretted. More questionable has been the way that street furniture has been 'themed' with nautical symbolism and the casual, take-it-or-leave-it quality of the town has gradually been eroded. The cultural change is apparent in the way that Britten himself has been physically commemorated. The 'official' monuments were a classically severe gravestone cut by Reynolds Stone, an artist connected at many points to the Festival circle, and a stained-glass window in the parish church by John Piper, depicting the 'Church Parables' in each of the three lights. The town proposed a statue as being potentially good for business, but strenuous protests succeeded in squashing the project as unsuitable. In its place, the architect H.T. Cadbury-Brown, whose house of 1964 is, so far, Aldeburgh's only listed modern building, devised an alternative in the form of a baulk of timber standing on the beach, with two holes through which the wind might, at times of storm, blow the two notes used by the chorus in the opera to call the name 'Peter Grimes!' Cadbury-Brown's intention was that the monument should be almost invisible, but that it would entice residents to come down to the beach and share the experience of the storm, in order to find out whether it was sounding as intended. The proposal was never taken up.

Twenty-five years on, Britten did receive his memorial, in the form of a sculpture by the local painter Maggi Hambling, sited on the long shingle beach between Aldeburgh and the slightly bizarre neo-Tudor holiday village of Thorpeness to the north. The monument takes the form of a scallop shell of welded sheet iron, with a line from the *Peter Grimes* libretto cut out of the rim. In the controversy that accompanied the sculpture's early life, Hambling, probably the best-known lesbian artist in Britain, defended it as a statement about Britten's sexual politics; she attributed opposition to homophobia. Does it fulfil the artist's intention, or merely contribute to the further transformation of Aldeburgh into a Benjamin Britten theme park? Is there a generational difference between the restraint of Cadbury-Brown's proposal and the highly visible Hambling piece? If the landscape could speak, what would it say? Perhaps one winter a storm will make the final decision.

Alexandra Harris

Alexandra Harris is a Lecturer in English at the University of Liverpool. She studied history of art at the Courtauld Institute in London and holds a doctorate from the University of Oxford. She is working on a book about English culture in the 1930s and 1940s, investigating modernism's fascination with landscape, antiquarianism and the lure of 'home'.

Seaside Ceremonies

Coastal Rites in Twentieth-Century Art

WHEN CHAOS THREATENS, we tidy up. Inhabitants of the seafront are specialists in this patient art. High tides and salty squalls trespass on their property. Paint flakes, doors warp, roofs leak. But very soon order will return. The façades will be repainted, the doors straightened, the roofs repaired. Pass through any coastal town on the morning after a storm and there will be some determined restoration work going on. People will be getting themselves straight again – deleting the effects of the sea and reclaiming control of this border territory.

These are proud acts in the ongoing battle between man and the elements, and the coastline breeds this kind of ritual ordering. Formal gardens are planted along the seafront, with bright annuals planted in neat shapes as if to announce that uncontrollable nature ends with the high-tide mark on the beach, and here begins the organised human world of flower beds. The traditional seaside holiday is an elaborate sequence of rituals which, likewise, ensure the tidiness of things beneath the buzz of 'letting go': up the pier on one side, down on the other; fish and chips on that same bench; a rug spread beneath those particular dunes. Revisiting the Norfolk coast where he spent many childhood holidays, Philip Larkin surveyed the scene with a certain wonder that it was 'Still going on, all of it, still going on!' He watched the holidaymakers carefully carrying out their familial duties. This esplanade was where they came to lead the 'uncertain children' gently up and down, or 'wheel / The frigid old along for them to feel / A final summer'.[1]

Many of the essays in this collection have been about seaside liberation, whether it be sexual release, anarchic holiday spirit or the sense of wildness that comes from walking high on cliffs or through the spray of breaking waves. This last essay suggests that there is a very closely related tradition of seaside orderliness, and that artists throughout the twentieth century have interpreted it with a profound, almost religious, feeling for the rituals that we invent to hold back the tide. For Larkin, a trip to the sea was no improvised abandonment, but a ceremony: 'half an annual pleasure, half a rite'.[2] This essay is about these coastal rites and their presence in English art.

Tidying

Tidiness is powerful. It is a humble but remarkable form of resilience, a display of orderliness in the face of the elements. This is why Benjamin Britten put a tidy fisherman's hut at the still centre of his gale-force opera *Peter Grimes*, a work in which wildness and trim domesticity come into fatal collision. Grimes, the raging prophet of Aldeburgh, is viewed by the townspeople as the embodiment of chaos. He is in league with the storm against which they barricade their houses; he is a force to be eradicated if they are to continue with their respectable routines. So they march along the coast to arraign Grimes at his hut, but what they find there is not the scene of monstrous debauchery they expect. Grimes turns out to be a careful seaside housekeeper. The hut they find is empty but organised. 'Here's order', says the Rector in admiration, 'here's skill'.[3]

'The Borough' places a high value on such skills. In the poem which inspired Britten's opera, George Crabbe had invented an Aldeburgh narrator alert to the town's ethos of tidiness. Setting the scene in the 'General Description' he proudly makes a point of it: 'We prune our Hedges, prime our slender Trees.'[4] Britten, and his librettist Montagu Slater, translated these details into central symbols of order, and they imagined a Grimes who might keenly feel their influence. Grimes's housekeeping is his purposeful defence against the passions which rule him. Britten took the trouble to specify in the stage directions that the apprentice's fishing clothes should be 'neatly stacked' on Grimes's shelf, and he saw that the simple orderliness of Grimes's home could chasten the whole shouting, outraged crowd. It is enough to give the Borough its quietus, points out the town magistrate

Swallow: 'Here we come pell-mell / Expecting to find out – we know not what / But all we find is a neat and empty hut.' It is now the crowd which appears monstrous, and in quiet atonement the Rector asks that the last to leave 'please close the door'.[5]

The closing of the door is a ritual politeness which pays tribute to Grimes's own efforts at polite living. He longs for domesticity, but knows he cannot sustain it. The solitary visionary finds comfort in homely daydreams: he will get married, he tells Bulstrode; he will 'set up / Household and shop'. Alone, he allows himself to inhabit for a few moments this fantasy of building 'some kindlier home' where life is lived cleanly and purposefully:

> Fruit in the garden, children by the shore,
> A whitened doorstep, and a woman's care.[6]

He imagines order, and then tears it apart, unable to confine his imagination to the well-tended orchard and the seemly front door. He knows too much to conform to the Borough; it would be a lie for him to sing merry rounds with them at the inn. So he breaks through their chorus, transcending it with his own daemonic version of the song, and in doing so he breaches the unwritten human pact in which we agree to perform whatever orderly rites are necessary to keep the storm at bay.

Since Grimes has defected from society to join the sea, he must drown himself in his boat, and while he dies offstage, far out at sea, the Borough makes itself spick and span for the new day. 'Cleaners open the front door of the inn and begin to scrub the step [...] The Nieces emerge and begin to polish the brasses outside the Boar'.[7] There is something savage in this conspicuous carrying-out of the respectability rites that Grimes could not manage. Britten asks whether the restoration of order that traditionally completes a tragedy has, in this case, been achieved at too high a price. Are these cleaners smug in the knowledge that they have cleaned up Peter Grimes, disposing of him like the mess on the front step? Britten allows their tidying to be both a tyranny and a kind of heroism. It is exclusive and intolerant, but it is also, after all, what Grimes admired and what Britten respectfully acknowledges as a 'skill'.

Britten's strong feeling for housekeeping is part of a long tradition in English art, and one which is closely allied to the coast. While living in St Ives during the war, Ben Nicholson imagined himself more as a reliable cleaner than an erratic genius, telling Herbert Read that working on a painting was like 'scrubbing the top of a really well-used kitchen table': physical, familiar, domestic.[8] And Auden invoked the careful cultivation of England's edges in his poem 'Look, stranger'. He positions us at the meeting point between farmland and wilderness: 'Here at the small field's ending pause / Where the chalk wall falls to the foam'.[9] He goes against the cliché of rugged cliffs topped by ragged grass, and shows us instead the 'small field', a place of order and containment, beyond which is the indeterminate sea.

The aesthetics of trimness inflected the twentieth century's new coastal buildings. Many of the modernist architects interested in seaside design realised that the tradition of being 'Bristol fashion' could be adapted as part of the great modern move to whiteness, openness and purity. This meant that new architecture in the International Style could be promoted as in keeping with the long-established tidiness of maritime buildings. And perhaps, after all, the gleaming white walls of the Midland Hotel at Morecambe and the De La Warr Pavilion in Bexhill were not so far removed from the English vernacular as it would appear. They turn a confident, orderly face towards the elements, confronting wildness with tidiness. The architects knew these buildings would need a lot of 'keeping up'. The paint would need renewing, the great expanses of glass would need washing, the large chrome handles on the Pavilion doors would need to be polished – like the brasses at Britten's Boar Inn. To keep them sparkling would be to endorse an idea of clean, rationalised living, surrendering not an inch to the unpredictable elements. Mendelsohn and Chermayeff did not countenance any Ruskinian aesthetics of decay. Their buildings were not meant to age gently, crumbling picturesquely. They must look sea-worthy; they must be kept shipshape.

When John Piper described the unique merits of 'Nautical Style' (discussed in this book by Frances Spalding) he kept coming back to the word 'trim'.[10] He loved the bright white numbers on the sides of boats and the bulled-up lamps of lighthouses, and when he wrote a short book about Romney Marsh he began by evoking the coastal culture of pruning and priming: 'the weather-boarded houses, the trim fences and trimmer hedges'.[11] On the wide open Marsh, where the shingly land gets mixed up with the sea, these trim hedges signified the determined efforts of local people to carve out inhabitable spaces. They formed shelter and privacy; they defined the limits of a manageable domestic world.

One of the earliest heroes of the English novel was a trimmer of hedges, and – whether venerated or ridiculed – he has been a strong presence in the arts of this country since he first cultivated his island in the eighteenth century. Cast out into the wilderness, Robinson Crusoe became the most expert of seaside housekeepers and gardeners. Commuting regularly between his Country House and his Sea-Coast House, he managed his desolation by keeping shipshape. He made his kingdom knowable by dividing it up and building partitions. His fence-building grew to excessive proportions (more a fiercely defensive system of military barricades than a sheltering garden wall), but it took a certain stoic heroism to do such a patient job of keeping up appearances when there were no neighbours nearby to impress. Mowing and hoeing and arranging and tidying, Crusoe was able to feed himself. But his work was an act of survival in other ways too: Defoe had defined the human need to take control of alien wildness. Peter Grimes could not do so, or not for long. This was his tragedy and he did not survive.

Gardening

At the furthest point of Romney Marsh, in the humming shadow of Dungeness power station, Derek Jarman found that a trim fisherman's hut was for sale. He bought it in 1986, soon after being diagnosed HIV positive, and became one of the century's great interpreters of the shoreline. He loved this unforgiving landscape. As his biographer Tony Peake remembers, 'he relished openness, starkness, rigour; to be in the teeth of the wind'.[12] Deeply opposed to all forms of cosiness, Jarman was a *bête noire* of the avant-garde: his films were a perverse kaleidoscope of violence, erotica and kitsch. But he saw no contradiction between this and his passion for coastal trimness. He tidied Prospect Cottage, giving the windows a new coat of yellow paint, strikingly bright against the black-tarred weather-boarding. Most of all, he gardened, rearranging the wilderness in compelling patterns at his front door (see Plate 7).

Jarman worked in the exuberant tradition of Gertrude Jekyll, and he admired Christopher Lloyd's herbaceous profusions at Great Dixter. 'If a garden isn't shaggy, forget it', he said, knowing that purposeful shagginess is its own form of tidiness because it depends on there being little walls for plants to flop over and a strong underlying pattern to define the digressions above.[13] Jarman designed a formal garden in front of his cottage and a less formal garden behind, but both were meticulous works of art, labour-intensive and encouraging in the visitor a respectful attentiveness to detail. Like Crusoe (who spent several weeks making a spade) Jarman revered his tools, observing the patina on the wooden handle of a well-used garden fork and (when it reached the end of its useful life) displaying it in the garden as a memorial of past work. But where Crusoe wanted clear markers delimiting his patch, Jarman wanted to dissolve the line between art and nature. 'There are no walls or fences,' he wrote in his journal *Modern Nature*, 'my garden's boundaries are the horizon'.[14] He picked up the remains of wartime anti-tank fences, relics of a time when barricades were needed, and put them to happier use as climbing frames for his plants.

Jarman cultivated species native to the shingle (sea kale, yellow poppies, gorse, viper's bugloss) and he brought home choice pieces of debris from his walks over the Ness. A compulsive beachcomber with a fine eye for accidental sculptures, he accumulated 'anchors from the beach, twisted metal, an old table top', old railway sleepers, pots, stakes, and hundreds of pebbles.[15] These pebbles were arranged in squares and circles, or standing upright in rings like miniature megaliths. Jarman performed these building rites with the seriousness of an ancient druid; he studied the history of ley-lines and stone circles, and the dedication with which he made his own circles ensured that force fields adhered around them. These were mystic ceremonies which (more than any fence) protected him from the elements and sanctified his relation to them. The garden was, as Peake writes, 'an area of magic, where its alchemist of a creator could take sanctuary from the outside world and heal himself'.[16] Jarman's own poetry explored the workings of this sanctuary: 'Here at the sea's edge,' he wrote,

> I have planted my dragon-toothed garden
> To defend the porch.[17]

His house did not have a porch: it was as plain and four-square as houses come. But the word was his tribute to more orthodox ideas of homeliness which, like the 'whitened step' that haunted Grimes, both attracted and terrorised Jarman.

The pagan rites of his protective stone circles mixed with Christian iconography in Jarman's 1990 film *The Garden*. Prospect Cottage and its bleak landscape became both an Eden of innocent pleasure and a fallen Gethsemane in which savage punishment awaits those who do not conform. Jarman made a ghostly, fractured gospel of the shingle in which Tilda Swinton appeared as the Madonna, holding the baby Jesus outside a rusty fisherman's hut, and in which the risen Christ walked down the avenue of pylons carrying power from Dungeness to England. Jarman was claiming the company of other lonely visionaries. Blake had seen the resurrection in his Felpham garden; Stanley Spencer had peered over his wall in Cookham to see the day of judgement. Learning from these local prophets, for whom the mundane and transcendent were inextricable, Jarman intercut his apocalyptic shots of the power station burning in the sunset with quiet footage of himself digging vegetable beds. An open bag of compost flaps at his feet; the worn spade is as much an icon as the crucifix.

The film was an elegy for friends who had died. It was full of anger at their loss, but attempted also to be a horticultural gift to their memory. Jarman gave himself the role of Ophelia going to her death and said his farewells by giving out flowers carefully selected from his garden:

> My gilly flowers, roses, violets blue
> Sweet garden of vanished pleasures.
> Goodnight boys, goodnight Johnny, goodnight.[18]

Like Ophelia's herbs, these were peaceful tokens of orderliness in what seemed like a mad world.

'At first', wrote Jarman about his early months at Dungeness, 'people thought I was building a garden for magical purposes – a white witch out to get the nuclear power station'.[19] His magic had no such practical, definable aims but, collecting his sacred objects and arranging stone circles, Jarman was a seaside wizard nonetheless. He filmed his muse Tilda Swinton as a beachcomber in *The Garden*, equipping her with a giant sieve for the sifting of shingle. The stones jump up to meet the sieve, as if Swinton were charming or hypnotising them. She, too, is a white witch. As she examines the hole of a large pebble, and plucks from it a golden ring, it appears that she is holding a philosopher's stone; the alchemists' long hunt seems to have ended at the sea.

Totems

All strollers along beaches like to perform the simple alchemy of taking a pebble from among millions and making it a little sculpture which will catch the light on a window-sill. But artists and writers have been especially alert to the strange powers of these found objects. Jarman's stones owed some of their magic to the work of modernist predecessors who had sifted the shingle before him.

One such predecessor was Paul Nash, who picked up a piece of driftwood on Romney Marsh in 1933 and called it Marsh Personage because it so evidently had a life of its own. Nash developed a passion for found objects and when in 1934 he went to live at Swanage on the Dorset coast, there were many objects waiting to be found. Wherever Nash looked, the small seaside town seemed to be undergoing surreal metamorphoses. He imagined giant pebbles floating past cliffs, and the benches on the esplanade turned into

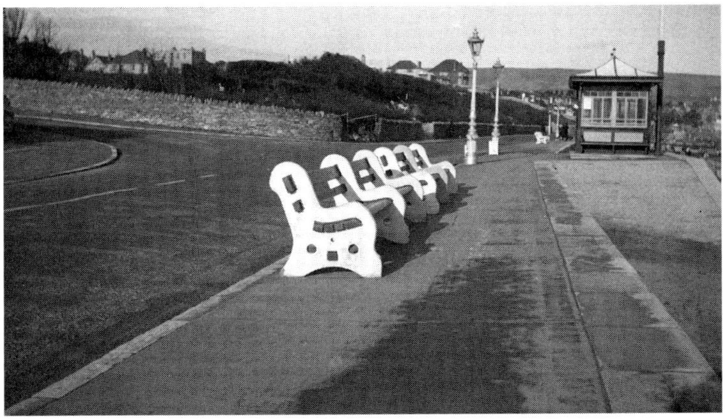

Figure 32 Paul Nash, *Benches at Swanage*, 1935. To Nash, even the benches on the Swanage seafront looked surreal

swans (see Figure 32 and Plate 8). In his 1934 painting *Event on the Downs* (see Plate 9) the chalk paths over the cliffs became the white lines around a tennis ball, and threatened to roll away. The whole county seemed to be alive with archaeological oddities. His *Shell Guide to Dorset* was illustrated with all manner of fossils; one of the region's biggest dinosaurs stalked the front page, and the book's selection of haunting photographs included an old boat on the shingle, reduced to its hull timbers, and looking like the beached skeleton of some ancient Dorset beast.[20]

Best of all, though, were the Victorian bedposts, bollards and door-knockers that were to be found in surprising places all over Swanage. The Victorian entrepreneur George Burt, mayor of Swanage in the 1870s, had imported architectural salvage from London to provide ornamentation for his native town. And here it still stood: ornate ironwork leaning in fields, and Hanover Square lamps on the quay.[21] Nash photographed these transplanted objects and wrote an essay called 'Swanage, or Seaside Surrealism', in which he declared this small coastal town to be 'a surrealist dream'.[22]

Nash's article launched a brief craze for seaside surrealism; the *Architectural Review* even ran a holiday competition for the best surrealist photographs taken by the sea. But there was nothing faddish about the growing prominence of the coast in English modernism. In 1936, John Piper dreamt up a 'beach engine' which was a fantastic agglomeration of bits and bobs, including nautical marker-posts, and the silhouettes of washed-up bottles.[23] His admiration for tidiness did not stop him from loving the flotsam of the water's edge. For him, the distinct aesthetics of the coast were characterised by the coming together of trimness and detritus. In his beach paintings and collages, Piper relished the interaction of neat, strong nautical shapes, and the inspiringly eccentric assortment of driftwood, old boxes, fishing nets and the relics of picnics.

In St Ives, Alfred Wallis was painting on driftwood, making pictures with all the physicality of found objects, and Barbara Hepworth was carving large, sensuous pebbles which exposed their interior spaces, or turned themselves into female forms. H.S. Ede, who acquired many of these St Ives works, would later arrange them at Kettle's Yard in Cambridge, interspersed with rings of pebbles that were so precisely placed as to become objects of worship, as if – like the stone circles in Jarman's garden – they might be capable of magic.

Virginia Woolf wondered whether beach finds might have the power to take over one's life. She imagined in her 1920 short story 'Solid Objects' that they could prove extremely dangerous.[24] The story is about a successful politician who one day finds a smooth piece of glass buried in the sand and becomes entranced by it. He is compelled to seek out more objects, so that his life becomes an obsessive series of scrabblings, diggings and siftings. The chosen pieces accumulate on John's mantelpiece, exerting their hold over him, and stealing him away from his former life. Eventually John gives up his job, and yields entirely to the world of shards and pebbles. The story is partly a comedy, making fun of infatuated collecting and the attention so often lavished on clutter. But Woolf probes disturbingly at the allure of these found objects, sensing that they might come to haunt one.

Certainly they haunted the novel Woolf was beginning to write and in which, a decade before *objets trouvés* were officially appropriated by the surrealists, she examined the way that things lost and things found might work on the mind. *Jacob's Room* introduces such an object in its first pages, stumbled upon by the young Jacob playing on the beach: 'lying among the black sticks and straw under the cliff, he saw a whole skull – perhaps a cow's skull, a skull, perhaps, with the teeth in it'.[25] Adventuring alone through the vast world of rocks and seaweed, suddenly lost and about to cry out, Jacob spots this skull and is captivated by it. He takes its jaw under his arm and back to the lodging house, leaving the rest on the sand where, after a short eulogy, it is condemned to its fate:

> clean, white, windswept, sand-rubbed, a more unpolluted piece of bone existed nowhere on the coast of Cornwall. The sea holly would grow through the eye-sockets; it would turn to powder; or some golfer, hitting his ball one fine day, would disperse a little dust.[26]

The rescued jaw, with its yellow teeth, knocks against Jacob's bedstead in the night, and it rattles on through the novel, which contains at least fourteen different kinds of bone and which sends its x-ray vision right though the flesh of daily life down to the skeleton beneath. Chicken bones, nose bones, bones on the moor in moonlight: these signs of mortality in a book about a man who dies young are not grotesque but beautiful, mostly glowing white, or – like the ram's skull carved into the wood over the doorway in Jacob's elegant London rooms – small works of art. The animal bones return to haunt Cam in *To the Lighthouse*, who cannot go to sleep with a boar's skull on the wall, and James, her brother, who cannot go to sleep without it.[27] It is an object of fantasy, as is the brooch which Minta loses on the beach and which Paul dreams of finding for her. The brooch has been lost before: in *Jacob's Room* Mrs Flanders's brooch fell among the pebbles on the moor above Scarborough. But lost in the sand at Skye it becomes a hidden grail, which Paul imagines he will find, heroically, alone, on the beach at dawn, thereby proving his love for Minta.

These treasures of the shoreline, which are jewel-like – or which are in fact jewels – in Woolf's fiction, become gothic burials in the writing of Elizabeth Bowen. Woolf finds a clean, white sheep's jaw; Bowen finds the whole gruesome corpse of the sheep. She began her autobiography with a walk on the wooded cliff path above Seabrook, and vividly remembered the shock many years ago of finding a dead sheep there, 'blood rusting its clotted wool'.[28] The found sheep had already been a disturbing off-stage presence in her 1963 novel *The Little Girls*, where a schoolgirl boasts that she knows where there's a wood with a dead sheep in it. *The Little Girls* is Bowen's novel of seaside totems, obsessively burying and unearthing strange objects in the thickets along the coast of the fictional Southstone. 'I like looking for things ... or hiding things', announces Dinah, and the novel conducts the ceremonial digging up of the things she hid as a child.[29]

With two of her school friends Dinah buries a coffer in the grounds of their seaside school, St Agatha's, each girl secreting in it some meaningful token. As grown women they go back one evening to find the coffer, which is now in a private garden, the school having long since been closed down. They gather like revenants in the dusk, enacting their exhumation rites. In a novel so haunted that a homely boiling kettle becomes a medium exhaling ectoplasm, the three figures in the garden are descendants of Macbeth's witches, relocated to the south coast. Positioning them here, on the ghostly border between the tidy Southstone gardens and the dark, unknown sea, Bowen brilliantly orchestrates the collision between genteel external trimness and chaotic interior lives. These three women, who might by day appear to be quite shipshape, are to be found with their spades at twilight, in a stranger's garden, digging up a pot.

They trespass down the 'well-kept drives', past the 'trimmed escallonia hedges', on an imaginative journey into a messier past.[30] This is Bowen's version of beachcombing, and the 'finds' are suitably extraordinary. The coffer turns out to be empty, but the novel hunts down the items which once filled it: a gun, a pickled toe and a copy of Shelley (this being a second beach cremation for the poet drowned at sea). This is seaside surrealism at its height, concealing outlandish fantasies between the escallonias. 'We prune our Hedges, prime our slender Trees', as Crabbe said, but we keep being haunted by the bits (like the pickled toe) which have had to be pruned off.

Travellers

Beach objects are the souvenirs of seaside journeys; they are the relics which reward the pilgrim for his efforts and they have some of the dubious powers associated with the bones of medieval saints. Jarman's totems perform miracles, summoning angels to the beach; Bowen's perform the no less mysterious duty of summoning up the past. In the summer of 1982, Jonathan Raban went hunting for fossils on the Dorset coast. As he chipped at the limestone, he was 'knocking [his] way back into 1952' when, as a boy, he had come to this same spot with his father. Raban's fossil-hunting, then, was a doubly archaeological activity, a quest for remains from the early years of the earth and for embedded traces of his own early life.

Raban was on an elaborate and very extended pilgrimage, sailing around Britain in his small boat, the *Gosfield Maid*, and hoping along the way to get a new perspective on his country and his past:

> home is always the hardest place to get into sharp focus. If only it could be *encompassed* ... by a slow, stopping, circular voyage ... if only one could go back to all the stages and places of one's own life, as a stranger, out of the blue ... couldn't one emerge at the end as a domestic Columbus, the true discoverer of a doorstep empire?[31]

There had been many of these journeys before Raban's (he carefully researched the travels of his predecessors) and there have been many since – such is the ceremonial appeal of following the coast of Britain. There was even one going on at exactly the same time: Paul Theroux was doing a British orbital on foot and by bus. They were going in opposite directions (Theroux clockwise, Raban anti-clockwise), and they were equally at odds in their imaginative approach. Theroux's journey, written up as *The Kingdom by the Sea*, was the antithesis of Raban's, which was recorded, in its turn, in a stretchily hybrid memoir-travelogue-political diary called *Coasting*.[32] Theroux was in a rush. He whizzed round in three months, no detours, no dawdling. He did not quite get back to his starting point, finishing on Southend Pier rather than crossing the estuary back to Margate. Raban, by contrast, was coasting. He spent four years over it, passing the finish mark after one year and going round again. The American Theroux saw himself as a visitor, and accordingly he played the part of the detached anthropologist, watching as if through binoculars (he carried a pair with him) as the elderly arranged themselves on the decks of the De La Warr Pavilion. He itemised the objects people choose to keep in beach huts, and enjoyed the 'surrealistic' derangements of Weston-super-Mare. Raban was standing at a distance too, trying to spring up by surprise on his own past, but he travelled with intimate knowledge of his country and with a coastal history behind him. His was an interior journey as much as an outer one, so Raban packed a whole library onto his boat and hung English watercolours on the walls, housing himself within a tradition. The wandering Theroux, meanwhile, travelled light with a small backpack and no detritus from the past to worry him.

Hunting for fossils between Lyme Regis and Charmouth (places with rich literary as well as geological history), Raban was following his younger self: 'the ten-year-old raced on ahead; the thirty-nine-year-old plodded behind, trying to remember the way.'[33] His father had been a devoted history-hunter and genealogist, collecting remains from all ages: ammonites, Roman pots and most particularly family ancestors. It was a Shandean preoccupation this, and in tribute Raban carried a ten-volume 1780 edition of Sterne on his boat. But 'where would it end?' Would the family tree be traced right back to the fossils? The collecting of relics made Raban think of T.S. Eliot's fragments shored against ruins. His father's fossil-hunting – his 'great antiquarian truffle hunt' – looked, from a distance of thirty years, like 'just such a shoring-up job' but none the less potent for that.[34]

Pilgrims

On the 11.33 to Margate, Paul Theroux met a fellow passenger who suggested that he go to Canterbury instead. 'Full of history [...], beautiful old cathedral'.[35] Unimpressed, Theroux carried on to his seaside destination, but he did not invest it with any of the sacredness or ritual drama that would make it a viable alternative to Canterbury for the modern pilgrim. This was left to Graham Swift, one of the greatest writers of contemporary seaside rites.

In his 1996 novel, *Last Orders*, Swift imagined the journey of four friends from Bermondsey to Margate, where they loyally fulfil Jack's puzzling request that his ashes be scattered from the end of the pier. Swift ensures that Margate ousts Canterbury Cathedral from its elevated position as chief goal of pilgrimages. The Bermondsey ash-scatterers pay an apologetic visit to the cathedral, but their mission takes them elsewhere and this is only a sideshow. Canterbury is used to being the end point, the culmination. Ray notes that it looks like 'a town you're meant to arrive at, at your journey's end'. But his journey is not going to end there. No, he says, with a note of quietly iconoclastic triumph, 'we're going on to Margate, by the sea'.[36]

The novel's hybrid of solemnity and holiday spirit is established by two brilliantly juxtaposed epigraphs: the first from *Urn Burial*, Thomas Browne's book of man's elaborate funerary rites, and the second starting up a sing-song: 'I do like to be beside the seaside.' The funeral and the holiday are rolled together: Jack's 'gift' is 'to give them a day out by the sea – like we're off on a jaunt, a spree, and the world looks good'.[37]

Jack had dreamed of starting life afresh, and this meant buying a bungalow in Margate. 'It's not exactly the promised land', Ray points out, but it was Jack's idea of making good, coming clean. He was destined for the seaside – before being interrupted by cancer – and his friends finish the journey for him. Swift reworks the pilgrimage described in *As I Lay Dying*, revising Faulkner's narrative to make it suitable for modern Londoners. The mule-drawn cart with its precariously balanced coffin is replaced by a leather-lined Mercedes and the more sanitary cargo of ashes. The journey feels just as strange and just as sacred, although in both novels there is a distinct possibility that the troublesome last orders were in fact a bad joke played by the dying.

One of Swift's more subtle inheritances from Faulkner is a profound investment in the value of domestic craftsmanship, a feeling for getting things just right. So, where Faulkner respectfully describes Cash's making of the coffin – the wheezy 'snoring' of his sawing and the purposeful solidity of his carpenter's tools – Swift imagines the pride and care with which Vince drives the funeral car, and the concern with which Vic checks the pier. Vic is an undertaker: he does ritual for a living. And he carries with him an air of authority for which, on this occasion, the others are grateful. He knows, as much as anyone, how things should be done, and so it is he who decides the order of ceremonies. Ray watches him stride ahead to the appointed scattering spot: 'It seems right that Vic's there first, to inspect the pitch, check the facilities, it wouldn't do if something wasn't up to scratch'.[38]

It sounds a romantic idea: scattering ashes into a rough sea while rain lashes down and a gale blows across the pier. But in this case the wind is not properly fierce (more blustery), the rain is more a drizzle, and the ashes are shaken out of something that looks like an instant coffee jar. This is Swift's response to the customary incongruities of the English seaside, its mixture of exhilaration and ordinariness. The Margate pilgrims are doing something primal and deeply emotive; their walk down the pier is so intricately described that it feels like an epic journey. But the whole process is firmly down-to-earth, refusing any sublime abandonment to the moment. 'Keep your hands as dry as you can', says Vic, wiping his own hands on a handkerchief so that the ashes won't stick.[39]

Swift's coast, like Piper's, is both messy and bright. The 'niff of the seaside' is oxymoronically defined: 'tarry and bilgy and mucky, same time as it's zingy and clean'.[40] This is the fascination of it. It turns out that Jack's seaside history is mucky too, despite his efforts to erase it by making a zingy clean start. As the scattering is performed in Margate, Jack's wife Amy sits elsewhere, remembering a prewar visit to that same pier. She and Jack should have walked down it as lovers, but instead they are disappointed in each other, and angry. He wins a teddy-bear for her and brutally throws it off the pier.

Amy, following the road to Margate in her head, reckons 'they must be there by now, they must have done it'.[41] She is Swift's version of Lily Briscoe, who stands painting on the lawn while Mr Ramsay and his children sail, at last, to the lighthouse. Both women synchronise their own imaginative journeys with the physical pilgrimages they know are taking place. Lily thinks back over her life with the Ramsays, full of violent loves and loathings. It is exhausting to try and make sense of it and pull it all into a definable shape, so it is a tremendous relief to look out to sea and sense that Mr Ramsay must be at the end of his journey, thus allowing her to conclude her own: '"He must have reached it" said Lily Briscoe aloud, feeling suddenly completely tired out.'[42]

Both Woolf and Swift orchestrate the confusion of registers so integral to a seaside outing – the comedy of it all, the tragedy, the mundanity of a holiday packed-lunch, the elusive, inestimable significance of reaching the lighthouse or the pier. Cam sits peeling her hard-boiled egg but imagines herself, at the same time, to be a fearless adventurer. Learning that sailors drowned in just the place the boat is now passing, Mr Ramsay performs the scattering of ashes, except that it is only the crumbs from his sandwich paper. Nobody in the boat to the lighthouse wants very much to be there. It is painful and embarrassing, but it is a necessary act of symbolic reparation. The seaside is the place for such ceremonies; it encourages feelings of ritual.

The arrival at the lighthouse in Woolf's novel is the completion of a family ritual proposed and postponed many years before. When Lily and Mr Ramsay return to the seaside they pay homage not only to what has gone but to what remains, and to what can, with effort, be reconstructed. And here again it is the housekeeper whose patient art makes it possible for life by the sea to go on – which is why Woolf makes Mrs McNab, with her mops and pails, the guardian of the 'Time Passes' section, cleaning up after the years of decay and delivering the house to a new life.

As Woolf knew so well, annual trips to the coast are made up of repetitions, recognitions, the joy and the boredom of familiarity. When this continuity is broken, the sense of desolation is intense. John Betjeman watched as the seaside routine was shattered by another war. He established the jaunty repeated rhythms of his 'Margate, 1940' before making a line of asterisks across the page and writing four desolate wartime lines:

> Beside the Queen's Highcliffe now rank grows the vetch
> Now dark is the terrace, a storm-battered stretch,
> And I think, as the fairy-lit sights I recall,
> It is those we are fighting for, foremost of all.[43]

Much later, in 'Beside the Seaside', when the lights had come back on, Betjeman wrote about the miracle of finding things 'still there'. The little word 'still' is repeated appreciatively, and with simple wonder:

> Still on the terrace of the big hotel
> Pale pink hydrangeas turn a rusty brown
> Where sea winds catch them, and yet do not die.
> The bumpy lane between the tamarisks,
> The escallonia hedge, and still it's there –
> Our lodging house, ten minutes from the shore.[44]

Against all the odds these things have survived. The hydrangeas and the lodging house have been battered by war and storms, but they persevere. Larkin's use of the word 'still' in his poem 'To the sea' enacts its own seaside tribute to Betjeman. 'Still going on, all of it, still going on!' Larkin marvels at the 'miniature gaiety' of the scene with all its pleasures and duties. Still going on, but only because we keep acting out the rituals, firm in the belief that they have a certain kind of magic.

Notes

Introduction

1 T.S. Eliot, *The Waste Land* (1922), ll. 300–3.
2 Iain Sinclair, *Dining on Stones* (London: Penguin, 2004), p. 415.
3 John K. Walton, *The British Seaside: Holidays and Resorts in the Twentieth Century* (Manchester: Manchester University Press, 2000), p. 7.
4 John Piper, 'Abstraction on the Beach', *XXe Siècle* 1 (1938), p. 41.
5 Elizabeth Bowen, *Pictures and Conversations* (New York: Knopf, 1975), p. 28.
6 Ibid.
7 Peter Maitland, contribution to 'Leisure at the Seaside', *Architectural Review* 80 (1936), pp. 7–28.
8 For the life-story of the Pavilion, see Alistair Fairley, *De La Warr Pavilion: The Modernist Masterpiece* (London: Merrell, 2006).
9 Ted Hughes, 'The Beach', *Birthday Letters* (London: Faber & Faber, 1998), p. 154.
10 Ibid.
11 *The Journals of Sylvia Plath*, ed. Karen V. Kukil (London: Faber & Faber, 2000), p. 286.
12 Stevie Smith, *Over the Frontier* (1938; London: Virago, 1980), pp. 44–5.
13 Sinclair, *Dining on Stones*, pp. 435, 212.
14 Graham Swift, *Last Orders* (London: Macmillan, 1996), p. 239.
15 John Piper, *British Romantic Artists* (London: Collins, 1942), p. 7.
16 W.G. Sebald, *The Rings of Saturn* (1998; London: Vintage, 2002), p. 175.

Kiss Me Quick: The Aesthetics of Excess in 1930s Literature and Film

1 Tom Harrisson, Humphrey Jennings and Charles Madge, 'Anthropology at Home', *New Statesman and Nation*, 30 January 1937, p. 155.
2 Stephen Jones, *The British Labour Movement and Film, 1918–1939* (London: Routledge & Kegan Paul, 1987), p. 8.

3 See Gary Cross (ed.), *Worktowners at Blackpool, Mass-Observation and Popular Leisure in the 1930s* (London: Routledge, 1990), p. 9.
4 C. Delisle Burns, *Leisure in the Modern World* (London: George Allen & Unwin, 1932), p. 19.
5 Friedrich Nietzsche, *The Will to Power*, trans. Walter Kaufmann and R.J. Hollingdale (London: Weidenfeld & Nicolson, 1968), p. 77; Yeats, conversation with Herbert Grierson, 1906, quoted by Grierson, Preface to V.K. Narayana Menon, *The Development of W.B. Yeats* (Edinburgh: Oliver and Boyd, 1942), p. x.
6 Walter Benjamin, 'The Work of Art in the Age of Mechanical Reproduction' (1936), *Illuminations, Essays and Reflections*, ed. Hannah Arendt, trans. Harry Zohn (New York: Schoken Books, 1968), p. 241.
7 Walter Benjamin, 'Theses on the Philosophy of History' (1950), *Illuminations*, p. 258; for mass-produced art see 'The Work of Art in the Age of Mechanical Reproduction'.
8 See John Carey, *The Intellectuals and the Masses* (London: Faber & Faber, 1992).
9 Tom Gunning, 'The Cinema of Attractions: Early Film, Its Spectator and the Avant-Garde', in Thomas Elsaesser and Adam Barker (eds), *Early Cinema, Space, Frame, Narrative* (London: BFI Publishing, 1990), pp. 57–8.
10 J.B. Priestley, *English Journey* (Harmondsworth: Penguin, 1977), pp. 252–3.
11 Gary Cross's book presents these reports in the order originally intended by Harrisson (see Cross, *Worktowners at Blackpool*), p. 49.
12 Priestley, *English Journey*, p. 252.
13 James Barke, *Major Operation* (London: Collins, 1936), p. 434.
14 Cross, *Worktowners at Blackpool*, p. 61.
15 Ibid., p. 90.
16 Ibid., p. 89.
17 62C, *The Mob*, Mass-Observation Archive, Sussex University.
18 Cross, *Worktowners at Blackpool*, p. 162.
19 Stuart Laing, 'Presenting "Things as They Are"', in Frank Gloversmith (ed.), *Class Culture and Social Change, A New View of the 1930s* (Sussex: Harvester Press, 1980), p. 155 (my italics).
20 Mass-Observation, *Britain by Mass-Observation*, by Charles Madge and Tom Harrisson (Harmondsworth: Penguin, 1939), p. 175.
21 Mass-Observation, *Britain*, p. 182.
22 Cross, *Worktowners at Blackpool*, p. 124.
23 Priestley, *English Journey*, p. 251.
24 Walter Greenwood, *Love on the Dole* (Harmondsworth: Penguin, 1981), p. 120. Subsequent references are incorporated in the text.

25 Graham Greene, *Ways of Escape* (London: Lester & Orpen Dennys, 1980), p. 62.
26 George Orwell 'The Sanctified Sinner' (1948), *Collected Essays, Journalism and Letters*, vol. iv (Harmondsworth: Penguin, 1970), p. 499; Carey, *The Intellectuals and the Masses*, p. 83
27 Graham Greene, 'Frederick Rolfe: Edwardian Inferno' (1934), in *Collected Essays* (London: Bodley Head, 1969), p. 175.
28 Graham Greene, *Brighton Rock* (London: Vintage, 2007), p. 83. Subsequent references are incorporated in the text.
29 Randall Swingler, *Selected Poems*, ed. Andy Croft (Nottingham: Trent Editions, 2001), p. 30.
30 Patrick Hamilton, *Hangover Square* (Harmondsworth: Penguin, 1990), p. 141. Subsequent references are incorporated in the text.
31 Quoted in Nigel Jones, *Through a Glass Darkly: The Life of Patrick Hamilton* (London: Abacus, 1993), p. 228.

Morecambe: The Sunset Coast

1 Parts of this essay appeared in slightly different form in *Cabinet* magazine. Graham Greene, *Journey Without Maps* (London: Penguin, 2006), p. 19.
2 T.S. Eliot, *The Waste Land* (1922), l. 300; Paul Nash, 'Swanage, or Seaside Surrealism', *Architectural Review* 79 (1936), pp. 151–4; W.H. Auden, 'Get there if you can' (1930), *The English Auden*, ed. Edward Mendelson (London: Faber & Faber, 1977), p. 49.
3 Frank Kermode, *The Sense of an Ending* (New York: Oxford University Press, 1966).
4 John Betjeman, 'Margate 1940', *Collected Poems* (London: John Murray, 2003), p. 100.
5 Ibid., p. 101.

London to Brighton: The Indian Summer of the Camden Town Group

This essay is based upon a previous paper, '"Poor abraded butterflies of the stage": Sickert and the Brighton Pierrots', *Tate Papers*, spring 2006, and research undertaken for Tate's online catalogue of works by the Camden Town Group.

I would like to thank the following for information and assistance: Thomas Ardill, Wendy Baron, David Beevers, Frederick Gore, David Fraser Jenkins and Robert Upstone.

1 Walter Richard Sickert, letters to Nan Hudson, both 1907, Tate Gallery Archive.

2 For comprehensive histories of the Fitzroy Street and Camden Town groups see Wendy Baron, *Perfect Moderns: A History of the Camden Town Group* (Aldershot and Burlington, Vermont: Ashgate, 2000), and Robert Upstone (ed.), *Modern Painters: The Camden Town Group*, exhibition catalogue (London: Tate, 2008).

3 Ironically, the family could have been even richer were it not for the fact that Taylor's father was persuaded to sell his shares in Wills Tobacco, convinced by his financial advisers that the passion for cigarettes could not last. Information supplied to the author by Frederick Gore, C.B.E., R.A, March 2004.

4 Osbert Sitwell (ed.), *A Free House! Or the Artist as Craftsman: Being the Writings of Walter Sickert* (London: Macmillan, 1947), pp. xxxv–xxxvi.

5 Marjorie Lilly, *Sickert: The Painter and his Circle* (London: Elek, 1971), p. 78.

6 Quoted in David Buckman, *Brighton Yesterdays: Douglas Fox Pitt 1864–1922 and Walter Taylor 1860–1943*, exhibition catalogue (Maltzahn Gallery: London, 1973), p. 1.

7 See for example Buckman, *Brighton Yesterdays* and *Brighton Revealed: Through Artists' Eyes c. 1760–c. 1960*, exhibition catalogue (Brighton: Royal Pavilion, Art Gallery and Museums, 1995).

8 Sickert wrote to Nan Hudson, 'I saw a lovely etching of yours in Fox Pitt's little house in Brighton. That man is rather touching. He wears old pea jackets of the eighties over his no longer 1880 tum to buy our pictures!' See Nicola Moorby, 'Biography of Douglas Fox Pitt', Tate online catalogue of works by the Camden Town Group, www.tate.org.uk.

9 Wendy Baron has also suggested that Brighton subjects by John Doman Turner (c. 1870–1938) suggest a link with Taylor. See Baron, *Perfect Moderns*, p. 208. Turner, who was deaf, was a student of Spencer Gore's by correspondence and a minor figure amongst the Camden Town Group. The style of his watercolours resembles those of Taylor and Fox Pitt.

10 For example, see *The Balcony at the Alhambra*, c. 1911–12 (York City Art Gallery) and *'The Mad Pierrot' Ballet at the Alhambra*, 1911 (private collection).

11 The invitation was almost certainly the result of the close friendship between Gore and Walter Taylor, who was on friendly terms with a member of Brighton town council. Information from Frederick Gore, C.B.E., R.A., February 2004.

It is also possible that Douglas Fox Pitt had some influence. He served on the Fine Arts Committee of the gallery at some point between 1911 and 1918.

12 *Brighton Herald*, 20 December 1913. Also the *Brighton Gazette*, 17 December 1913: 'it can be claimed that nothing like it has ever been seen locally before.'

13 For a full discussion of the evolution of the London Group see Baron, *Perfect Moderns*, pp. 62–8.

14 See the *Newcastle Journal*, 18 December 1913, the *Chronicle*, 13 January 1914, the *Sunday Times*, 18 January 1914 and the *Athenaeum*, 17 January 1914.

15 Reported in the *Sussex Daily News*, 17 December 1913.

16 *Sussex Daily News*, 16 December 1913.

17 Exhibitors in the exhibition were: Bernard Adeney, Walter Bayes, Robert Bevan, David Bomberg, Ruth Doggett (misspelt Duckett in the catalogue), Malcolm Drummond, Jacob Epstein, Frederick Etchells, Jessica Etchells, Fanny Eveleigh, Renée Finch, Douglas Fox Pitt, Harold Gilman, Charles Ginner, Spencer Gore, Sylvia Gosse, C.F. Hamilton, J. Hamilton Hay, Nan (Anna Hope) Hudson, Stanislawa de Karlowska, Mervyn Lawrence, Thérèse Lessore, Wyndham Lewis, James B. Manson, John Nash, Paul Nash, C.R.W. Nevinson, Martin Ogilvie, Lucien Pissarro, William Ratcliffe, Ethel Sands, Harald Sund, Walter Sickert, Harold Squire, Walter Taylor, Edward Wadsworth.

18 As described by Baron, *Perfect Moderns*, p. 68.

19 James Bolivar Manson, 'Introduction: Rooms I.–II.', *Exhibition of the Work of the English Post-Impressionists, Cubists and Others*, exhibition catalogue (Brighton: Public Art Gallery, 1913), p. 8.

20 Percy Wyndham Lewis, 'Introduction: Room III (The Cubist Room)', *Exhibition of the Work of the English Post-Impressionists, Cubists and Others*, exhibition catalogue (Brighton: Public Art Gallery, 1913), p. 10.

21 *Sussex Daily News*, 16 December 1913.

22 *Brighton Gazette*, 17 December 1913.

23 *Brighton and Hove Society* newsletter, 25 December 1913.

24 *Brighton Herald*, 20 December 1913.

25 Reported in the *Sussex Daily News*, 17 December 1913.

26 *Sussex Daily News*, 16 December 1913.

27 *Brighton Herald*, 20 December 1913. Similar sentiments were expressed by the *Lady's Pictorial* and the newsletter of the *Brighton and Hove Society*.

28 The approximate average price for a work from the first two rooms was £19, and £13 from the third room. The older, more established artists such as Sickert and Lucien Pissarro generally commanded the higher prices although the most expensive

pieces were two works at £85 each by virtual unknown, Mervyn Lawrence. The cheapest meanwhile was by Renée Finch, probably a work on paper, at £2 2s.

29 Annotated catalogue in records of Brighton Museum and Art Gallery.

30 André Germain of Paris purchased a work by James Bolivar Manson whilst Clifton bought works by Ethel Sands and Douglas Fox Pitt.

31 James Bolivar Manson, 'Introduction: Rooms I.–II.', *Exhibition of the Work of the English Post-Impressionists, Cubists and Others*, exhibition catalogue (Brighton: Public Art Gallery, 1913).

32 Walter Richard Sickert, letter to Nan Hudson and Ethel Sands (1914), Tate Gallery Archive. Ironically, twenty years later, Sickert resigned from the Royal Academy as a protest in defence of the work of Jacob Epstein; see James Fenton, *School of Genius: A History of the Royal Academy of Arts* (London: Royal Academy of Arts, 2006), p. 26.

33 See Baron, *Perfect Moderns*, pp. 70–2.

34 Sickert had also stayed with Taylor in April 1914.

35 Sickert, letter to Ethel Sands (1915), Tate Gallery Archive.

36 Walter Sickert, letter to Ethel Sands (1914), Tate Gallery Archive. Richard Shone has identified the subject of Sickert's painting, *The Rehearsal, Brighton*, 1915 (Ashmolean Museum, Oxford), as a dress rehearsal for the play *Mr Wu*, which opened at the Theatre Royal in September 1915; see Baron, *Perfect Moderns*, p. 442, no. 473.

37 The first version was bought by Morton Sands, brother of Fitzroy Street artist Ethel Sands.

38 Bill Pertwee, *Pertwee's Promenades and Pierrots: One Hundred Years of Seaside Entertainment* (Newton Abbot: Westbridge Books, 1979), pp. 12–14.

39 Wendy Baron and Richard Shone (eds), *Sickert: Paintings*, exhibition catalogue (London: Royal Academy of Arts, 1992), p. 252.

40 Judy Middleton, *Brighton and Hove Volume 1: A Portrait in Old Picture Postcards* (Market Drayton: S.B. Publications, 1991), p. 36.

41 Pertwee, *Pertwee's Promenades*, p. 26.

42 Sir Claude Phillips, 'Walter Sickert's Paintings', *Daily Telegraph*, 28 November 1916.

43 See Upstone, *Modern Painters*, p. 167.

44 *Brighton Herald*, 14 August 1915, p. 5. See Douglas Fox Pitt's oil painting, *The Indian Hospital, the Dome, Brighton* (Imperial War Museum).

45 See Nicola Moorby '"Poor abraded butterflies of the stage": Sickert and the Brighton Pierrots', *Tate Papers*, spring 2006.

46 Sickert, 'A Perfect Modern', *The New Age*, 9 April 1914, reprinted in Anna Gruetzner Robins (ed.), *Walter Sickert: The Complete Writings on Art* (Oxford: Oxford University Press, 2000), pp. 353–6.
47 Reproduced in Baron, *Perfect Moderns*, p. 127.
48 Wendy Baron, *Sickert: Paintings and Drawings* (New Haven and London: Yale University Press, 2006), reproduced p. 444, no. 475. Sickert also painted a study in oil of the balcony of Bedford Square, p. 444, no. 476.
49 The earliest signs of his new technique can be seen in the Tate's version of *Ennui*, 1914, revealed during cleaning in 2008.
50 Stephen Hackney, Rica Jones and Joyce Townsend (eds), *Paint and Purpose: A Study of Technique in British Art* (London: Tate, 1999), pp. 123–5.
51 See for example, Lynne Lawner, *Harlequin on the Moon: Commedia dell'Arte and the Visual Arts* (New York: Abrams, 1998).
52 Martin Green and John Swan, *The Triumph of Pierrot: The Commedia dell'Arte and the Modern Imagination* (New York: Macmillan, 1986), p. 1.
53 For a full discussion see Moorby, 'Poor abraded butterflies of the stage'.
54 She is also the one figure whom Sickert seems to have taken most pains to get right. There are two known extant compositional sketches related to the painting and one is devoted solely to her (Walker Art Gallery, Liverpool).
55 Sickert was born in Germany to a father who was Danish and a mother who was Anglo-Irish. For periods of his life he lived in France and Italy.
56 Sickert, letter to Ethel Sands (1914), Tate Gallery Archive.
57 Sickert, letter to Ethel Sands (1914), Tate Gallery Archive.
58 Sickert, letter to Ethel Sands (1915), Tate Gallery Archive.

'Remember Scarborough': The Sitwells on the Sands

1 Sacheverell Sitwell, 'A Sketch of the Scarborough Sands', in *The Homing of the Winds and other passages in prose* (London: Faber & Faber, 1942), p. 11.
2 Ibid., p. 12.
3 Sacheverell Sitwell, *For Want of the Golden City* (London: Thames & Hudson, 1973), p. 160.
4 Osbert Sitwell, *Left Hand, Right Hand!* (London: Macmillan, 1945), p. 81. Subsequent references are incorporated in the text.
5 Jack Binns, *The History of Scarborough* (Pickering: Blackthorn Press, 2003), p. 232.

6 Osbert Sitwell, *Laughter in the Next Room* (London: Macmillan, 1949), p. 85. Subsequent references are incorporated in the text.
7 Charles Altieri, *The Particulars of Rapture: An Aesthetics of the Affects* (New York: Cornell University Press, 2003), p. 2.
8 Ibid.
9 Sacheverell Sitwell, *All Summer in a Day* (London: Duckworth, 1926), p. 10. Subsequent references are incorporated in the text.
10 Osbert Sitwell, *The Scarlet Tree* (London: Macmillan, 1946), p. 217.
11 Ibid., pp. 224–5.
12 Osbert Sitwell, *Before the Bombardment* (1926; London: Penguin, 1938), p. 64. Subsequent references are incorporated in the text.
13 Osbert Sitwell, *Triple Fugue* (London: Grant Richards, 1924), p. 18. Subsequent references are incorporated in the text.
14 Jeff Malpas, *Place and Experience: A Philosophical Topography* (Cambridge: Cambridge University Press, 1999), p. 191.
15 Sacheverell Sitwell, 'A Sketch of the Scarborough Sands', p. 13.

'A Good Time Was Had By All'? Stevie Smith Beside the Seaside

1 Stevie Smith, *Collected Poems* (London: Penguin, 1978), p. 303. Subsequent references are incorporated in the text. Courtesy of the Estate of James MacGibbon.
2 For a biographical reading of this period of her life, see Frances Spalding, *Stevie Smith: A Critical Biography* (London: Stroud Publishing, 2002), p. 16.
3 Stevie Smith, *Over the Frontier* (1938; London: Virago, 1980), pp. 123–4. Subsequent references are incorporated in the text.
4 Stevie Smith, 'Beside the Seaside', reprinted in *Me Again*, ed. Jack Barbera and William McBrien (London: Virago, 1981), pp. 13–26, p. 21.
5 Stevie Smith, *Collected Poems* (London: Penguin, 1978), p. 174. Subsequent references use the abbreviation *CP*.
6 A further blurring will come post-publication. Smith's eponymous volume is personified via the same means when she thanks the reviewer Daniel George for 'kindness to Harold in his leaping' in a letter dated 9 February 1951, quoted in Jack Barbera and William McBrien, *Stevie* (London: Heinemann, 1985), p. 177.

7 See, for example, her poem 'The Celts' (*CP*, p. 350), which imagines the Celts as 'rather a whining lady'.

8 Stevie Smith, *Novel on Yellow Paper* (1936; London: Virago, 1980), p. 76. Subsequent references are incorporated in the text.

9 Celia further aligns herself with sailors in *The Holiday* when discussing *Les Désenchantées* (1906) by Pierre Loti, a French sailor, and his description of the 'cemetery bordering the sea-walk' (Stevie Smith, *The Holiday* (1949; London: Virago, 1999), p. 46).

10 Stevie Smith to Denis Johnston, 28 June 1937, University of Dublin, as quoted in Spalding, *Stevie Smith*, p. 193.

11 See also *Over the Frontier*, p. 63: 'Ah pain, ah wilderness of pain and war and death. And throughout and outside of it all in the awful aloofness of the artist, the mind that creates and is aloof and by itself, alone with the loneliness that is so cold as death, more cold than the salt sea water lapping and sucking beneath the icebound waves of northern Russia.'

12 Joseph Conrad, *Heart of Darkness and Other Tales* (Oxford: Oxford University Press, 1998), p. 150.

13 This illustration was first published by the author in 'Drawing in the Reader: Looking at Illustrations in the Work of Stevie Smith', *Jubilat* 12, pp. 71–82.

14 This book is now in the Stevie Smith Collection at the McFarlin Library, University of Tulsa. Every effort has been made to find the copyright holder for this image – please contact the author in case of query.

15 The lines quoted from the poem also begin Smith's story 'Beside the Seaside: A Holiday with Children' in *Holidays and Happy Days*, ed. Oswell Blakeston (London: Phoenix House, 1949), pp. 147–61, reprinted in *Me Again*, pp. 13–25.

16 'Advice to Young Children', *CP*, p. 174.

17 This obsessively repeated farewell provokes comparisons with her closing 'Adieu, adieu, adieu' in the poem 'Fuite d'Enfance', *CP*, p. 158.

'The Purest Ecstasy': Virginia Woolf and the Sea

1 John Bourke, *The Sea as a Symbol in English Poetry* (Eton: Alden and Blackwell, 1954).

2 Roberta Gefter Wondrich has noted that 'Joyce's work literally overflows with water and sea-imagery: as early as 1959 W.Y. Tindall pointed out its importance and, among most recent studies, Katharina Hagena has devoted an entire volume

to the subject of the sea in Joyce's masterpiece and Robert Adams Day a perceptive essay on Joyce's "acquacities", in which he reminds the reader that "the sea embraces the text of *Ulysses*". Roberta Gefter Wondrich, '"All the Seas of the World": Joycean Thresholds of the Unknown: A Reading of the Marine and Watery Element from *Dubliners* to *Ulysses*', in Caroline Patey, Giovanni Cianci and Francesca Cuojati (eds), *Anglo-American Modernity and the Mediterranean* (Milan: Cisalpino, 2005), pp. 227–43 (pp. 227–8).

3 *The Diary of Virginia Woolf*, ed. Anne Olivier Bell, assisted by Andrew McNeillie, vol. ii, 1920–1924 (London: Hogarth Press, 1978), p. 103.

4 Virginia Woolf, *Moments of Being*, ed. Jeanne Schulkind, rev. Hermione Lee (London: Pimlico, 2002), pp. 78–9.

5 Virginia Woolf, *A Passionate Apprentice: The Early Journals and 'Carlyle's House and Other Sketches'*, ed. Mitchell A. Leaska (London: Pimlico, 2004), pp. 281–2.

6 Ibid., p. 282.

7 Virginia Woolf, *Jacob's Room*, ed. Kate Flint (Oxford: Oxford University Press, 1992), p. 6. Subsequent references are incorporated in the text.

8 *The Essays of Virginia Woolf*, vol. ii, 1912–1918, ed. Andrew McNeillie (London: Hogarth Press, 1987), p. 143.

9 Virginia Woolf, *The Voyage Out*, ed. Jane Wheare (1915; Harmondsworth: Penguin Books, 1992), p. 20. Subsequent references are incorporated in the text.

10 John Milton, *Comus* (1634), l. 861.

11 Virginia Woolf, *To the Lighthouse*, ed. David Bradshaw (Oxford: Oxford University Press, 2006), p. 150. Subsequent references are incorporated in the text.

12 In Virginia Woolf, *The Mark on the Wall and Other Short Fiction*, ed. David Bradshaw (Oxford: Oxford University Press, 2001), pp. 54–9 (p. 54). Subsequent references are incorporated in the text.

13 Sir Arthur Eddington, *The Nature of the Physical World* (1928; London: J.M. Dent, 1955), p. 13.

14 See Michael H. Whitworth, 'The Atom and Woolf's Idea of Fiction', in *Virginia Woolf* (Oxford: Oxford University Press, 2005), pp. 178–80.

15 See 'Character in Fiction', in Virginia Woolf, *Selected Essays*, ed. David Bradshaw (Oxford: Oxford University Press, 2008), pp. 37–54.

16 *The Diary of Virginia Woolf*, ed. Anne Olivier Bell, assisted by Andrew McNeillie, vol. iii, 1925–1930 (London: Hogarth Press, 1980), p. 34.

17 *Diary*, iii, pp. 236, 285.

18 Virginia Woolf, *The Waves*, ed. James M. Haule and Philip H. Smith, Jr (Oxford: Blackwell, 1993), pp. 3, 18, 47. Emphasis added. Subsequent references are incorporated in the text.
19 *Diary*, iii, p. 209.
20 *Diary*, iii, p. 229.
21 Julia Briggs, *Virginia Woolf: An Inner Life* (London: Penguin, 2006), p. 243.
22 Virginia Woolf, *The Waves: The Two Holograph Drafts Transcribed and Edited by J.W. Graham* (London: Hogarth Press, 1976), Draft 1, p. 62.
23 Virginia Woolf, *Night and Day*, ed. J.H. Stape (Oxford: Blackwell, 1994), p. 6.
24 Virginia Woolf, *Mrs Dalloway*, ed. David Bradshaw (Oxford: Oxford University Press, 2000), pp. 121, 118.
25 Henry Newbolt, *Sea-Life in English Literature from the Fourteenth to the Nineteenth Centuries* (London: Thomas Nelson, 1925).
26 Virginia Woolf, *Between the Acts*, ed. Gillian Beer (London: Penguin Books, 1992), pp. 48, 114.
27 *Diary*, iii, p. 208.
28 *Diary*, ii, p. 246.

Survivals of Ariel: Sea and Form in Sylvia Plath's Poetry

1 William Shakespeare, *The Tempest*, Act 1, Scene 2, ll. 400–5.
2 Alfred, Lord Tennyson, *Tennyson: A Selected Edition*, ed. Christopher Ricks (Edinburgh: Pearson Longman, 1969), p. 165.
3 Sylvia Plath, *Collected Poems*, ed. Ted Hughes (London: Faber & Faber, 1981), p. 21. Subsequent references are incorporated in the text.
4 Virginia Woolf, *The Waves* (London: Penguin, 1998), p. 287.
5 *The Journals of Sylvia Plath*, ed. Karen V. Kukil (London: Faber & Faber, 2000), p. 286.
6 Karen Kukil, personal communication to the author.
7 Ezra Pound, 'In a Station of the Metro' in *Ezra Pound: Poems Selected by Thom Gunn* (London: Faber & Faber, 2000), p. 23.

In the Nautical Tradition: John Piper

1 *Blast* 1 (1914), p. 23.
2 Le Corbusier, *Towards a New Architecture*, trans. Frederick Etchells (London: John Rodker, 1927), pp. 102–3.
3 John Piper, 'The Nautical Style', *Architectural Review* 83 (1938), pp. 1–14 (p. 1); revised and reprinted in John Piper, *Buildings and Prospects* (London: Architectural Press, 1948).
4 Piper, 'Nautical Style', p. 4.
5 John Piper, 'Younger English Painters – II', *Listener* 9 (1933), p. 492.
6 John Piper, 'English Sea Pictures', *Listener* 20 (1938), p. 180.
7 Piper, *Buildings and Prospects*, p. 18.
8 John Piper to Myfanwy Evans, 13 July 1934, Tate Gallery Archive.
9 John Piper to Myfanwy Evans, 26 July 1934, Tate Gallery Archive.
10 John Piper to Ben Nicholson, 9 April 1934, Tate Gallery Archive.
11 Piper, 'Nautical Style', p. 1.
12 Piper, *Buildings and Prospects*, pp. 18–19.
13 Peggy Angus to Myfanwy Piper, 29 April 1942, Tate Gallery Archive.
14 Myfanwy Piper, address delivered at the Architectural Association at a memorial event for J.M. Richards, transcript in Architectural Association archives, File 25.
15 J.M. Richards, *Memoirs of an Unjust Fella* (London: Weidenfeld & Nicolson, 1980), p. 138.
16 J.M. Richards, 'Black and White', *Architectural Review* 82 (1937), p. 166.
17 Piper, *Buildings and Prospects*, p. 12.
18 Ibid., p. 18.
19 Ibid., p. 12.
20 Timothy Mowl, *Stylistic Cold Wars: Betjeman versus Pevsner* (London: John Murray, 2000), p. 7.
21 Le Corbusier, *Towards a New Architecture*, p. 95.

Modernism at Sea: Ocean Liners and the Avant-garde

1 Le Corbusier, *Towards a New Architecture*, trans. Frederick Etchells (London: John Rodker, 1927), p. 93.
2 Mardges Bacon, *Le Corbusier in America: Travels in the Land of the Timid* (Cambridge, Mass.: MIT Press, 2001), pp. 32–3.

3 Offrey Foucart and Fullers Robichom, *Normandie: Queen of the Seas* (New York: Vendôme Press, 1985), p. 56.
4 N.R.P. Bonsor, *North Atlantic Seaway* (Prescot: Stephenson, 1955), p. 214.
5 'A Fine Romance', written by Dorothy Fields and Jerome Kern for the 1936 film *Swing Time*, starring Fred Astaire and Ginger Rogers.
6 John Maxtone-Graham, *The Only Way to Cross* (New York: Macmillan, 1972), p. 248.
7 Letters from Erich Mendelsohn to Luise, on board the *Deutschland*, 3 and 9 October 1924, in *Erich Mendelsohn: Briefe Eines Architekten*, ed. Oskar Beyer (Munich: Prestel-Verlag, 1961), pp. 55–6.
8 Erich Mendelsohn to Luise, 11 October 1924, in *Briefe Eines Architekten*, p. 56.
9 *New York Times*, 23 April 1939.
10 D.N. Wallace, 'Queen Elizabeth 2: Some Design Considerations', *Shipping World and Shipbuilder*, January 1969, p. 88.

1930s Architecture and the Cult of the Sun

1 This essay develops ideas in Fred Gray, *Designing the Seaside: Architecture, Nature and Society* (London: Reaktion Books, 2006). For contextual information about the English seaside and its architecture between the wars see: Steven Braggs and Diane Harris, *Sun, Fun and Crowds: Seaside Holidays Between the Wars* (Stroud, Gloucestershire: Tempus, 2000); Allan Brodie and Gary Winter, *England's Seaside Resorts* (Swindon: English Heritage, 2007); John K. Walton, *The British Seaside: Holidays and Resorts in the Twentieth Century* (Manchester: Manchester University Press, 2000); and Ken Worpole, *Here Comes the Sun: Architecture and Public Space in Twentieth-Century European Culture* (London: Reaktion Books, 2000).
2 Contrasting English, French and American accounts of the relationships between the seaside and seaside fashion include: Avril Lansdell, *Seaside Fashions 1860–1939* (Princes Risborough, Buckinghamshire: Shire, 1990); Marie-Christine Grasse, *Coups de Soleil & Bikinis* (Toulouse: Éditions Milan, 1997); and Lena Lencek and Gideon Bosker, *Making Waves: Swimsuits and the Undressing of America* (San Francisco: Chronicle Books, 1989).
3 See, for example, John R. Gold, *The Experience of Modernism: Modern Architects and the Future City 1928–1953* (London: Spon, 1997); Andrew Higgott, *Mediating Modernism: Architectural Cultures in Britain* (Abingdon, Oxon: Routledge,

2007); and Alan Powers, *Britain: Modern Architectures in History* (London: Reaktion Books, 2007).

4 Quoted in Harold Tomlinson, 'Towards a New Architecture', *The Architects' Journal* (1927), p. 379.

5 George Ryley Scott, *The Story of Baths and Bathing* (London: Werner Laurie, 1939), p. 218.

6 Grasse, *Coups de Soleil*, p. 63.

7 Worpole, *Here Comes the Sun*, p. 14.

8 Wesley Dougill, 'The British Coast and its Holiday Resorts', *Town Planning Review* 16/4 (1935), pp. 265–78.

9 Edmund Vale, *North Country* (London: Batsford, 1937), p. 49.

10 'Leisure at the Seaside', *Architectural Review* 80 (1936), pp. 7–27.

11 Stephen V. Ward, *Selling Places: The Marketing and Promotion of Towns and Cities, 1850–2000* (London: Spon, 1998).

12 David Scurrell, Felicity Stafford and John Whyman, *Margate: A Resort History* (Margate: Margate Charter Trustees, 1986), pp. 57–8.

13 Scurrell et al., *Margate*, p. 62.

14 'Developments at Poole', *The Municipal Review* (1932), pp. 378–9; Poole Borough Council, *Official Guide to Poole* (Poole, 1934).

15 Ward, Lock & Co., *A Pictorial and Descriptive Guide to Bournemouth, Poole and District* (London, 1937), p. 67.

16 The most comprehensive account of seaside pools is Janet Smith, *Liquid Assets: The Lidos and Open Air Swimming Pools of Britain* (London: English Heritage, 2005). See also Braggs and Harris, *Sun, Fun and Crowds*.

17 Weston-super-Mare Borough Council, *The New Swimming Pool Weston-super-Mare: Souvenir Programme* (Weston-super-Mare, Somerset, 1937), p. 15.

18 Hastings Corporation, *Hastings and St Leonards: Official Handbook 1935* (Hastings, Sussex, 1935), p. 25; Hastings Corporation, *Hastings For Health: Official Handbook 1939–40* (Hastings, Sussex, 1939), p. 5.

19 Scott, *The Story of Baths and Bathing*, p. 181.

20 Southport Corporation, *Sunny Southport: Official Guide 1938–39* (Southport, 1938), p. 17.

21 S.D. Adshead and H.V. Overfield, *The Further Development of Scarborough* (Scarborough, Yorkshire: Borough of Scarborough, 1938), p. 42.

22 John Hassan, *The Seaside, Health and the Environment in England and Wales Since 1800* (Aldershot, Hampshire: Ashgate, 2003), pp. 109–11.

23 For example, Margate's 1927 open-air swimming pool, later to be called Cliftonville Lido, is described in Felicity Stafford and Nigel Yates, *The Later Kentish Seaside* (Gloucester: Sutton for Kent Archives Office, 1985), pp. 116–17.

24 *The Municipal Review* (1933), p. 263.

25 *Hasting and St Leonards Observer*, 10 June 1933.

26 See Alastair Fairley, *De La Warr Pavilion: The Modernist Masterpiece* (London: Merrell, 2006) and Alan Powers, *Serge Chermayeff: Designer, Architect, Teacher* (London: RIBA Publications, 2001).

27 'Leisure at the Seaside', *Architectural Review*, p. 23.

28 Fairley, *De La Warr Pavilion* and Powers, *Serge Chermayeff*, p. 77; Russell Stevens and Peter Willis, 'Earl De La Warr and the Competition for the Bexhill Pavilion, 1933–34', *Architectural History* 33 (1990), pp. 134–65 (p. 143).

29 Ward, Lock & Co., *A Pictorial and Descriptive Guide to Margate and North-East Kent* (London, c. 1933), p. 15.

30 Quoted in Stafford and Yates, *The Later Kentish Seaside*, p. 149.

31 Quoted in Stafford and Yates, *The Later Kentish Seaside*, p. 120.

32 See, for example, Vale, *North Country*.

33 James Laver, 'Blackpool', in *Beside the Seaside*, ed. Yvonne Cloud (London: Bodley Head, 1934), pp. 145–84 (pp. 171–2).

34 Quoted in Peter Bennett, *Blackpool Pleasure Beach: A Century of Fun* (Blackpool: Blackpool Pleasure Beach, 1996), p. 62. See also Gary S. Cross and John K. Walton, *The Playful Crowd: Pleasure Places in the Twentieth Century* (New York: Columbia University Press, 2005).

35 Barry Guise and Pam Brook, *The Midland Hotel: Morecambe's White Hope* (Lancaster: Palatine Books, 2007).

36 Ian Nairn and Nikolaus Pevsner, *The Buildings of England: Sussex* (Harmondsworth: Penguin, 1965), p. 528.

37 The most thoughtful history of the British holiday camps is Colin Ward and Dennis Hardy, *Goodnight Campers! The History of the British Holiday Camp* (London: Mansell, 1986). For a recent case study of one small camp see Bertha Wood, *Fresh Air and Fun: The Story of Blackpool Holiday Camp* (Lancaster: Palatine Books, 2005).

38 Sue Read, *Hello Campers!* (London: Bantam Press, 1986).

39 See, for example, Johnny Lancaster, *If It Hadn't Been Hi-de-Hi, It Wouldn't Have Been Funny!* (London: Glastonbury Publishing, 1994).

40 *Holiday Camp Review*, 21 May–3 June 1949, p. 4.

41 Prestatyn Holiday Camp, *Souvenir and Guide* (1953), p. 7.

42 Godfrey Winn, *Holiday Camp* (London: World Film Publications, 1947), postscript.

43 See the early postwar discussion of holiday camps in J.A.R. Pimlott, *The Englishman's Holiday: A Social History* (Hassocks: Flare Books, 1976), pp. 246–53. See also George Orwell, 'Pleasure Spots', in *Collected Essays, Journalism and Letters*, vol. iv (Harmondsworth: Penguin, 1970), p. 102.

44 English Tourist Board, *Turning the Tide: A Heritage and Environment Strategy for a Seaside Resort* (London, 1993); English Tourism Council, *Sea Changes: Creating World-Class Resorts in England* (London, 2001); English Heritage and Commission for Architecture and the Built Environment, *Shifting Sands: Design and the Changing Image of English Seaside Towns* (London, 2003).

45 Kaye Webb, 'By the Sea', *Leader Magazine*, 10/29 (1948), pp. 20–1.

46 *The Independent*, 4 August 2001; *The Guardian*, 16 April 2002; *The Observer*, 19 March 2000.

The Seaside *Flâneuse* in Elizabeth Bowen's *The Death of the Heart*

1 See Michael Bracewell's essay in this volume.

2 Martin Easdown, *Victoria's Golden Pier: The Life and Times of the Victoria Pier, Folkestone and Other Seafront Attractions of 'Fashionable Folkestone'* (Kent: Marlin Publications, 1998), p. 33.

3 Patricia Craig, introduction to Elizabeth Bowen, *The Death of the Heart* (1938; London: Vintage, 1999), p. 4. Subsequent references are incorporated in the text.

4 Elizabeth Bowen, *The House in Paris* (1935; London: Vintage, 1999), p. 134.

5 Easdown, *Victoria's Golden Pier*, p. 32.

6 T.S. Eliot, 'Marie Lloyd' (1923), in *Selected Essays* (1932; London: Faber & Faber, 1999), pp. 456–9.

7 Eliot, 'Marie Lloyd', p. 456.

8 Eliot, 'Marie Lloyd', p. 458.

9 Friedrich Nietzsche, 'Third Essay on Aesthetics', *On the Genealogy of Morals: A Polemic* (1887), trans. Douglas Smith (Oxford: Oxford University Press, 1996), p. 101.

10 The letter was published posthumously by Leonard Woolf, who deemed it one of his wife's significant essays. Virginia Woolf, 'Middlebrow' in *The Death of the Moth and Other Essays* (New York: Harcourt Brace Jovanovich, 1942), p. 178.
11 Woolf, 'Middlebrow', p. 180.
12 Easdown, *Victoria's Golden Pier*, p. 35.
13 Bowen, *Pictures and Conversations: Chapters of an Autobiography* (London: Penguin, 1975), pp. 3–63.
14 Easdown, *Victoria's Golden Pier*, p. 51.
15 Bowen, *Pictures and Conversations*, p. 32.
16 Bowen, *Pictures and Conversations*, pp. 24–5.
17 Neil Corcoran, *Elizabeth Bowen: The Enforced Return* (Oxford: Clarendon Press, 2004), p. 102.
18 Janet Wolf, 'The Invisible Flâneuse: Women and the Literature of Modernity', *Feminine Sentences* (Cambridge: Polity Press, 1990), pp. 35–50.
19 Charles Baudelaire, 'The Painter of Modern Life' in *The Painter of Modern Life and Other Essays*, trans. and ed. Jonathan Mayne (London: Phaidon, 1995), pp. 1–41.
20 Walter Benjamin, *The Arcades Project*, trans. Howard Eiland and Kevin McLaughlin (Cambridge, Mass.: The Belknap Press of Harvard University, 1999), p. 427.
21 Declan Kiberd, 'Elizabeth Bowen: The Dandy in Revolt', in *Inventing Ireland* (Dublin: Vintage, 1999), pp. 364–79.
22 Maud Ellmann, *Elizabeth Bowen: The Shadow Across the Page* (Edinburgh: Edinburgh University Press, 2004), p. 128.

The Margin of the Printable: Seaside Postcards and Censorship

1 George Orwell, 'The Art of Donald McGill', in *The Collected Essays, Journalism and Letters of George Orwell*, ed. Sonia Orwell and Ian Angus, vol. ii (London: Secker & Warburg, 1968), pp. 161–2.
2 See Elfreda Buckland, *The World of Donald McGill* (Poole: Javelin, 1984), p. 133.
3 See Noel Perrin, *Dr. Bowdler's Legacy: A History of Expurgated Books in England and America* (London: Macmillan, 1970).
4 See Jerry Palmer, *Taking Humour Seriously* (London: Routledge, 1994), p. 129.
5 Obscene Publications Act 1959, Section 1.

6 Listed in Ted Goodman, *Censorship: The Current Legal Position in Britain, March 1991* (London: Libertarian Alliance, 1991).

7 'Some Borough Bye-Laws', in *A Blackpool Miscellany*, ed. Bob Dobson and Doreen Brotherton (Blackpool: Landy, 1988), p. 76.

8 *Censorship in the Arts: A Freedom of Vision Report*, ed. Jean Straker (London: Academy of Visual Arts, 1967), p. 20.

9 Buckland, *McGill*, p. 193.

10 Gary Cross (ed.), *Worktowners at Blackpool: Mass-Observation and Popular Leisure in the 1930s* (London: Routledge, 1990), p. 190.

11 Orwell, *Collected Essays*, p. 163.

12 See Chapters III, IV and VI of Sigmund Freud, *Jokes and Their Relation to the Unconscious*, trans. and ed. James Strachey (Harmondsworth: Penguin, 1983).

13 Orwell, *Collected Essays*, p. 155.

14 *The Weekly Law Reports*, 9 July 1954, pp. 1002–3.

15 Richard Alderson, *The Comic Postcard in English Life* (Newton Abbot: David and Charles, 1970), pp. 100–10.

16 Buckland, *McGill*, p. 122.

17 Buckland, *McGill*, p. 193; Alderson, *Comic Postcard*, p. 100.

Postwar Promenade: Pleasure, Reconstruction and the Festival of Britain

1 Alain Corbin, *The Lure of the Sea* (London: Penguin, 1994), p. 95.

2 Darren Webb, 'Bakhtin at the Seaside', *Theory, Culture and Society* 22 (2005), pp. 121–38 (p. 134).

3 'Leisure at the Seaside', *Architectural Review* 80 (1936), pp. 7–28.

4 Gordon Cullen, 'Westminster Regained', *Architectural Review* 102 (1947), pp. 159–70; Gordon Cullen, 'Bankside Regained', *Architectural Review* 105 (1949), pp. 15–24.

5 For a complete account of Cullen's riverside plans, see David Gosling, *Gordon Cullen* (London: Academy, 1996), pp. 23–50.

6 These routes are detailed in the official Festival souvenir: Ian Cox, *The South Bank Exhibition* (London: HMSO, 1951).

7 On Spence's design see Louise Campbell, *Coventry Cathedral* (Oxford: Oxford University Press, 1996), pp. 75–6. The pavilions and displays of the Festival are listed in *Twentieth Century Architecture* 5 (2001), ed. Elain Harwood and Alan Powers, p. 67. See also *Architectural Review* 109 (1951), pp. 123–34.

8 For more on the typographic identity see Paul Rennie, 'Fat Faces all Around' in Harwood and Powers, *Twentieth Century Architecture*, p. 109.

9 The televisual significance of the Coronation far outweighs that of the Festival. Accordingly, and especially in relation to television broadcast history, the Festival is more or less invisible. See Paul Rennie, *Design: Festival of Britain 1951* (Woodbridge: Antique Collectors' Club), pp. 70–4.

The Destructive Element: Benjamin Britten and Aldeburgh

1 Britten, Diary, 29 June 1937, cited in Donald Mitchell and Philip Reed (eds), *Benjamin Britten, Letters from a Life*, vol. i, 1923–1939 (London: Faber & Faber, 1991), p. 496.

2 Julian Tennyson, *Suffolk Scene* (London: Blackie, 1939), p. 124.

3 Imogen Holst, *Britten* (London: Faber & Faber, 1966), p. 15.

4 E.M. Forster, 'George Crabbe: The Poet and the Man', reprinted in Ronald Blythe (ed.), *An Aldeburgh Anthology* (Aldeburgh: Snape Maltings Foundation in association with Faber Music, 1972), pp. 3–7.

5 'Britten Looking Back', *Sunday Telegraph*, 17 November 1963, p. 9.

6 Christopher Palmer, 'Embalmer of the Midnight: The Orchestral Song-cycles' in Christopher Palmer (ed.), *The Britten Companion* (London: Faber & Faber, 1984), p. 315.

7 Christopher Palmer, 'Chaos and Cosmos in *Peter Grimes*' in Palmer, *Britten Companion*, pp. 108–19.

8 Benjamin Britten, 'England and the Folk-Art Problem' in Paul Kildea (ed.), *Britten on Music* (Oxford: Oxford University Press, 2003), p. 34.

9 Ibid.

10 See Alan Powers, 'The Reluctant Romantics: Axis Magazine 1935–37' in David Peters Corbett, Fiona Russell and Ysanne Holt (eds), *The Geographies of Englishness: Landscape and the National Past 1880–1940* (New Haven and London: Yale University Press, 2002), pp. 248–74, for a discussion of some of the relevant figures, especially Geoffrey Grigson.

11 See Andrew Causey, 'English Art and "The National Character", 1933–34' in Corbett et al., *Geographies of Englishness*, pp. 275–302.

12 Hans Keller, in Hans Keller and Donald Mitchell (eds), *Benjamin Britten: A commentary on his works by a group of specialists* (London: Rockliff, 1952), p. 350.

13 Humphrey Carpenter, *Benjamin Britten: A Biography* (London: Faber & Faber, 1992), p. 254.

14 Benjamin Britten to Edith Sitwell, 3 March 1959, quoted in Carpenter, *Britten*, p. 379.

15 Philip Brett, *Music and Sexuality in Britten: Selected Essays* (Berkeley, Los Angeles and London: University of California Press, 2006), *passim*.

16 *The Songs of Michael Flanders and Donald Swann* (London: Elm Tree Books and St George's Press, 1977), p. 114. The Earl of Harewood, a cousin of the Queen, was President of the Festival from 1948 to 1965.

17 Brett, *Music and Sexuality*, p. 122.

18 Ibid., p. 170.

Seaside Ceremonies: Coastal Rites in Twentieth-Century Art

1 Philip Larkin, 'To the Sea' in *High Windows* (London: Faber & Faber, 1974), p. 9.

2 Ibid.

3 Benjamin Britten, *Peter Grimes* (1945), libretto by Montagu Slater, Act II.2.

4 George Crabbe, 'The Borough' (1810) in *George Crabbe: The Complete Poetical Works*, ed. Norma Dalrymple-Champneys and Arthur Pollard, vol. ii (Oxford: Clarendon, 1988), p. 364.

5 Britten, *Grimes*, Act II.2.

6 Britten, *Grimes*, Act I; Act II.

7 Britten, *Grimes*, Act III.

8 Ben Nicholson to Herbert Read (1944), cited in Lee Beard, '"Gentle Nest" or "Modernist Cell"?', unpublished doctoral thesis, Courtauld Institute of Art, London, 2003, p. 59. Nicholson used an old kitchen table-top as his palette, and dutifully scrubbed it clean at the end of each day's painting (see David Lewis, 'Scratching the Surface', *Tate Etc* 13 (2008), pp. 102–5 (p. 102).

9 *The English Auden*, ed. Edward Mandelson (London: Faber & Faber, 1986), p. 158.

10 John Piper, 'The Nautical Style', *Architectural Review* 83 (1938), pp. 1–14.

11 John Piper, *Romney Marsh* (Harmondsworth: Penguin, 1950), p. 7.

12 Tony Peake, *Derek Jarman* (1999; London: Abacus, 2001), p. 395.

13 Derek Jarman, *Derek Jarman's Garden* (London: Thames & Hudson, 1995), p. 41.

14 Derek Jarman, *Modern Nature* (London: Century, 1991), p. 3.

15 Jarman, *Jarman's Garden*, p. 109.

16 Peake, *Jarman*, p. 429.

17 Jarman, *Jarman's Garden*, p. 82.
18 *The Garden*, 1990, directed by Derek Jarman.
19 Jarman, *Jarman's Garden*, p. 47.
20 Paul Nash, *Shell Guide to Dorset* (London: Faber & Faber, 1936).
21 See Pennie Denton, *Seaside Surrealism: Paul Nash in Swanage* (Swanage: Peveril Press, 2002).
22 Paul Nash, 'Swanage, or Seaside Surrealism', *Architectural Review* 79 (1936), pp. 151–4.
23 Described and reproduced in Piper's essay 'Lost, A Valuable Object' in *The Painter's Object*, ed. Myfanwy Evans (London: Gerald Howe, 1937), pp. 69–73.
24 Virginia Woolf, 'Solid Objects' (1920), in *A Haunted House: The Complete Shorter Fiction*, ed. Susan Dick (London: Vintage, 2003), pp. 96–101.
25 Virginia Woolf, *Jacob's Room* (1922; London: Vintage, 1990), p. 4.
26 Woolf, *Jacob's Room*, pp. 4–5.
27 Virginia Woolf, *To the Lighthouse* (1927; London: Penguin, 1992), p. 124.
28 Elizabeth Bowen, *Pictures and Conversations* (New York: Knopf, 1975), p. 6.
29 Elizabeth Bowen, *The Little Girls* (1963; London: Vintage, 1999), p. 90.
30 Bowen, *Little Girls*, p. 155.
31 Jonathan Raban, *Coasting* (1986; London: Picador, 1987), pp. 152, 22.
32 Paul Theroux, *The Kingdom by the Sea* (1983; London: Penguin, 1984).
33 Raban, *Coasting*, p. 151.
34 Raban, *Coasting*, p. 152.
35 Theroux, *Kingdom*, p. 21.
36 Graham Swift, *Last Orders* (London: Picador, 1996), pp. 194, 192.
37 Swift, *Last Orders*, p. 18.
38 Swift, *Last Orders*, pp. 291–2.
39 Swift, *Last Orders*, p. 293.
40 Swift, *Last Orders*, p. 287.
41 Swift, *Last Orders*, p. 228.
42 Virginia Woolf, *To the Lighthouse* (1927; London: Penguin, 1992), p. 225.
43 John Betjeman, 'Margate, 1940' in *Collected Poems* (London: John Murray, 2003), p. 101.
44 John Betjeman, 'Beside the Seaside' (1948), in *Collected Poems*, p. 129.

Index

References in italics indicate figures